Social Constructionist Identity Politics and Literary Studies

Also by Suman Gupta

AESTHETICISM AND MODERNISM: Debating Twentieth Century Literature 1900–1960 (*co-editor with Richard Danson Brown*)

CORPORATE CAPITALISM AND POLITICAL PHILOSOPHY

DISCOURSES AND TEXTS OF ECONOMIC MIGRATION: International Perspectives (*co-editor with Tope Omoniyi, forthcoming*)

INDIA IN THE AGE OF GLOBALIZATION: Contemporary Discourses and Texts (*co-editor with Tapan Basu and Subarno Chattarji*)

INDIA AND GLOBALIZATION: Contents and Discontents (*co-editor with Tapan Basu and Subarno Chattarji*)

MARXISM, HISTORY AND INTELLECTUALS: Toward a Reconceptualized Transformative Socialism

NIGERIA AND GLOBALIZATION: Discourses on Identity Politics and Social Conflict (*co-editor with Duro Oni, Tope Omoniyi, Efurosibina Adegbija and Segun Awonusi*)

THE REPLICATION OF VIOLENCE: Thoughts on International Terrorism after 11 September 2001

RE-READING HARRY POTTER

THE THEORY AND REALITY OF DEMOCRACY: A Case Study in Iraq

A TWENTIETH CENTURY LITERATURE READER (*co-editor with David Johnson*)

TWO TEXTS AND I: Disciplines of Knowledge and the Literary Subject

V.S. NAIPAUL (Writers and their Works Series)

Social Constructionist Identity Politics and Literary Studies

Suman Gupta
Open University, UK

First published 2007 by
PALGRAVE MACMILLAN
Houndmills, Basingstoke, Hampshire RG21 6XS and
175 Fifth Avenue, New York, N.Y. 10010
Companies and representatives throughout the world

PALGRAVE MACMILLAN is the global academic imprint of the Palgrave
Macmillan division of St. Martin's Press, LLC and of Palgrave Macmillan Ltd.
Macmillan® is a registered trademark in the United States, United Kingdom
and other countries. Palgrave is a registered trademark in the European
Union and other countries.

ISBN-13: 978-0-230-50047-1   hardback
ISBN-10: 0-230-50047-1   hardback

This book is printed on paper suitable for recycling and made from fully
managed and sustained forest sources.

A catalogue record for this book is available from the British Library.

A catalog record for this book is available from the Library of Congress.

10   9   8   7   6   5   4   3   2   1
16   15   14   13   12   11   10   09   08   07

Printed and bound in Great Britain by
Antony Rowe Ltd, Chippenham and Eastbourne

Contents

Acknowledgements   vi

1   Introduction: Prelude to Definitive Elaborations   1

Part I   Social Constructionist Identity Politics   **5**

2   Identity-Based Political Positions   7

3   Embodying Identity-Based Political Positions   22

4   Analogues and Equivalences   48

5   Identity Politics at Work   81

Part II   Literary Studies   **97**

6   Theory, Institutional Matters, Identity Politics   99

7   Self-Announcements and Institutional Realignments   137

8   Theory Textbooks and Canons   179

9   Conclusion: Questions and Prospects   216

Notes   221

Bibliography   241

Index   255

Acknowledgements

I am particularly indebted to David Johnson, Open University, and Mark Turner, King's College London, for reading initial drafts of this book and giving most perceptive and helpful comments. Facilities which I have used for writing this were extended by the Open University and Roehampton University – for these I am grateful. I routinely run ideas and thoughts past Cheng Xiao before committing them to paper, and have done so for this study. To say I am grateful to her for her attention and responses would be a far from adequate return.

1
Introduction: Prelude to Definitive Elaborations

Anti-essentialist social constructionist identity politics is becoming institutionalized in literary studies. The same could be said of other areas of academic study, across the humanities and the social sciences. Indeed the same could be said of a wide range of political, social, and cultural formations in our time. That the second part of this book is addressed primarily to the institutional practice of literary studies is a convenience, or rather is to demarcate an examinable ground on which such institutionalization can be demonstrated. I am convinced that it can also be demonstrated for other grounds; the case of literary studies in this regard is symptomatic of a larger phenomenon.

This book is written because I have misgivings about the implications of institutionalizing identity politics, as understood here, anywhere at all. These misgivings do not arise from an essentialist position; the critique of identity politics offered here is from *within* anti-essentialist commitments and social constructionist convictions. By 'identity politics' I always mean the anti-essentialist social constructionist variety in this study.

Identity politics is understood here in a rather narrow sense which needs delineation. Part I of this book is devoted, at some length, to clarifying what I understand by identity politics. This part is not addressed specifically to literary studies or to literary analysis; this discussion is undertaken mainly in terms of political and cultural analysis. Part II examines the institutionalization of identity politics in literary studies and the implications thereof.

Identity and identity politics are prodigiously discussed and debated terms, with an enormous variety of philosophical, social, and political nuances and applications. Though customary in academic writing, I do not attempt to provide a survey here of so complex a field. I begin

1

instead with a brief statement of what I think identity politics is, in the narrow sense which applies here. This statement of identity politics may or may not conform to prevailing expectations – I expect, at some level, it will, or at any rate will resonate with current expectations.

Identity politics works through perceived analogues and equivalences between different identity-based political positions, and seeks thereby to extend its reach across and embrace different identity-based political positions. Identity-based political positions that are thus embraced within identity politics are centred on and among those who can embody those political positions. To embody an identity-based political position implies the following: only those who can identify themselves with or are identified with a particular identity-based collective can authentically and authoritatively assume the political position appropriate to that particular collective. Identity-based political positions are thus largely confined to those who can embody those positions; identity politics extends across such confines by exploring analogues and equivalences between different identity-based political positions, but without disturbing the logic of embodiment in identity-based political positions.

A crucial distinction is made, and relationship is drawn, here between 'identity politics' and 'identity-based political positions'. In everyday communication the phrase 'identity politics' is often used – approvingly and pejoratively – to connote what I call 'identity-based political positions' here. In academic writings 'identity politics' is usually interchangeably and confusingly used for both what I call 'identity-based political positions' and what I think of as 'identity politics' here. This study departs from the obfuscations of both current common usage and academic usage by insisting on the distinction between 'identity politics' and 'identity-based political positions'. The above statement presents the distinction but does not in itself fully explain what the distinction consists in or why it is crucial. The explanation comes hereafter.

That brief italicized statement may look and sound like a definition, but is not one. It seems to be conventional to give definitions in emphatic brief statements like that, employing an abstract and decontextualized register – whereby, as Alvin Gouldner had observed, a powerful social stratum of intellectuals validates and extends its cultural capital and assumes a (new) class character.[1] That the play of identity can be attributed where it seems to be most explicitly disavowed is a widely debated problem that this study addresses at the appropriate juncture. More to the moment, it seems to me arguable that such a brief italicized statement exacerbates rather than alleviates incomprehension, and appears to confine its address to select cognoscenti (smaller than Gouldner's new intellectual class). Elaboration is necessary, and it is in the elaboration rather than the italicized sentences that the definition of identity politics assumed here rests.

I understand identity politics, as briefly but incompletely delineated above, to be inevitably *social constructionist* and *anti-essentialist* in character. Identity politics cannot embrace different identity-based political positions by invigorating the analogues and equivalences between them without arguing against and overcoming the essentialisms within those identity-based political positions or without mobilizing the possibilities of social constructionism. Identity politics is, therefore, in itself social constructionist in character, and seeks to purge essentialisms from the identity-based political positions that it incorporates while maintaining the logic of embodiment. The rationale behind this understanding becomes clearer in the following elaboration of the brief italicized statement (particularly in Chapters 3 and 4).

This elaboration occurs in the following consecutively arranged chapters of Part I: Chapter 2, Identity-Based Political Positions; Chapter 3, Embodying Identity-Based Political Positions; Chapter 4, Analogues and Equivalences; and Chapter 5, Identity Politics at Work.

Part I Social Constructionist Identity Politics

2
Identity-Based Political Positions

The philosophical approach

Identity-based political positions are taken with regard to specific groups and are exercised by or for their particular memberships and, sometimes, through concordant institutions; in other words, these are positions taken with regard to, for, on behalf of, and by specific identity-based groups. For identity-based political positions, the political prerogatives of group identity generally supersede those of individual identity. The practice of politics with regard to specific group identities – national, ethnic, religious, class, race, gender, etc. – obviously precedes, usually by a long way, their being brought together under the umbrella term 'identity politics'.

The emergence of identity politics as a way of embracing all sorts of specific identity-based political positions has a fairly recent linguistic and socio-political history. One of the first, and still useful, efforts at coming to grips with this history – going back to the etymological roots of identity as sameness, and tracing the evolution of identity as formal recognition and identity as characterizing collectives – was made by W.J.M. Mackenzie (1978).[1] He traced the modern connotations of collective identity and therefore political identity to the 1950s and 1960s, to formulations of social psychology being brought to bear on the invention of area studies in the United States. It is a history that has since been rather sadly neglected. Though I do not attempt to give a systematic rendering of that history here, I do touch upon some of the significant points in it below.

Let me repeat though, the first point I wish to emphasize here is that different identity-based political positions (such as nationality-, ethnicity-, religion-, class-, race-, gender-, and sexuality-centred political positions) place individual identity as a secondary or separate matter. Insofar as this study goes, identity-based political positions are centred on group identities as superseding considerations of individual identity. Some alignment of equivalences and analogues between these devolves into what I call identity politics here.

This observation has necessary corollaries which are germane to understanding identity-based political positions. Focusing on collective identity as superseding individual identity entails the over-determination of what we may think of as individual identity markers. Each individual has (is) a unique combination of identity markers: physiognomic features, linguistic ability, sexual proclivities and gendered experiences, education and socialization, professional abilities, history of locations and memories, cultural habits and religious beliefs, etc. A unique combination of identity markers constitutes an individual identity. Collective identity is demarcated by taking one or some such markers as a common denominator joining members of the collective, and by accepting that such markers confer a commonality of experience for members, a particular mutual understanding, an ambit of joint aspirations, and therefore some sort of allegiance. Thus, racial politics involves an over-determination of physiognomic features to demarcate collective identity; feminist politics grows through an over-emphasis of the experience and condition of being a woman; concentration on territorial location could take the form of national or regional politics; particular focus on linguistic ability and participation in communal activities and rituals coalesce into ethnic politics; and so on. Such over-determination of identity markers could also be thought of as the reduction of individual identity to an aspect (or some aspects) of itself – to become an identifiable member of the identity-based collective – for political purposes.

In presenting identity-based political positions as collective over-determinations of individual identity markers, I have acceded in some measure to a philosophical convention (especially where philosophical systems open political possibilities). With Descartian inspiration lurking in the background, philosophers sometimes habitually move from the conceptualization of individual identity to the conceptualization of collective (in various senses, simple or complex group, or simply human) identity. This occurs, for instance, in existentialist philosophy, where the individualized condition of being in-itself and for-itself is extended to a political conceptualization of freedom (a process that is best exemplified in Sartre's quest for an accommodation between existentialism and Marxism[2]). For another instance: the most uncompromising focus on individual identity with political repercussions derives, it seems to me, from analytical philosophy. A familiar analytical philosophical question about individual identity is: what are the reasonable and sufficient conditions under which an individual I1 at a time T1 can be regarded as the same person as the individual I2 at a later time T2? It is an obdurately enclosed question, which resists and pushes consideration of collectivity to an after-the-fact prospect. Nevertheless, addressing this question opens up political positions too (where individual identity precedes collective identity), which can be regarded as the opposite of identity-based political positions (where collective identity precedes individual identity). Neo-liberals take such a position up when asserting the primacy of individual identity most single-mindedly: in Frederick Hayek's understanding of political freedom as an extension of individual freedom,[3] for instance, or Robert Nozick's visualization of the minimal state which accepts the inviolability of the individual.[4] And such a political presumption feeds into liberal politics where fairness is sought for a collective of individuals: e.g., in John Rawls's well-ordered liberal democracy drawing on an ideal contract,[5] or Derek Parfit's examination of the individual identity question to argue against self-interest propositions without offering a prescriptive political framework.[6]

I have outlined identity-based political positions so far by briefly following the philosophical convention of moving from individual to collective identity. However, importantly, identity-based political positions are markedly different from existentialist or neo-liberal or liberal political positions which follow that philosophical convention rigorously (though, confusingly, it is increasingly found that liberal politics merges into identity politics). Indeed the former are the opposite of the latter, and seek to reverse the precedence of individual identity to collective identity. Perhaps it would have been more apt to assume a different convention (not a philosophical approach) to delineate identity-based political positions. A sociological convention may be better suited, and I take that up briefly too – soon. For the moment though, the formulation of identity politics as a collective over-determination of individual identity markers is a useful one to develop this elaboration. Besides, this is a familiar way of understanding this matter. Kathleen Wallace, for instance, has examined from a philosophical perspective the relationship between the concept of an autonomous and unitary self and that of, what she calls, 'an intersectional self (typically made up of race, class, gender, occupation, ethnicity, language, and so on)',[7] to conclude that:

'I' functions in a location: it (partially) detaches from a location and in so doing generates the possibility of a new location or perspective. [...]

Autonomous agency [...] is possible because through reflexive communication a self can project itself into the future by articulating self-perspectives; its function is *its* not because it is unrelated to or undetermined by its social and other locations, but because it has the capacity to partially detach itself from some perspective(s) in some respect and articulate another perspective from itself.[8]

Novelists like Caryl Phillips and Amin Maalouf, who self-consciously occupy a position between several collective identities, also maintain a need to resist the distortions of identity-based political positions and express complex, true, tangible individual identities.[9]

It might be averred that there is another end to this equation: that of universal human interests and the politics thereof, or the identity, so to say, of society or humanity in general. This is most familiarly raised as the aspiration of old left politics when it is straightforwardly hostile to the new left's embracing of identity-based political positions (which it has commonly dubbed 'identity politics'), memorably expressed by Eric Hobsbawm as follows:

Let me state firmly what should not need restating. The political project of the Left is universalist: it is for *all* human beings. However we interpret the words, it isn't liberty for shareholders or blacks, but for everybody. It isn't equality for all members of the Garrick Club or the handicapped, but for everybody. It is not fraternity only for old Etonians or gays, but for everybody. And identity politics is essentially not for everybody but for members of a specific group only.[10]

Along similar lines was Todd Gitlin's critique of the thickening of identity politics in the new left, and the taking over of the language of universals by the academic right:

[...] there has been a curious reversal since the nineteenth century. Then, there were aristocracies who unabashedly stood for the privileges of the few. Today, the aspiring aristocrats of the Academic Right tend to speak the language of universals – canon, merit, reason, individual rights, transpolitical virtue. By the same token, they hold the Left guilty of special pleading – a degradation of standards, affirmative action (which it considers racial preference), diehard relativism. Seized by the psycho- and sociologic of polarization, committed to pleasing its disparate constituencies, an Academic Left obsessed with differences fails to reckon with commonalities.[11]

The new left response to such arguments is pithily charted in an essay by David Palumbo-Liu, who feels that they have 'a stake in both down-playing the pervasive significance of racism, sexism, homophobia, and other violent manifestations of prejudice against those who are particu-larly *identified* [...], and overplaying the economic as an isolatable space outside the racial, gendered, and otherwise identified social and politi-cal spheres'.[12] Despite the association of universal claims with the old left, and the alignment of identity-based political positions with the new left, the idea of universality (and concordant claims) obviously has wider application and is contested territory itself. The desire to uphold universal interests could as well be a liberal or neo-liberal claim as a socialist one. In the sense that universality refers to society or humanity in general (everybody), the clarification of identity-based political posi-tions from that direction is best undertaken by a sociological (rather than philosophical) approach to the question of identities – which, as I said, I come to soon. But an immediate, and important, caveat should be inserted here. Though identity-based political positions are often – almost customarily now – understood as inherently opposed to univer-sal political conceptualization (are not 'homogenizing', 'unitary', or 'totalizing', in the prevailing jargon of postmodernism), they do not remain so when encapsulated by social constructionist identity politics. Separate identity-based political positions may be exclusive in a fashion that does not recognize the universality of human political interests and rationality, but when conjoined under the banner of identity politics – chained together by analogues and equivalences – we are presented with a particular kind of (disquieting) universal political conceptualiza-tion which contains and even valorizes exclusions. I am aware that this contention goes against the grain of current orthodoxies, and needs careful justification. My reasons for saying this are given below in Chapter 4, 'Analogues and Equivalences'.

There is naturally an implicit fluidity or instability in the construction of collective identities as over-determinations of individual identity markers for political purposes. Overlapping of identity markers can lead to different kinds of fractures and shifts within any identity-based polit-ical position, as can conflicting allegiances operating on overlapping members of two or more identity-based political positions. This is evi-denced continuously in the histories of different identity-based political positions. Feminist politics, for instance, has been constantly interro-gated and recast from within along the fissures of race, class, ethnicity, religion, etc., among women. Similarly, to take another kind of instance, feminist and religious politics have often tested allegiances of overlapping memberships. The same could be said for all kinds of identity-based political positions. Indeed, the instability of identity-based political positions has come to be one of the foci of critical and theoretical attention of late, focused in discussions of multiple identities, shifting identities, contingent identities, hybridity, diaspora, etc. It is now understood that the instabilities of collective identity reveal more about the processes and power relations in identity construction than apparent stabilities, and emphasize the social constructionist rather than essentialist character of collective identities. Unsurprisingly, in attempting to introduce the current vogue of thinking about collective identities (as cultural identities), Stuart Hall observes that it is now generally accepted that:

> identities are never unified and, in late modern times, increasingly fragmented and fractured; never singular but multiple and constructed across different, often intersecting and antagonistic, discourses, practices and positions. They are subject to radical historicization, and are constantly in the process of change and transformation.[13]

Nevertheless, the constant ebb and flow of fractures and reconstitutions of identity-based political positions does not collapse into the pre-eminent emergence of individual identity in political terms. Nor do separate identity-based political positions, in themselves, merge and disappear into universal human interests and the politics which extends to all. However fractured and reconstituted, an identity-based political position remains with regard to some collective – members identified through over-determined identity markers – a smaller, or larger, or overlapped one. Identity-based political positions are always with regard to collectives, and it is as such that they are encapsulated within the (as I soon explain) all-embracing reach of social constructionist identity politics.

The sociological approach

In registering the implicit instability and fluidity of identity-based political positions, an obvious question arises: why is it that nevertheless identity-based political positions are successfully maintained and evidence high effectiveness in themselves (indeed there is increasing evidence of this)? There are several reasons for this. A more or less abstract reason has to do with the manner in which such positions are constituted. As I have remarked already, in introducing identity-based political positions above I moved from individual identity to collective identity, and correspondingly from the unique complex of identity markers that is an individual to the over-determination of one or some identity markers to demarcate collective identity. In other words, I acceded in some measure to a philosophical convention. Arguably, however, the identity markers in terms of which both individual identity (a unique combination) and collective identity (an over-determination) are discerned above are distinguishable and available entirely at the level of the collective – at the level of social perceptions and distinctions. Race, gender, sexual orientation, class, religious convictions, ethnicity, etc., are each understood as collective matters; these terms only make sense in the continuum of collective social existence where identity is perceived, constructed, allocated, claimed, instituted, acted upon ... When I approached individual identity above as a unique combination of identity markers, I was effectively characterizing the individual through given lenses of the collective, while claiming to approach the collective through the individual. So, integrity and veracity demand that the abstraction of the individual be always recognized for what it is: a sort of inference made from social discourses, perhaps even no more than nodal points constructed in the continuum of the merging and dispersing and separating of collective identities. If that account is accepted, identity-based political positions are *effective* if not stable because they derive from the social reality and experience of all individuals – the fact that all individuals are constantly being perceived, constructed, allocated, claimed, instituted, acted upon, etc., in collective identities which precede and indeed enable an apprehension of self, of individual identity. Identity-based political positions are effective, in brief, because they are closer to the bone of everyone's immediate collective existence; they are more immediately real.

This twist in the philosophical convention is perhaps most self-consciously expressed by Kwame Anthony Appiah when he seeks to insert an ethics of identity within the liberal tradition (drawn particularly from John Stuart Mill) that privileges notions of individual autonomy. He presents the individual's self-understanding as inevitably in relation to society, as constituted by 'tell[ing] a story of one's life that hangs together', and entails ethically effective 'soul making' with reference to extant models of social identity.[14] For Appiah the models of social identity that are available are precisely collective identities like race, gender, nationality, class, religion, etc. Appiah's is effectively a self-conscious insertion of a more defined *social* (as collectives) in liberal philosophical conceptions of the individual than is conventional.

However, and problematically, Appiah then strives to adhere to the liberal philosophical notion of individuality by taking the given collectives, the given society, as simply that – presumptively *given*. It is no longer necessary, it seems to be suggested, to ask 'what sort of society' or 'society in what context' or 'what kinds of social relations'; society is already prefigured by collective identities. A curious ahistoricism sets into Appiah's argument; resonant socio-historical episodes are thereafter plucked out by him in a bland soup of philosophical rationality that is indifferent to their social and historical contexts. He paradoxically reaches from a philosophical to a sociological convention and withdraws from the latter at the selfsame moment.

Despite that sort of liberal compromise, implicit in the notion that individual identity is an inference made from given collective identity-positions, whereby the precedent emphasis falls on collectivity rather than on individuality, are a range of sociological debates – or rather, the notion exposes an emphatically sociological convention (rather than a philosophical one). In choosing society as the primary object of analysis, social scientists have structured collectives and approached the individual in several ways, and in every instance with a releasing of political possibilities. Identity-based collectives and identity-based political positions are implicitly theorized in terms of discernments of different modes of division of labour, social stratifications and fluidities and tensions, dispositions of boundaries, characterization of social systems, etc., since sociology's 19th-century self-constitution and academic institutionalization. But sociology cannot and should not be regarded (though it now often appears so) as naturally inclined to a releasing of identity politics. In the sociological convention, society or collectivity is often regarded as a universal (*within* which agents, actions, boundaries, hierarchies, systems, etc., are discernible), and the consideration of individuality (if at all necessary) has often occurred in relation to society and collectivity as a universal notion. The equation between the individual and the collective in sociology, in other words, is usually understood as being mediated in various ways (including through identity-based collectives), but ultimately regarded as an equation between two universal poles: individual and society. This is amply evidenced in attempts to conceptualize individual identity sociologically. The fact that *identity* as a link between certain individuals and specific collectives had seldom been a matter of sociological reflection before the Second World War is indicative in itself. As Niklas Luhmann had argued, within the all-encompassing sociological focus on the continuous, ongoing, endlessly replicative or reproductive nature of social systems and processes in general, there is no place to comprehend the individual except as an element that is in itself mortal.[15] However, Norbert Elias's work provides a good example of a long-drawn (from the 1930s to the 1980s) attempt to mediate precisely between individual and society, or later between 'I-identity' and 'we-identity',[16] and illustrates the use of *identity* at both ends as sociological universals.

Sociological perspectives of collective identity as incorporating individual identity in a contemporary sense (the one that applies to this study) seem to me to be formatively rooted in sociological psychology: in a pioneering fashion in George Herbert Mead's consideration of social processes that mediate understanding of self and assuming of roles;[17] in Marcel Mauss's attempt to discern the social construction of the self or person in various cultural contexts;[18] and in Erik Erikson's formulations of identity.[19] In 1975, Kenneth Hoover attempted to draw a 'politics of identity' based on these social psychological sources, but his was a very different understanding of that politics from this study's, mainly to do with invigorating the liberal political project of maximizing individual freedom while retaining a sense of community in general.[20] By 1980, however, though following similar liberal commitments as Hoover's, Peter du Preez adopted a contemporary view of identity politics as collective identity-based political positions with reservations. He felt identity-based political positions involved some agents persuading individuals to subscribe to collective 'identity frames' (similar to what I have described as an over-determination of identity markers), which he regarded as a con. He defined ideology accordingly as: 'a system of ideas adapted to the lives of some particular group of people, with some particular identity or set of identities'.[21] The 1980s also saw the growing influence of social psychological studies such as Henri Tajfel's[22] (based on intergroup discrimination experiments conducted in the 1970s), and of sociolinguistic research on collective identity construction such as John J. Gumperz's[23] (brought to notice through his BBC programme of 1 May 1979, *Crosstalk*[24]). Increasingly since the 1980s a greater body of sociological research – or greater employment of the sociological convention in political understanding – has tended towards or provided a base for identity politics as understood here (the maintenance of analogues and equivalences between different identity-based political positions). It would be tedious and unnecessary to chart this tendency closely here.

Political imperatives

An abstract argument about the immediacy of social experience to explain the effectiveness of identity-based political positions, however, should always be regarded with a healthy measure of scepticism. The nature of political reality can be argued in several ways, and where primary emphasis should be laid for effective political theory and action is as ever a moot point. Much stronger and more contingent explanations can be adduced to understand the effectiveness of identity-based political positions. A comparatively more persuasive reason is available not so much in their constitutive characteristics as in the results of adopting such positions. Usually, once (through whatever process) an identity-based political position is assumed, it enables a political apprehension of a very large perceptual field – much larger than the confines of membership with regard to which, for which and on behalf of which it is addressed. Most identity-based political positions, in other words, enable an apparently comprehensive political explanation and analysis, embracing not only the inside of relevant collectives but also their outsides, yet always with the interests of the inside at heart. A symptomatic example may help clarify this point. A political position addressed to ameliorate the marginalization and oppression of women, for instance, must begin by understanding what it is up against. It would justifiably find that it is up against a patriarchal orientation of political discourse, whereby the modes of marginalizing women are implicitly held as based on universal and obvious truths. Such patriarchal orientation is so deep-seated that it is embedded into the very syntax of language and is normalized through any attempt at expressing oneself. Seeking redress under these circumstances means trying to undermine that through which expression itself is framed – an understandably complicated affair that has exercised feminist politics and generated numerous debates and strategies. The point that interests me at this moment is that in this argument a scope of engagement has revealed itself which is enormous, which extends in all directions and to unexpected corners. It defamiliarizes the apparently obvious, it gives a key to the world at large, it comes with the force of a revelation, and opens up a political purpose that is as enticing as it is exciting. Feminist politics takes over the perceptual field and defines the agenda of the feminist in extensive ways:

> To destroy the categories of sex in politics and in philosophy, to destroy gender in language (at least modify its use) is therefore part of my work in writing, as a writer. An important part, since a modification as central as this cannot happen without a transformation of language as a whole. It concerns (touches) words whose meanings and forms are close to, and associated with, gender. But it also concerns (touches) words whose meanings and forms are furthest away.[25]

I do not quote Monique Wittig here to privilege her particular brand of feminist politics, but to give a taste of the realization and sense of agency expressed here: a taste that most of those committed to identity-based political positions would recognize. Enunciating the conditions of and agendas for an inside of racial, ethnic, gay, national, religious, etc., identity-based political positions involves apprehension of the outside – extends to disposing the entire outside in terms of the preoccupations of the inside – and often enables exhilarating political perceptions (and naturally misperceptions) and realizations and motivations.

The kind of invigorating political apprehension and purpose that is often released through identity-based political positions has another aspect, and one that provides the most likely reason for their strength and effectiveness. This has to do emphatically with the inside and out-side (continuing the conceit from the last paragraph) on the basis of which identity-based political positions extend their scope. Such political positions are of course devoted to the interests of those inside – members bearing/claiming over-determined collective identity markers – over or against the interests of those who are outside. The efficacy and strength of identity-based political positions depend on their being able to generate a sense of those inside being *threatened* or being *marginalized* (or dominated, oppressed) from without. Indeed, it would not be too far off the mark to say that identity-based political positions invariably build upon and are consolidated by a perception of being threatened or marginalized. Supremely confident dominant collectives are apt to represent themselves as humanity itself and expect all to not only endorse but also integrate. Insofar as rationality is given a geopolitical character (erroneously, for reason has more dispersed conceptual roots), as some how defining Western identity (and rooted in European Enlightenment[26]), it is sometimes understood as the absorbent and simultaneously hegemonic instrument of an imperially dominant and self-satisfied West – drawing all into itself, Westernizing in all directions. The West as representing a dominant and universalizing collective iden-tity seems to be a commonplace of identity politics, figuring consis-tently with roughly similar geopolitical and ideological configurations as much in the work of the Frankfurt School (still held in place by Habermas[27]), as in that of American neo-conservatives, liberal global-ization champions, and liberal post-colonial postmodernists. That a frame of dominance so pervasive across ideological zones has not yet been sufficiently interrogated and undermined is probably indicative of the need for a dominant signifier to let loose the sway of identity poli-tics. Further, obliviousness to the fact that conjoining this signifier with something as pervasive as rationality effectively dispossesses many developed and carefully organized civilizations and histories of rational self-understanding (along Hegel's explicitly racist lines[28]) tangentially reveals, I feel, no more than a desire to revel either in imperial self-satisfaction or in the righteousness of the marginalized and threatened.

A sense of being marginalized or being threatened, through which identity-based political positions consolidate themselves, naturally pulls in contrary directions. The contrary directions are marked by the distinction between being marginalized and being threatened.[29] The identity-based political position that is consolidated through marginalization pits itself against the dominant establishment wherein marginalization occurs. Working against marginalization is an emancipative step, equivalent to striving for an egalitarian prospect, and is usually regarded as the precinct of the left. In different ways, the working-class movement, anti-colonial nationalisms, civil liberties struggles, women's movements, gay rights movements, etc., have sometimes been in that mould (much of the politics associated with those terms are *not* identity-based, as I explain in Chapter 3, 'Embodying Identity-Based Political Positions'). Working against threats from outside, on the contrary, is a conservative step; protecting itself from infiltration by a numerous and undesirable other is the arena of a dominant but not-too-confident right. Identity-based political positions that consolidate themselves against threats are protectionist rather than emancipationist. White supremacists, male chauvinists, fundamentalists identified with dominant religions in different contexts (Christianity in USA, Islam in Saudi Arabia, Hinduism in India, etc.), homophobes, fascist nationalists, etc., are usually associated with identity-based political positions that consolidate themselves against threats. There are, of course, many intermediate shades of identity-based political positions. When George Bush and Tony Blair speak of the need to protect the West (or *our* people) from the threats of the outside, they are dominant and not-too-confident protectionists playing on rightist identity-based politics. When they simultaneously proclaim the need to integrate (by force) the world into liberal democracy, they assume the garb of the supremely confident dominant imperial alignment which eschews identity-based political positions and speaks for all humanity. When, at the same time, they champion the causes of what passes as pluralism and multiculturalism, they play with leftist identity-based politics against marginalization. It is clearly possible to unite these contrary and immiscible strains in political practice. But, at least conceptually, these strains should be held apart – and as far as this study goes, are held apart here.

To many, my bringing together of the leftist and rightist identity-based political positions within the same conceptual space would seem unwarranted. Emancipationist and protectionist impulses obviously seem to belong to opposite ends of the political spectrum, implacably opposed to each other. But insofar as these opposite ends subscribe to identity-based political positions, they are joined by a structural similarity – they simply reflect each other and are defined by each other. This is a very well-known phenomenon: anti-colonial nationalism could, with a change of circumstances, turn into fascist nationalism; black supremacism (negritude) may become a mirror image of white supremacism; radical feminists may exercise a similar sort of exclusionist violence as male chauvinists; proletariat revolutionaries can become governing elites and indistinguishable from their bourgeois forebears; reform religions can be as oppressive and repressive as the dominant religions they seek to replace; and so on. Under the banner of emancipative identity politics – where equivalences and analogues between different (particularly marginalized) identity-based political positions are played up – efforts to oppose this kind of mirroring of right and left identity-based political positions are understood as opposing 'essentialism'. Anti-essentialist identity politics exhorts amenable marginal identity-based political positions not to become reflexive of their conservative opposites. However, the critique of essentialism within identity politics, against the essentialist tendency of specific identity-based political positions, appears to me to be a red herring – a simplistic misdirection to draw attention away from a complex and widely accepted and disturbing strategy. The critique of essentialism is addressed squarely in Chapter 3, 'Embodying Identity-Based Political Positions'.

A final point remains in these remarks on identity-based political positions, and one that takes me away from reasons for their effectiveness despite their inherently unstable nature. The articulation of an identity-based political position – articulation that is poised somewhere in the balance of being for, on behalf of, to, in the interests of an identity-based collective – inevitably involves the acceptance of something outside the field of articulation. It comes with the weight of something that is beyond interaction between individuals (in principle, anyone who happens to be there and knows the language and the idiom and context in question), and is greater than the cohabited arena that is mapped and constituted and apprehended through a mesh of such communicative processes (discourses). The articulation of an identity-based political position emanates as if from/of/to/for an identity-based collective *itself*. This is a condition whereby the emanation of such articulation comes always with the weight of the collective itself behind it, as greater than he/she who speaks and anyone who may hear and respond. I think of this excessive and inarticulable weight that pushes the articulation of identity-based political positions forth – emanating as if from the collective itself, from beyond personal feelings and a pervasive ability to think and understand – as the manifestation of a claim to authenticity. This mode of enforcing the weight of an abstraction as if it speaks itself, as if it has a sentient presence, is far from being confined to the expression of identity-based political positions alone. Other kinds of political positions do this too, but rarely. It occurs, I suppose, wherever the articulation of a politics resists open debate and interrogation. In fact another kind of political articulation which was charged with a similar manoeuvre may be cited here to make this point clearer. I have in mind Adorno's critique of the existentialist (primarily addressed to the work of Buber, Heidegger, and Jaspers) 'jargon of authenticity', particularly in the following general observation:

> The resonant directive of the jargon, that its thought should not be too strenuous, because otherwise it would offend the community, also becomes for these people the guarantee of a higher confirmation. This suppresses the fact that language itself – through its generality and objectivity – already negates the whole man, the particular speaking individual subject: the first price exacted by the subject is the essence of the individual. But through the appearance that the whole man, and not thought, speaks, the jargon pretends that, as a close-at-hand manner of communication, it is invulnerable to dehumanized mass communication – which is precisely what recommends it to everyone's enthusiastic acceptance. Whoever stands behind his words, in the way in which these words pretend, is safe from any suspicion about what he is at that very moment about to do: speak for others in order to palm something off on them.[30]

For Adorno 'the whole man' – existential being in-itself – is the abstraction to which existentialists seek to give a political voice, to derive a 'higher confirmation' from, at the expense of thought and the nature of language. The identity-based collective is a smaller abstraction which assumes similar proportions in identity-based political positions, and thereby in identity politics. Adorno's references to 'the essence of the individual' and to 'dehumanized mass communication' are themselves drawn from a critical jargon which does not need immediate elucidation. They are close enough to discussions of individuals and collectives, with both philosophical and sociological conventions, which I have referred to already, to be comprehensible.

If at the moment the presentation of that last point appears to be too abstruse, I hope that as I progress through Chapter 3, on 'Embodying Identity-Based Political Positions', the idea becomes clearer.

3
Embodying Identity-Based Political Positions

The argument of this chapter can be summarized as follows. Within different identity-based political positions a great deal of energy has gone into the debate between essentialism and social constructionism. In embracing different identity-based political positions through analogues and equivalences, social constructionist identity politics has derived from and has assumed the terms of that debate to maintain certain limits within itself, and has thereby constrained the potential and reach of social constructionist and anti-essentialist thinking. The logic of this is examined in the first section of this chapter. It is also maintained here that inordinate attention to the essentialism vs. social constructionism debate within identity-based political positions is a distraction from a deeper problem. This problem has to do with the logic of *embodiment* which works in both essentialist identity-based political positions and social constructionist ones. Because it works in the latter too, it slips through into the identity politics which tries to embrace different identity-based political positions, with worrying results. The distinctive logic of embodiment in identity-based political positions, which is transferred into social constructionist identity politics, is examined in the second section of this chapter. There have been and it is possible to have, I observe later, identity-based political positions that are not premised on being embodied; *this critique is particularly addressed to identity politics that embraces identity-based political positions insofar as such positions are embodied.*

Going beyond the social constructionist vs. essentialist bind

Two tasks are implicit in that preliminary summary of this chapter. First, the main points of the debate between essentialism and social constructionism are worth reviewing briefly. This is needed to clarify why I regard the focus on this debate in identity politics (as embracing different identity-based political positions) to be more distracting than illuminating. Second, elaboration of what I mean by embodying identity-based political positions is needed. It naturally becomes easier to present the notion of embodiment with the main points of the essentialism vs. social constructionism debate in mind. I begin with the first by briefly outlining what political essentialism usually alludes to, and then move to how social constructionism can be understood accordingly.

Political essentialism draws into political theory and practice the philosophical tradition that presumes that things have an intrinsic and unchangeable nature (have essences). This could involve discerning an essence of individuality for members of a polity (inalienable rights discourses derive from this), or an essence of humanity (arguments from human nature draw upon this), or discrete essences for politically recognizable collectives (this is relevant to identity-based political positions) which are politically determinative. Insofar as essentialism applies to identity-based political positions, the conviction that there is a biogenetically embedded character to how an identity-based collective behaves or conducts itself is usually asserted. This entails maintaining that there is something biogenetically embedded that unites all women, or all blacks, or all gays, or all members of a particular ethnicity or religion or nationality or even class (there are numerous examples of bloodlines being recruited to consolidate each of these), etc. That is, all members of such groups have common denominators or essential features that characterize every member of each of these groups, which are constitutionally engrained, probably inheritable, possibly perpetuated through biological kinship, sometimes anatomically manifest, and can always be called upon to explain group allegiance and the political behaviours or conducts of such groups as a whole and of each member therein. In the essentialist argument it appears then that there are inalienable and essential differences between different identity-based collectives, especially when these are mutually defined: racially black and white; male and female; homosexual and heterosexual; Jews and Gentile, etc. Unsurprisingly some of the most pernicious forms of racist, nationalist, sexist, homophobic politics are associated with essentialism. Identity-based political positions with emancipative aspirations are generally eager to either qualify their particular brands of essentialism or (usually) to distance themselves from essentialism altogether.

There are two ways of trying to adopt a decisive political stance vis-à-vis essentialist identity-based political positions. One, by examining the evidence for and against biogenetic embeddedness in identity-based collectives with a view to discerning whether such embedded characteristics should be taken into account for political purposes if discernible. Despite the unsavoury reputation of such essentialism, this has proved to be an inconclusive affair. Some areas of so-called evidence are easily shown to be self-fulfilling ideologically led affairs (e.g., a vast amount of research on the relationship between race and IQ, or research on gender and mathematical ability); some are shown to be indeterminately poised between social environment and 'natural' proclivity (e.g., varying athletic abilities of different races, archetypal behaviour according to sexual orientation); and a few identity-based collective features are shown to be biogenetically embedded in ways that cannot be politically neglected, if only as a matter of risk prevention and compensation (e.g., with regard to a range of female bodily experiences that men do not have access to, certain racial or ethnic groups that have a much higher probability of carrying certain genetically transmitted diseases than others). It is impossible to adopt a general attitude towards *all* forms of political essentialism on the grounds of existing evidence. Two, the political place of essentialism can also be gauged by examining the consequences of accepting biogenetic embeddedness in identity-based collectives for political purposes. From a political perspective, the most productive arguments have taken place in such a consequentialist vein – and, again, with inconclusive results. On the one hand, this has led to rejection of essentialist identity-based political positions because of the exclusions that are implicit in them. The exclusions of essentialist identity-based political positions have resulted in the violence and repression that dominant collectives have often exercised against minorities, opened up the possibility of minority identity-based political positions reflecting the characteristics of that which they seek to oppose, or released the possibility of a political ethos of unbridgeable fragmentations and petty fascisms. On the other hand, both emancipative and protectionist identity-based political positions often acknowledge the need for contingent and strategic essentialism – as, for instance, in a political assertion of pride or a bid for political recognition in the face of established odds.

What that brief summary of arguments shows is that these are muddy waters: for identity-based political positions the dangers of essentialism are well known, and so are its advantages and, in some (on the whole minor) respects, inevitability. The articulation of a sweeping anti-essentialism therefore is not a self-evident matter, but a construction itself which it is prudent to be aware of. Most importantly, the construction of comprehensive essentialism is complicit with comprehensive social constructionism: these polarize against each other so that both gather a kind of mutually defined and correlative dynamic which actually draws analysis away from the nuances of identity politics (I have called this a red herring above). My main argument here is that the mutually exacerbating spiral of the debate between essentialism and social constructionism, egging each other on (so to say) conceptually, draws attention away from the heart of the matter: that irrespective of that debate, and through both poles of that debate, identity politics embraces identity-based political positions that are *embodied*.

The over-determination of the polarization between essentialism and social constructionism is evidenced in a tendency on the part of anti-essentialists to conceptually over-endow essentialism. An example is probably the best way to convey this observation. Stephan Fuchs prefaces a sustained sociological and philosophical critique of essentialism with certain definitive formulations about what essentialism is and entails. These include the following consecutive statements:

(1) Essentialism searches for the intrinsic 'nature' of things as they are, in and of themselves.[1]
(2) Essentialism makes either/or distinctions, rather than variable distinctions in degree.[2]
(3) In essentialism, the preferred mode of operation is static typologies and rigid classifications, whose grids separate things that are everywhere, and under all circumstances, really separate.[3]
(4) [...] essentialism is the failure to allow for variation.[4]

It can be observed that each subsequent statement is a hardening of the formulation of essentialism in ways that remove it gradually from the field where political essentialism seems to apply. The first statement is roughly where I begin my summary of essentialist arguments above too. The second corresponds to the observation of mutually defined exclusions in identity-based political positions that I touch on above – but generalizes this in a puzzling way against variable distinctions of degree. Mutually defined exclusions following an either/or logic is widely evidenced in identity-based political terms (as in either black or white; either male or female; either straight or queer, etc.), but it is difficult to see why that should be regarded as being the same as not having variable distinctions of degree. In fact, it seems obvious that essentialism can fluidly apply to levels of political engagement with a significant variability of degree: for instance, one can be essentialist in a particular way insofar as she is a woman; and essentialist at the same time in a different way inso-far as she is also black; and again at the same time essentialist in a distinct way insofar as, say, she is lesbian, and so on. The same person can claim variable essentialist positions depending on what level of political engagement is demanded: as a feminist, as a black feminist, as a black les-bian feminist, as a black lesbian Christian working-class feminist … . It is, at any rate, clearly understood in philosophy that essentialism is related to level of conceptualization – one can discern a macrocosmic essence and a distinct microcosmic essence with reference to the same things – and there is every evidence that this occurs in political essentialism too. Having, however, over-endowed essentialism in this fashion in the second statement, Fuchs proceeds to concretize the asserted lack of variability in essentialism further in the third and fourth statements, by endowing essentialism with static typologies and failure in the face of variations. But essentialist typologies are anything but static: arguably, essentialist poli-tics is sustained by an endless proliferation of typologies in response to perceptions of variations in politically effective ways. The ongoing and long-standing persistence of political essentialism is inexplicable if its pro-cessive and responsive character is lost sight of, and if it is endowed with a static and unresponsive character. It may be apt to say that essentialist politics *resists* hybridity and miscegenation, but equally it also promptly absorbs these when it becomes expedient; so that it becomes possible to have an essentialist identity-based political position for transsexuals, bisexuals, mixed-race persons, mixed ethnicities, itinerant nationalities, etc. – or these can all be given a space in some essentialist schema.

Fuchs's kind of over-endowment of essentialism serves its purpose not in illuminating social and political phenomena which are currently rec-ognized and understood as manifesting political essentialism, but in enabling the polarization of its opposite – the variable, the 'networked', as its other. The formulation of essentialism is not derived with reference to the social and political field as available; the formulation is con-structed to enable a mutually defined opposite (concretizable ultimately as social constructionism) to spin out, and subsume attention in that mutually defined performance, so that the dialectical argument *becomes* (rather than *refers to*) the field.

The mutually defined polarization of essentialism and social construc-tionism in relation to identity-based political positions operates as much in formulating social constructionism as in formulating (and over-endowing) essentialism: they are part of the same game. To demonstrate how ideas of social constructionism fit into this picture I do not attempt to summarize the arguments in question, as I did for essentialism. Suffice to say, to a significant degree this has meant an inversion of the essentialist approach, along the lines of Marx's lucid words: 'The human essence is no abstraction inherent in each individual. In its reality it is the ensemble of social relations'.[5] Instead, I take up a couple of strong and particularistic formulations of social constructionism which convey this mode of conceptualizing identity-specific political positions more effectively than a summary of arguments. Social constructionism is necessarily sensitive, in its self-formulations, to the specific socio-cultural histories that it addresses and derives from. Both the following quotations are contextualized against the history and culture of race relations, primarily black and white, in the United States. Glenn Loury's summary of the process through which the social construction of racial identity becomes culturally and politically effective is exemplary:

A field of human subjects characterized by morphological variability comes through concrete historical experience to be partitioned into subgroups defined by some cluster of physical markers. Information-hungry agents hang expectations around these markers, beliefs that can, by processes I have discussed in some detail, become self-confirming. Meaning-hungry agents invest these markers with social, psychological, and spiritual significance. Race-markers come to form the core of personal and social identities. Narrative accounts of descent are constructed around them. And so groups of subjects, identifying with one another, sharing feelings of pride, (dis)honor, shame, loyalty, and hope – and defined in some measure by their holding these race-markers in common – come into existence. The vesting of reasonable expectation and ineffable meaning in objectively arbitrary markings on human bodies comes to be reproduced over the generations, takes on a social life of its own, seems natural and not merely conventional, and ends up having profound consequences for social relations among individuals in the raced society.[6]

Loury goes on in the final passages of his book to envisage a condition of race-blindness, but maintains the need to achieve race-egalitarianism before that. Similarly indicative (but with slightly different emphases) is Paul C. Taylor's statement of his 'radical constructionist' perspective of race, amidst a thoughtful philosophical analysis of the linguistic, historical, and metaphysical aspects of racism:

My view, which I promised to call 'radical constructionism,' extends the insights of social naturalism by emphasizing the array of conditions that connect the morphological prerequisites for racial identity to social goods like erotic and romantic interest. For the radical constructionist, our social practices create populations as well as breeding groups, by connecting certain bodies and bloodlines to certain locations and modes of treatment. On this view, races are probabilistically defined populations. If we pick out subsets of the US population by focusing on bodies and bloodlines in the way that race-thinking suggests, we'll find that the members of these subsets tend to be – *tend to be* – similarly situated with regard to certain social conditions, including the mechanisms of social stratification. Since these mechanisms assign meaning – a statistical relation to certain measures of social stratification, for example – to bodies and bloodlines, we can speak of them as racializing, and the populations they create as races.[7]

Taylor immediately contextualizes this constructionist characterization of modern race-thinking as rooted in white supremacism.

Now, both of these are strong statements of social constructionism which implicitly open up thinking and understanding of the issue to general consideration – and, as such, I am sympathetic to these. And it is because these are strong statements that (even) their being bound in the essentialism vs. social constructionism debate is all the more indicative. Despite their implicit opening up of the issue against the exclusionary tendency of a particular essentialist political position, by being bound to a position against this particular form of essentialism, these statements limit that opening up. I need to be cautious here: I do not wish to suggest that such social constructionism thereby plays into essentialism itself (it laudably does not), but it does limit itself – its field of application and effect, its rational potential – by being locked in a continuous struggle against the pull of a particular essentialism. This is what happens in both quotations. Both deliberately and systematically seek to invert the explanative logic of race essentialism: instead of seeing social effects as being caused by or explicable through underlying essentialized racial distinctions, these explain the genesis and pervasiveness of race-thinking as *built* (comprehensively) upon social and material interests which have no intrinsic relation to biogenetic constitution (bodies and bloodlines, cluster of physical markers). Put differently, biogenetic constitutions are, in these views, instrumentalized and disseminated through and in the interests of agents and processes that are not biogenetically constituted. So far so good – and the argument more or less stops there. The point of course is that it need not and should not. Social constructionism of this sort cannot contain itself to a particularistic field; the bent of this explanative discourse is towards the unravelling of other constructions, and the relation between the construction of race and the construction of other political subgroups (into identities, strata, alignments), and of constructionism itself. Its emancipative impetus seems able to embrace more than is addressed or acknowledged, just as the essentialism it opposes denies the possibility of an increasing embrace. The self-imposed limitation of what is addressed and acknowledged leaves questions behind: why is social constructionism particularly addressed to race? Can it be addressed to other mappings of humanity? If so, what is the basis of social constructionism that enables that reach (the general applicability of materialist analysis? The comprehensiveness of rationality? The universality of certain ethical norms? ...)? At least an acknowledgement of that reach, it seems to me, is left tantalizingly unsaid.

As it stands here, these social constructionist statements confine their emancipative gestures within the 'raced society', the constructed racialized population, to race-identified subjects, as arbitrarily as the essentialist politics they implacably oppose exclude racial others. Actually more arbitrarily, since the logic of this selection is determined by the preexistence of essentialized racial politics and against the grain of its own – always tendentiously expansive – reach. That can be generalized: social constructionism as it stands now arbitrarily limits itself by pitching itself against the logic of particularization that is rooted in specific identity-based essentialist politics, and therefore along those lines of particularization of essentialist identity-based collectives. Thus, at present, against racial essentialism there is the social constructionism that addresses race, against feminist essentialism there is the social constructionism that addresses women, and so on. There are, in fact, different social constructionisms that are locked in battle against different identity-based essentialisms, each confined to their own areas of exchange, each defined by its opposite and spiralling into inward-looking autonomous discourses ... expanding to an ever-growing dynamism of identity-based political positions that are inwardly focused. These discrete identity-based social constructionisms are brought together under identity politics, can be brought together only because these are social constructionist, but are nevertheless held apart as separate areas caught in a bind with different essentialisms. After all, identity politics is such because it recognizes different identity-based political positions and their different imperatives as such, and tries to find common ground or a coherent space through that recognition.

To be really politically effective, social constructionism should acknowledge its own expansive mechanism. That is, social constructionism

should break away from engagement simply with particular essentialisms – with their manifestations in specific identity-based political
positions – and engage critically with that which contains those particularities (by discerning analogues and equivalences) to reify them: social
constructionist identity politics itself. Ultimately, as observed above,
political essentialism is able, despite its exclusionist bent, to respond to
variations and seep through them. Social constructionism can only
finally stamp out that divisive persistence by expanding beyond particular identity-based essentialisms in a bind with identity-based anti-
essentialisms, and overcoming their shadow in social constructionist
identity politics itself.

It is with regard to the limitations of social constructionism that
obtain now, derived from its being constantly pitched against essentialism, *apropos* identity-based political positions that Kenneth J. Gergen
(2001) perceives a 'love affair between identity politics and social constructionism'.[8] By 'identity politics' here he means different identity-
based political positions. The 'love affair' alludes to the manner in
which social constructionism has operated persistently in tandem with
and against essentialism *within* different identity-based political positions to strengthen their effectiveness and often give them a radical
force. And it is with regard to the limitations of this kind of social constructionist invigoration of identity-based political positions that he
goes on to call for an extension of social constructionism towards 'relational politics' (of which I have more to say in the next chapter). On a
related note, it is pretty obvious that the enormous steps taken by different identity-based political positions, and thereby identity politics,
especially since the 1980s, were derived from the social constructionism
of postmodernist thinking. Many identity-based political formulations
and identity politics in general have together come to be regarded as
coeval with postmodernism's focus on discourse construction and the
constitutiveness of discourses; interrogation of holistic and universal
systems and ideologies; assertion of the centrality of difference; and
focus on the provisional, pluralistic, contradictory, or ambivalent, and
slippery nature of social, political, and cultural existence (if something
as unitary as existence can be posited at all). In other words, identity-
based political positions and identity politics have to a great degree
become jointly associated with the implicitly social constructionist formulations of Derrida, Foucault, Althusser, and a few others. It is not
uninteresting that a collection of essays, edited by Nicholson and
Seidman (1995), registering the impact of postmodernism on 'identity
politics' (meaning identity-based political positions here),[9] is also a

testimonial to the fillip that it gave 'identity politics' (in the sense of social constructionist identity politics here) from *within* different identity-based political positions. The volume in question was presented in the title as going 'beyond identity politics' (meaning, I think, essentialist identity-based political positions), and included essays by well-known theorists/activists of specific identity-based political positions (Kwame Anthony Appiah, Rosemary Hennessy, Shane Phelan, and others) as well as by proponents of the overarching social constructionist identity politics (Chantal Mouffe, Stanley Aronowitz, and others). The bind of social constructionism vs. essentialism has meant that identity-based political positions and social constructionist identity politics have cohered in a positively friendly and mutually enhancing fashion. Social constructionism is seldom as strongly and rebelliously presented as in the quotations from Loury and Taylor given above; anti-essentialist social constructionist identity politics has become a broad school where different identity-based political positions now rest as happily as they ever did with essentialism.

But I am pre-empting myself, for these observations should rightly belong to the next chapter on 'Analogues and Equivalences'. There are more immediate issues to address.

The logic of embodiment

In this second section, I elaborate on the notion of *embodying* identity-based political positions, and therefore the logic of embodiment in social constructionist identity politics. This elaboration itself consists in a social constructionist approach to identity-based political positions which, without losing sight of the particularity of specific identity-based political positions, looks *across* them, because that is what *happens* in identity politics.

In fact, let me start off here by registering in a sweeping and panoptic fashion some of the particularities of specific identity-based political positions (the number of exchanges and debates involved here are so prolific that references would be redundant). Biogenetically embedded identifications of individuals as belonging to identity-based collectives, though theoretically often discredited, continue in many ways to be the most powerful mode of such identification. This has as much to do with objectively arbitrary markers on the body as with evidence or claims of bloodlines. Gender- and race-centred collectives are most strongly associated with biogenetic attributes/claims: even when the arbitrariness of such attributes is accepted, and the constructedness of power discourses around them is understood, the anatomized perception and claim has its strength. Even for the strongly constructionist feminist the question of whether a man can be a feminist is an agonizing one, at best conceded under logical duress (and in a conditional fashion) and more often deferred on the grounds of pragmatism; and this is similar for the question of whether a white person can adopt a black emancipative position. But the reach of biogenetic embeddedness is obviously larger and more pervasive in the construction of collective identities for political purposes. Behaviouristic biogeneticism is a not insignificant factor where the evidence of anatomy and bloodlines is unclear, often introduced at the level of metaphor which can blend into materiality. I do not just mean the kind of thing Nazi race-detectives did when they looked for the well-disguised Jew. Biogenetic embeddedness in behaviour is sometimes attributed and accepted in the identification of being gay or lesbian. National (when it is not understood in terms of racial homogeneities) or ethnic (when that is not just a euphemism for race, but refers to collectives in an environment which is culturally and locationally specifiable) identity is often presented as being a matter of akinness or heritage in a biogenetically metaphorical fashion. Class is often understood as an inheritance too with biogenetic echoes, and upper classes have often explicitly claimed bloodlines as determinative. The proselytizing or non-proselytizing nature of religions is a matter of biogenetic import. Biogenetic considerations are simply too intimately entwined with, or constructed into, every social and institutional function to be easily overlooked, from naming to schooling to property rights to death and thereafter.

The protean forms of biogenetic attributions/claims in identity-based collectives apart, there are of course other very important ways of identifying individual members as part of specific identity-based political positions – in some cases, rather more important. Cultural practices and rituals that are assumed by individuals, are presented and received accordingly, have a like role. Speaking a particular language, dressing in a particular fashion, following certain cultural rituals or codes of conduct, being located within a geopolitical space, etc., are key in the attribution/claiming of national or ethnic identity. These are also hugely significant in the construction and formation and assertion of racial and gender identities: as in using Ebonics or doing rap, in using female pronouns, in wearing hijab, cross-dressing, etc. The great importance of discerning a history of cultural expressions and codes, inventing and performing a series of cultural practices with a view to making visible a significant and proud collective presence is at the heart of gay- and lesbian-identity-based political positions. Religious identity is thoroughly intermeshed with such practice, following both inward and outward religious rituals and forms. This mode of attributing/claiming a position within an identity-based collective can work in as tendentiously exclusive a fashion as biogenetic embedding. Can a Christian speak authoritatively about Islam and on behalf of Muslims? Can a straight man be a participant in gay culture? These are as agonizing as asking whether a man can be a feminist, and are conceded far less often. Can someone who has left his/her country of origin for good be considered *of* that country, and if so in what sense? No answer to this can be conclusive.

Shouldering against and sometimes with these modes of attributing/ claiming collective-identity membership, exercising identity-based political positions, is the unqualifiable performative articulation of identity. I use "performative" here more or less in J.L. Austin's sense,[10] but less saying-as-doing and more saying-as-being. The performative articulation of being part of a collective identity is of the greatest significance when it is exercised not simply through a socialization process, or through an objectively visible biogenetic marker. This has a particular bearing on the attribution/claim of religious identity (especially with regard to proselytizing religions). To say 'I am Christian' or 'I am Muslim' is to assume religious identity in a way which cannot be easily reduced to any kind of biogenetic association or institutional form – it means something like 'I *believe* in the metaphysical truth of the Gospels/Qu'ran', with the emphasis on 'believe' as the unqualifiable performative articulation of just having faith. There is no point asking (as Kierkegaard pertinently observed) why or how to the statement of belief, the assumption of faith: belief simply unnegotiably, inexplicably, unqualifiably is there or is not there, everything else is after the fact. The performative articulation of religious identity can extend into other kinds of collective identity attributions/claims: national identity has, it is sometimes observed, powerful sacerdotal roots (though nationalism has more emphatically been theorized in secular ways, as imagined in various ways, deriving from print culture, the consolidation of modernist rationality, etc.). But it is not just the assumption of religious identity which is strongly based on unqualifiable performative articulation. Other identity-based political positions are exercised on those terms too. And since this is a mode of collective identity attribution that appears to be comparatively less remarked and debated, I am inclined to throw in just one quotation in this panoptic view of identity-based collective particularities – an elegant expression of the unqualifiably performative articulation of being Queer:

Actual sex with another man can thus be for the individual man exclusive or occasional, permanent or temporary, and this is likely to

be even more complex, fluid, variegated, fleeting and even unno-
ticed, in relation to sexual attraction, fantasy and speculation. A
strong notion of queers runs counter to this – queer is something you
are, constitutively, rather than something you might do (have done),
feel (have felt), mainly, sometimes, once, maybe. It is this latter
range and fluidity (which goes far beyond another fixing notion, the
bisexual) that analytical notions of homoeroticism and Queer seek to
address (and throughout my discussion capital letter Queer will indi-
cate the latter conceptualization).[11]

The conceptualization of capital letter Queer here, as distinct from
queer, is the conceptualization of an unqualifiable performative articulation. It is also illuminatingly that which concretizes the assumption of
a queer identity-based political position. Withdrawing the unqualifiable
performative articulation would entail another unqualifiable performative articulation (therefore always possible), and a betrayal of the
identity-based political position from which the withdrawing is performed. That is like someone who said 'I am gay' yesterday, saying 'I am
straight' today. Similar to someone who said 'I am a Muslim' last year,
announcing 'I am a Christian' this year.

The use of Austin's sense of 'performative', rooted as it is in the
neuterness of analytical philosophy, possibly does not convey the sheer
investment of identification, the totality of identification, which the
unqualifiably performative articulation of an identity conveys. Perhaps
some of this is conveyed if the unqualifiable performative articulation
is conflated with the sense (not the precise content) that Derrida allo-
cates to Heidegger in presenting 'being' as a 'transcendental signified' –
whereby, according to Derrida, 'the thought of being, as the thought of
this transcendental signified, is manifested above all in the voice: in a
language of words [*mots*]'.[12] Derrida's observation is regarding the linguistic logic that constitutes Heideggerian formulation; the *emphasis* of
signification as being there, seems to me analogous to what happens in
the unqualifiable performative articulation of identity. Whatever identity is claimed – whatever membership in a specific identity-based
collective is voiced/assumed – takes on at the self-same moment the
proportions of a 'transcendental signification'. The member who does
this becomes thereby embodied as/for/of/with regard to that identity-
based collective. But I have not elaborated on the notion of embodying identity-based political positions yet, to which I turn immediately.

By *embodying* an identity-based political position, I mean an aggregate
of the processes mentioned above, whereby an individual is identified as

(attributed as/claims to be/is claimed as being) a member of a specific identity-based collective (or set of collectives), and can therefore assume (with, for, to, on behalf of, with regard to that collective) the relevant identity-based political position effectively. At least, that is the sense in which 'embodying' is understood for the purposes of this study. Embodying an identity-based political position entails some such processes as presenting and/or being perceived as presenting, claiming and/or being understood to claim biogenetic association (usually to do with bodies and bloodlines, but also in metaphorically anatomized ways), association with cultural practices and rituals (in ways that can be exercised indicatively by persons), and unqualifiably performative articulations (as self-announcements). The conviction that individuals who thus embody an identity-based political position are the ones who can assume that identity-based political position effectively hardly needs an explanation. Embodying and assuming in relation to identity-based political positions are mutually sustaining aspects of this sort of politics. Thereby, the individual and the collective can merge into an identity-based configuration; by this logic, speaking about oneself becomes speaking about others who are identifiably similar, and expressing the individual becomes akin to expressing the collective, and individual acts becomes easily signified as of collective moment. Embodying thus, in other words, renders politics a simpler matter of constantly reductively signifying that which is of individual moment as being of immediate collective significance, and at the same time constantly expansively signifying that which is of collective import as being of immediate individual interest. It allows political theory and practice to proceed by a wilful denial of both ends of that time-honoured paradox: the coexistence of the inconvenient uniqueness of individuals on the one hand, and the unwieldy commonality of humanity on the other hand.

In the broadest sense, embodying a political position can be understood as registering a political presence. The embodiment of identity-based political positions is a particular mode of political embodiment – with peculiar implications that I am leading up to. The distinctness of the above-described mode of embodying identity-based political positions from other modes of political embodiment can be gauged by contemplating instances of the latter. The most familiar set of politically embodied relations – the body politic as related to the bodies of rulers and the bodies of subjects – was most incisively analysed by Foucault,[13] and does not need regurgitation. In a similar fashion, attempts at embodying the political agency of the populace as crowds or mass or multitude by Elias

Cannetti and José Ortega y Gasset[14] can be pondered. Ortega y Gasset's resentful reflections on this are also of tangential interest here in presenting an unusual dismissal of identity-based political positions by presenting these as disguised individualism. In a curious reflection on 'minorities', he maintains:

> In those groups which are neither mass nor multitude, the effective cohesion of the members is based on some desire, idea or ideal, which in itself alone exclude the majority of the people. In order to form a minority – of whatever kind it may be – it is first necessary that each member separate himself from the multitude for some *special*, relatively personal, reason. His agreement with the others who form the minority is, therefore, secondary, posterior to having adopted an individual attitude, having made himself *singular*; therefore, there is an agreement not to agree with others, a coincidence in not coinciding.[15]

The flawed argument here is that not to be in a political majority has to be a singular position. This is not only nonsense in itself, it is difficult to understand why it is at all proposed. It is possible that it is proposed for purely strategic reasons: the counterpoint of the embodied mass or multitude (especially when regarded as a political threat) is most conveniently the embodied political individual – anything that intervenes detracts from the anti-democratic rhetoric. It is, in brief, a strategy to limit discussion, to maximize the distance between individual agency and democratic agency (embodied in the mass).

Ortega y Gasset's views are irrelevant here, but that strategy of limiting discussion and communication is of some interest. The embodiment involved in identity-based political positions has a great deal to do with strategies of limiting communication. The questions (a very few of many such possible questions) I have remarked upon above in registering some of the particularities of identity-based political positions are all to do with limiting what one can or cannot do, should or should not apply him/herself to: Can a man be a feminist? Can a white person adopt a black emancipative position? Can a Christian speak authoritatively about Islam and on behalf of Muslims? Can a straight man be a participant in gay culture? Can someone who has left his/her country of origin for good be considered *of* that country, and if so in what sense? Such questions mark the tensions that arise through the embodiment of particularly social constructionist identity-based political positions, promise agonizing and inconclusive debate, lead most often to grudging concessions or pragmatic exclusions or provisional/ conditional inclusions. What these questions threaten is the logic of embodying identity-based political positions. The embodiment of an identity-based political position through the unqualifiable performative articulation is constitutively outside interrogation and criticism from those who cannot embody themselves as such. It is just impossible to cross those boundaries because they just *are* embodied in ways that cannot be qualified, elaborated, explained, or taken apart. The tension of not being able to discuss them is taut as a guitar string there, but out of tune. The logic of accepting these embodiments of identity-based political positions has a natural direction. If embodying and exercising an identity-based political position is a relatively paradox-free and immediately articulable and sustainable process, then it is best to maintain certain limitations to discussion and communication – it is best for those who can embody their identity-based political positions to exercise them, and for others to exercise their's, and for all to contain any desire to question what they cannot embody and simply accept what those who can embody, say and do in that regard – sure, it is good to understand each other (after all political efficiency demands maximum recognition), but do not question (and certainly do not challenge or refute) each other's views unless you can embody the same identity-based political position. Dissent and interrogation is best contained among discreet groups of identity-based collectives whose members embody their collectives, otherwise let all identity-based collectives agree not to turn a critical scrutiny on each other and let live. The raising of and agonizing around those and such questions and articulations have to do with the logic of embodying identity-based political positions, especially in a social constructionist mould, and maintaining them in an anxiety-ridden fragile environment.

Part of the anxiety of social constructionist identity-based political positions comes from the recognition that such limitations of communication smack of essentialist exclusion, with all its deeply reactionary and violent history, portending a world of a million fascisms now.

This is a misplaced anxiety, because limiting communication in social constructionism by the logic of embodiment is quite different from excluding through the essentialist logic. Political essentialism does not really allow the above questions to be raised. From an essentialist identity-based political position the answers to such questions are known before they can be raised, and the answer is always in the negative. There is no hesitation there: no need for debates, no uncomfortable concessions are necessary, no conditional allowances are permissible, no plea for strategic contingency need be offered. The kind of limitation of communication, critical engagement, interrogation, contestation described for identity-based political positions above is peculiar to the social constructionist perspective therein. It is less than the absolute and resolute exclusions of essentialist identity-based political positions; it could be thought of as the dispersal of that sort of exclusion into something more fluid – but nonetheless restrictive, limiting. Indeed, social constructionism is consensually now the dominant core of embodied identity-based political positions, whereby embodied agents can examine and analyse their social constructedness within the precincts of their identity-based collectives (and differ with each other there) and present their debates for the passive consumption of others who embody their other identity-based political positions, and should be polite enough not to focus too critically interrogative a glance on what is offered them from elsewhere. The logic of embodiment in fact sits particularly firmly within anti-essentialist social constructionist identity politics, which contains all those separately embodied identity-based political positions in a happy acquiescence of communication- and criticism-limiting differences, held together by equivalences and analogues (but more of that in the next chapter). But still of course those questions do exist and can be raised, so that these discrete zones of critical engagement and communication are constantly held against each other in an anxiety-ridden fragile environment.

The limitations on communication generated by the embodiment of identity-based political positions are always justified by that which gives identity-based political positions stability (and this also usefully distances that whiff of essentialism): the perception of being threatened or being marginalized. I have mentioned this before, associating being threatened with dominant identity-collectives and marginalization with the politics of identity-collectives that are dominated. That makes some sense, because it is evident that in the prevailing ethos of social constructionist identity politics there is a constant proliferation and reproduction of marginalized identity-based political positions. So prodigiously fertile has this proliferation been that the essentialized dominant collective itself is beginning to become blurred. The essentialized dominant was easily recognized in the early 1980s when identity politics in the sense used here came to be formulated and disseminated: it was something like the Western white upper/middle-class heterosexual male. This abstract entity's ability to have a critical and politically effective and ideologically justifiable position was entirely emptied. This empty abstract entity could only receive instruction from embodied agents in marginal identity-collectives, and simply could not critically engage or interrogate anything with political effect. Obviously there is no such entity, and the critical faculty is irrepressible, and the intelligent and ideologically sensitive existence of Western white heterosexual middle-class men, and indeed of any other rational individual (yes, rational – meaning able to understand, think, critically respond, question, communicate) itself raises some of those questions above, and keeps the anxiety-ridden fragile environment in place. Now this essentialized dominant is less often invoked; there are just marginalized embodied social constructionist identity-based political positions in restricted communication with each other and in ferment within themselves. Identity politics contains them. Perhaps identity politics is now a non-essentializable and non-embodiable abstraction that can be regarded as dominant. But, more of that in the next two chapters.

The logic of embodiment, I suggested above, is a dispersal of the exclusions of essentialism away from that and towards a generalization of limitations on communication and critical engagement. Limitations on communication spread out across different embodied identity-based political positions. I have already mentioned in the previous chapter that identity-based political positions are inherently unstable. The limitations on communication are spread out through the constantly emerging and disappearing fissures of this instability, and the constantly emerging and disappearing consolidations of embodiment. The constraints on free communication and critical engagement are thus constantly spread out – like butter on hot toast – but never erased. In the logic of embodiment, constraint on communication becomes a continuous condition of social constructionist political theory and practice. The black man's race politics can be listened to but should not be critically interrogated and undermined by the white man or woman. However, the black man's race politics can be effectively challenged by the black woman's feminist-race politics, which should not be interrogated beyond a point by either the black man or the white woman. The white woman's feminist politics can also be challenged by the black woman's race-feminist politics, but restraint is needed in the opposite direction. The black Muslim woman opens up a new dimension of embodiments and possibilities and restrictions of engagement, the poor black lesbian woman yet another. The Asian (in both American and British senses) person has certain embodied prerogatives, which the black or white man cannot really trespass very far upon, and Asian men and women have different prerogatives of where they should and should not critically engage ... and particular class and religious and national and ethnic and other identity embodiments open up new restraints and limited fields of critical engagements ... and so on, to form an enormously complex intermeshing, dimming and brightening, surfacing and drowning, of embodiments and consequent limitations on and restrictions of critical engagement and interrogation and communication of identity-based political positions, to encompass the entire field of social constructionist identity politics.

This fluidity and spreading of constraints is, however, always more than the politics of recognizing unique individuals as such and less than the politics of recognizing the commonality of humanity as a whole. These two ends are not enunciable in this arena at all, except as unqualifiable platitudes (of the 'universal human rights' sort) and tautologies (of the 'I am entitled to my opinion' sort). These *are* excluded from critical engagement; dual monoliths on the horizon that are dimly visible through the lenses of different identity-based political positions, the ultimate constraints.

Grasping the logic of embodiment as it operates with regard to specific identity-based political positions within social constructionist identity politics helps us to understand certain kinds of discomfort in the prevailing ethos. When one comes across a note of misgiving such as the following, expressing frustration about the:

> assumption that a person's racial or ethnic identity and views are one and the same. If people found what I said sympathetic or useful to blacks, I must be black. If minority women were frustrated or disappointed by an administrative decision, I, in my white skin, must be racist.[16]

I do not think we can infer that the author is accusing all those who have made these assumptions of biological essentialism. In fact this comes from a determinedly social constructionist position which is assured that the environment which produces these assumptions is a predominantly salutary social constructionist one. These misgivings, it seems to me, are about the logic of embodiment rather than about political essentialism.

But here is the key point: *the logic of embodiment ineradicably spreads a series of limitations on critical engagement and political communication through identity-based political positions, within social constructionist identity politics. The entire business undermines free political analysis and discussion and communication and exchange.* That is what embodying an identity-based political position means in this study.

The embodiment of different identity-based political positions characterizes political theory and practice in the prevailing ethos in interesting ways. One mode that demands attention is the sudden burst of
interest in bodies as a tangible aspect of em-*bodying* identity-based
political positions in the last decades of the 20th century. It is after all
identity markers on the body and bloodlines in the body, clothes on
the body and languages wrapping the body and the placement of the
body in institutions and geopolitical locations and the presence or
availability of the body in cultural and ritual practices, and mouths on
bodies announcing apparently with their whole bodies at stake their
unqualifiable performative articulations, that is, the stuff of embodying
specific identity-based political positions. The body is that usefully
fixed signifier which can be endlessly reiterated with different inflexions for different embodiments of identity-based political positions.
And endlessly reiterated it is. Books and papers on bodies with a deep –
almost mystical and yet tangible – political resonance occupy growing
numbers of shelves and indexes across academic humanities and social
sciences. The sophistication and numerousness of body-analysis that
concretizes and disseminates the embodiment of identity-based political positions is such that it would not be possible to dwell on this at
length here. But some sense of this can be conveyed by taking up a couple of characteristic instances in an illustrative fashion.

When the logic of embodiment takes the turn of becoming focused
on the trope of the body, the whiff of essentialism – that is obviously
not a part of this kind of social constructionism – turns up again. The
focus on anatomy and bloodlines in essentialist identity-based political
positions seems to become associated with the materiality of the body,
and naturally the distinction – the social constructivist validity of this
embodiment – has to be announced. These announcements (there are
numerous) are always of interest because these expose the strategy of
limiting communication clearly. The following quotation from Rosi
Braidotti could be taken as symptomatic of a larger discursive moment
in political thinking that accepts the logic of embodiment within social
constructivism and focuses it on bodies:

> The embodiedness of the subject is a form of bodily materiality, not
> of the natural, biological kind. I take the body as the complex inter-
> play of highly constructed social and symbolic forces: it is not an
> essence, let along a biological substance, but a play of forces, a sur-
> face of intensities, pure simulacra without originals. This 'intensive'
> redefinition of the body situates it within a complex interplay of

social and affective forces. This is also a clear move away from the psychoanalytic idea of the body as a map of semiotic inscriptions and culturally enforced codes. I see it instead as a transformer and a relay point for the flow of energies: a surface of intensities.[17]

This is an alluringly sophisticated distinction, but also a puzzling one. The redefinition offered here, whereby bodies are seen as 'pure *simulacra* without originals', 'a *surface* of intensities', 'a complex interplay of highly *constructed* social and *symbolic* forces', does not seem to leave much place for understanding why they should continue to be regarded as material – what does 'bodily *materiality*' mean here? Braidotti sticks admirably with this redefinition in the rest of her book, and offers interesting analyses of the anxieties and prejudices attached to the politics of sexual difference, and how these manifest themselves through significations of bodies, and the dangers that these anxieties and prejudices raise and how they should be redressed by the proper application of this redefinition – and nowhere does it become clear why any of this should be regarded as connected to bodily materiality. There is no suggestion anywhere that bodies bleed when they are cut, starve when they are hungry, suffer when they are whipped, sweat when they labour, are aroused when they are caressed, etc. In presenting her thoughts on political dispossessions and repossessions in that anti-essentialist constructionist vein, Braidotti might have had in mind that under all the social constructionism and discursive manoeuvres those political dispossessions and repossessions apply to and affect the visceral existence of individual bodies being perceived and articulated socially, and therefore what she says matters, and therefore 'bodily materiality' – but she does not say so, and it is far from obvious that this is what she had in mind. It seems very much more likely that she regards what she presents as the redefined body *as* the material body too: that the political abstraction *is* an articulation of, on behalf of, for, with regard to, to the politically embodied body – the abstract *is* in itself the material. This dislocates materialism not only from essentialist and psychoanalytical constructions, as she says, but also from the Marxist (which she touches on later) – or any other understandably materialist – political position. It is, however, analogous to the existentialist position in a limited way, at least to Adorno's understanding of that position.

This becomes clearer in other expressions of embodied body-centred thinking that concretizes (or apparently *materializes*) social constructionist identity-based political positions. A familiar agenda-setting understanding of embodied thinking, with reference to its significance for the continuation of identity politics (as understood here), in the words of Jamilah Ahmed can be contemplated here:

> The task of articulating the body ('the other' and/or 'the female') requires an interrogation of how the concept is framed within the language of sociology. A consideration of textual strategies enables a more embodied concept of the self to develop, and therefore challenges the assumption that a body marked by 'otherness' must necessarily occupy a position of weakness. Bodily markers of difference, and signifiers of 'otherness' (the body, the female, race, and difference), can instead offer a means of reaching new epistemological possibilities for an embodied self: the body can be explored as a platform for one's 'being-in-the-world'.[18]

Again, materiality seems invested in 'textual strategies' and 'epistemological possibilities' in a curious way that is expected to be politically enabling. But here the reason for that investment (and disinvestment from the visceral) is clearer: it is the rhetorical strategy that will allow marginalized identity-based political positions to overcome their marginality by positively *being* what they are, and speaking what they are. The line from the existentialist 'being-in-the-world' and the contemporary identity-based political position's embodied persons is drawn clearly here. Like Adorno, I feel tempted to note that as the existentialists tried to present the whole man and not thought speaking, in the identity politics that contains such embodied identity-based political positions apparently the whole identi(ty)fied person and not thought speaks. A similar 'jargon of authenticity' is produced. Only the existentialist jargon tried to break all limits on critical engagement and communication, and the jargon of embodied (literally em-*bodied*) identity-based political positions instils and disseminates limits in all directions. All the more so because, as Jamilah Ahmed noted earlier, from the latter perspective none can speak, think, critically contemplate anything without being understood as doing so with their bodies: 'the researcher *must* recognize the multiple subject positions that are evoked by the presence of their own body and the materiality of their fieldwork'[19] (my emphasis). Em-*bodiedness* becomes here the a priori condition of thought and is therefore inevitably contained in thought. Necessarily those who do not embody a particular identity-based political position can only attend to the political pronouncements of those who can within strict critical limits, and only critically engage openly within identity-based political positions that they can embody. But this process has to unfold without allowing a complete ghettoization of different identity-based collectives. A constant awareness of limits and others holds the whole field of identity politics together, and brings up uncomfortable questions and anxieties about avoiding essentialism and being constructionist.

Un- (not dis-) embodied identity-based political positions

I have mentioned in passing that I do not think social constructionist identity-based political positions necessarily need to follow the logic of embodiment, need to be em-*bodied*, as described above. In other words, I do not think identity-based political positions have to lead up to and be contained within social constructionist identity politics, within a field constituted by ever-present but well-spread and fluid limitations of communication and critical engagement. Identity-based political positions are possible within a field of open communication and without limit on critical engagement, in a matrix of social constructionist thinking that is beyond social constructionist identity politics. That the prevalence and pervasiveness of identity politics makes embodiment of identity-based political positions seem inevitable and desirable, at some expense to its democratic pretensions and the obviously always-open possibilities of critical engagement, is a characterizing feature of our time and ethos. It is not my business in this chapter to speculate on why this has come to be so, but to register that it has. If it evidently has come to be so, there are sound political reasons and vested interests at work, which I take up later in this study (in Chapter 4 and Chapter 5). What is immediately called for though, is some indication of what sort of identity-based political positions do not have to be embodied.

To register the very great social and political importance of prejudice and discrimination on the basis of race, gender, sexual orientation, class, ethnicity, nationality, religion, etc. – to recognize the deep roots and wide prevalence of the malaise of discrimination and prejudice – to chart the manner in which such discrimination and prejudice manifests itself and impacts upon societies where they are present – and to seek to oppose/attempt to erase prejudice and discrimination accordingly and demand redress – requires no more than unlimited critical engagement in terms of some sort of egalitarian commitment, or some desire for widespread well-being rather than pockets of prosperity, or some adherence to principles of justice, however contextually or universally apprehended. This sounds like a rather old-fashioned sentiment. And so indeed it is. Its appearance as old-fashioned is no more than another indication of the institutionalization of identity politics. Behind that bald sentiment lies a whole history of critical engagement and exchange which is now often regarded as finished, a precursor to embodied identity-based political positions contained within social construction-ist identity politics. To a great extent this allegedly finished business exercised a social constructionist view too, and attended to power rela-tions that negotiated through and with discourses: attended to ideas of representation (stereotyping, distancing, etc.), misrepresentation (infantalizing, primitivizing, etc.), and non-representation (silencing, erasing the presence of, etc.). And to a great extent such old-fashioned views extended to identity-based political positions with *materialist* analysis that was visceral and not embodied: sensitive to economic pos-session and dispossession, physical suffering and oppression, and straightforwardly set about to alleviate and erase them. The appearance of embodied identity-based political positions within identity politics, primarily in the 1980s, swept these modes of enunciating and acting upon identity-based political positions into a historicized whole precur-sive to itself. When Stuart Hall announced the need for 'new ethnicities' to unfold[20] – in many ways the announcement of identity-based politi-cal positions' incorporation into identity politics in Britain – he knew and therefore stated that this was necessary because representation-focused identity-based politics was old-fashioned, a thing of the past. Similar closures given to the second wave feminism of Simone de Beauvoir, Betty Friedan, Joan Kelly, Sandra Gilbert and Susan Gubar, Marilyn French, and others, also mark the incorporation of feminist identity-based political positions into the logic of embodiment and identity politics. In fact, insofar as a sweeping statement can be histori-cally applicable, it can be reasonably maintained that identity-based political positions prior to the 1980s were either biologically essentialist (sometimes) or social constructionist in a way that did *not* entail embodying that political position (frequently). Somewhere in the course of the last three decades of the 20th century embodied identity-based political positions and therefore social constructionist identity politics has captured the field comprehensively.

There is another way of taking up identity-based political positions that does not entail embodiment. One of the aspirations of embodied identity-based political positions (as described above) is that they seek to assert themselves through their members as embodying the relevant identity-based collective to perpetuity. Thus, the aspiration of an embodied feminist identity-based political position is to politically assert the agency of women as embodying the collective of women to perpetuity, and of embodied black identity-based political positions to assert the agency of blacks as embodying the black collective ever after, and so on. Each aspires to a condition of appropriate and lasting political recognition of its members *as* embodying that collective-identity. In a sense, therefore, the bent of embodied identity-based political positions is the reification of identity-based collectives (separately or in some combination), and the end of social constructionist identity politics as a whole is the recognition of all political positions as embodied on behalf of some identity-based collective or the other – the ideal of a world of well-balanced differences. The ideal is a world where politics can only be and is perpetually allowed to be spoken as one speaks one's own embodied identity-collective, and otherwise one should mind one's own (or one's identity-collective's) business. The identity-based political position that is resolved not to embody and assert a membership's identity-based collective for political recognition to perpetuity, but to dissolve itself when appropriate social and political arrangements (in ways that can be reasonably envisaged in specific contexts) come to exist, can be thought of as an identity-based political position that refuses the logic of embodiment. This can, of course, only be a rigorously social constructionist position: not a social constructionist identity politics, but a broader social constructionist politics. Here the identity-based political position is a gestural step taken by anyone with the critical were withal and ability to do so, with socially constructed identity-based collectives (who are subject to prejudice, discrimination, and systematic dispossession) in sight rather than embodied. It is a step that opens critical engagement and communication and does not limit these.

The latter kind of un-embodied (not *dis*-embodied, not embodied, and certainly not em-*bodied*) approach to identity-based political positions underlies affirmative action/positive discrimination wherever it has been instituted (e.g., with regard to scheduled castes and tribes in India, or with regard to race-defined groups in the USA or South Africa). But this is a tricky issue. Affirmative action is often regarded as complicit with the logic of embodiment, if not returning biological essentialism. The strands of the numerous debates here need separate and more extensive treatment that can only be a digression at this point.

Another un-embodied identity-based political position seemed to be configured in Marxist materialist class analysis. Insofar as I have included class among identity-based political positions above, I have done so because class has been embodied more often than not. Bodies and bloodlines (at the very least in a self-reproducing metaphorical biogeneticism), cultural rituals and practices, have attended the claiming/attribution/perception of class distinctions, in an enormous number of histories and contexts. The class politics of Marxism, however – which was reduced, deepened, and loosely described between two poles of capitalist/bourgeois and worker/proletariat, and set loose the identity-based political agency of the proletariat – was explicitly devoted to the dissolving of classes themselves along with the state itself. Again, this is a tricky area, not least because the mechanics of installing a Marxist communist state reconfigured and returned rather than dissolved classes in a variety of ways. In theoretical terms the agency of the proletariat became embodied in substantially the same kind of limiting ways as those described above for identity-based political positions generally. In pragmatic terms, the holding apart of a stratum of professional revolutionaries working on behalf of proletariat interests enabled the formation of elites (as self-interested as the bourgeois class it overcame) within communist states, held in place by a party structure. Occasionally, but rarely, these elites even asserted explicit biogenetically defined identity-based political positions (e.g., the initial phase of the Cultural Revolution in China was impelled by the claims of such elite revolutionary-born student groups). However, Marxist configurations of classes and class-conflict, and Marxism-inspired economic delineations of class, still present the possibility of an un-embodied identity-based political position.

I present these sketchy observations on un-embodied identity-based political positions only to give substance to that possibility. As far as this study goes, in referring to identity-based political positions I always mean that these are embodied in the manner described above, and are contained as such in the prevailing reign of social constructionist identity politics.

4
Analogues and Equivalences

Clusters of terms

To some extent the above elaborations have already conveyed what I mean by maintaining that social constructionist identity politics contains different identity-based political positions by spreading out limitations on communication and critical engagement. I have presented identity politics as the field within which identity-based political positions, with their in-built instabilities and constant embodiments, are held together; and I have suggested that what occurs thereby is a universalization of identity-based political expression and embodiment. The precise means through which identity-based political positions are contained in identity politics as defined here require further clarification.

I propose to examine this by focusing on three clusters of terms through and around which identity politics is largely constructed. These are: (1) *in-between* terms that mediate between different identity-based political positions – such as 'coalition' politics, politics of 'pluralism', politics of 'diversity', politics of 'difference', 'relational' politics, and 'networks'; (2) *encompassing* terms that appear to characterize the subject or object (depending how it is posed) of identity politics, enabling a synthetic consideration of different identity-based political positions – such as 'identity', 'ethnicity', 'multiculturalism', 'social movements'; and (3) *metatheoretical* terms that seem to provide a scaffolding upon and around and within which different identity-based political positions can be arraigned – primarily 'postmodernism', 'postcolonialism', 'globalization. These or such terms, with all their complex interconnections and cross-references, seem to me to delineate the field of, and provide foci of construction for, identity politics as understood here. The methodology of containing different identity-based political positions rests largely in allocating these terms with an ever-growing density of connotation or an ever-increasing intensity of significance. The centrality of these terms to the ethos of identity politics is evidenced in their, so to say, thickening and deepening. Contemplation of such thickening and deepening also mark out the context within which identity politics gradually takes over political understanding; all these terms have acquired new and distinctive connotations and significances since the late 1970s, and particularly in the 1980s and 1990s. There is another set of associated terms to do with this area that I take note of in passing, which have similarly thickened in this period, and acquired significances that distinguish them from other more familiar terms, and have come to dominate the field of political conceptualization at the expense of a formerly much-used register. I have in mind such words as: 'discourse' (as distinct from 'language'), 'articulation' (as distinct from 'expression' or 'perception'), 'marginalization' (as distinct from 'oppression'), 'hybridity' (as distinct from 'mixture'), 'diaspora' (as distinct from 'émigrés' or 'migrants'), 'toleration' (as distinct from 'accommodation', 'assimilation', 'integration'). The shifting nuances of 'representation' should be added to those, though it is slightly distinct in that it does not acquire currency over erstwhile near-synonyms but acquires multiple folds of associations (drawing closer to 'embodiment').[1] These are in constant play with the above three clusters. Indeed such is the thickening and deepening of these terms now, so densely loaded are these with debates and exchanges and illuminations, that naming these together is likely to be regarded as taking on more than anyone can comfortably chew.

I have entitled this subsection 'Analogues and Equivalences' precisely because these are words that are comparatively less evoked[2] in the register of identity politics, while describing fairly neatly what that register is about.

An immediate observation follows from naming those terms, and from the suggestion that the methodology of social constructionist identity politics' containment of different identity-based political positions derives from the negotiation of terms. It may be justifiably inferred that the methodology operates significantly at a communicative level. This seems to me to be the case for identity politics in several ways: in apprehending what is articulable from different embodied identity-based political positions; in pondering how communicative spaces may be explored between different identity-based political positions; and, in many ways most importantly, in trying to produce a vocabulary that allows the differently embodied positions to be articulated in relation to each other – not just as an interactive enterprise, but also to be able to gain a bird's-eye view that becomes identity politics, or just to be able to articulate identity politics as such. The latter is a fraught enterprise, since all articulations tend to slip into specifically embodied identity-based political positions. As I observed at the beginning of this study, every universalistic expression in identity politics is engaged within identity politics as emerging from particular identity-based political positions. The fact that the distinction between identity-based political positions and identity politics that I am labouring here is usually left confused, and that these are often regarded as interchangeable, is not a matter of oversight or an accident. The distinction *cannot* be laboured within identity politics without destroying the logic of embodiment, and therefore the fragile but pervasive environment of identity politics. Within the universalization of identity-based political expression and embodiment, any apparent expression of universal import (even of itself) has to be immediately reduced as issuing from an embodied identity-based source.

However, the emphasis on the communicative should not be taken as another postmodern reiteration of the constitutiveness of discourses, and of political agency and practice being available within and through discourse formations. That is certainly an enormously influential component of identity politics (hence the somewhat deified presence of Foucault and Derrida in identity politics and some identity-based political positions), but identity politics stretches well beyond such assumptions – into sociological and philosophico-political metatheorizations of systems and agents, ideology and economy.

But let me turn to those clusters of terms without more ado.

In-between terms

The first cluster (terms that mediate between different identity-based political positions) seem to mark relationships between things but are used in a manner that leaves the things in question open or unsaid. I think of these as *in-between* terms. In identity politics the things that are so mediated by these terms are identity-based political positions; but the important facet of the use of these terms is that it does not need to be said or clarified. It might seem natural to ask: 'Coalition between whom?'; 'Difference between what?'; 'Plurality of what?'; 'Diversity of what?'; 'Relation between what or whom?'; etc. But the point is that in identity politics the clarification of this is not necessary – it is presumptively understood. Just saying 'politics of difference' or 'pluralistic politics', and so on, immediately conveys that what is meant is 'difference between different embodied identity-based political positions' or 'a plurality of different embodied identity-based collectives'. In other words, these terms – denoting abstract relationships – have in identity politics also come to connote what they effectively relate. But it is not just that in this cluster, terms allude to more than they refer, connote more than seems syntactically plausible. Such terms also thereby assert that there is no need to be definite about what are mediated. By silently connoting embodied identity-based collectives in their loud mediating denotations, they assert a tendency of simply not having to – or generally not wishing to – articulate the identity-based political positions as being mediated. This is a convenient manoeuvre in identity politics: it suggests the universality of the mediating terms *as* identity politics without having to compromise the logic of embodiment of identity-based political positions, which would not allow any universalist utterance and which are nevertheless contained in identity politics. Or, another way of putting this: instead of allowing embodiments of different identity-based political positions to harden into essentialist positions, to keep the fragile social constructionist structure of embodied identities and fluid identities together the mediatory terms – which can shift locations according to shifts of embodiment and fluidities of identity – are essentialized. 'Coalition', 'pluralism', 'diversity', 'difference', 'relational', etc., in identity politics begin to glow with a luminous, autonomous, semi-mystical significance, and that itself allows identity politics to emanate and contain different identity-based political positions without touching their embodiments, and generalize the limits on communication and critical engagement that each embodied position assumes/is attributed.

Let us have a closer look at some of those terms. The story of identity politics as understood for this study begins, I think, primarily with 'coalition'. That is, insofar as 'coalition' is dislocated from its dominant use in electoral politics, and conceptualized as a mode of enabling different identity-based collectives to act together in a provisional, pragmatic, and temporary fashion without compromising their autonomous constituencies (the separate embodiments). With regard to identity-based political positions, a conceptually broadened notion of coalition politics emerged with the black solidarity and the feminist movements in the USA. Stokely Carmichael (later Kwame Ture) and Charles V. Hamilton's *Black Power* (1967) laid out certain conditions for biracial coalitions that stressed the autonomy of coalition alignments and the shared goals that are served by pragmatic coalition.[3] These have been extended to multiracial contexts, and reworked in various ways since.[4] The nuances of coalition building in political activism were discussed

influentially from the intersections of the black and feminist movements by Bernice Johnson Reagon in 1983.[5] Her views were integrated
from a lesbian–feminist position by Shane Phelan in her study of identity politics in 1989, expanding on not just the pragmatics but the
necessity of coalition building to bring different identity-based political
positions together within identity politics (and echoing Reagon):

> If coalition work is hard and painful, why do it? Simply because 'the
> barred rooms will not be allowed to exist. They will be wiped out'. The
> forces against people of color, against women, against gays and les-
> bians, against others, do not celebrate difference either; and they have
> never, will never, make us welcome without our pressure. None of us,
> then, can do without the others, not because our fights are the same,
> but because we can support each other's fights while waging our own.[6]

The importance of some such idea of coalition building among the
many strands of feminist politics continues to be asserted often.[7]

The refined sense in which 'coalition politics' is used for bringing
together different identity-based political positions, and constituting a
field of identity politics, fits well with the above-described logic of
embodiment and the consequent spreading of limitations in communication and critical engagement. The thrust of critical thinking in identity
politics thereby naturally draws away from open interrogation of specific
identity-based political positions from outside the *control* of their
embodied exponents, and admits its limits by focusing on the critical
spaces *in between* different identity-based political positions. The idea of
coalition politics, in other words, creates a space that is open to the critical attention and consideration of all (in-between space) to tacitly
emphasize the spaces that are outside the bounds of open scrutiny (those
that *are* the different identity-based political positions). It can be justifiably maintained that identity politics is very largely exercised as a
universal communicative and debating zone only in-between. Identity
politics becomes the theorization and practice of in-betweenness, by its
acceptance of the different embodiments of different identity-based
political positions. Only those who embody their identity-based political
positions can effectively consolidate, question, fracture, regroup, and
reconsolidate identity-based political positions pertinent to them; those
who wish to embrace more confine themselves to the mechanics of the
in-between spaces – whereby identity politics extends its grand embrace.
What I have understood as essentialism in the previous chapter is now a
straw man for all to burn; essentialism does not recognize in-between

spaces as politically effective. In essentialist identity-based political positions only the asserted position has prerogatives, and all in-between spaces are negligible compared to that.

The cluster of in-between terms in question here, therefore, marks the zone of communication and critical engagement in identity politics. Coalition politics sets up the tendency of identity politics, but the unrestrainable energy of identity politics could not be confined to the baggage of *coalition* alone. The very open-endedness of in-between areas, at the expense of openness with regard to embodied identity-based political positions, magnetically attracts and stimulates debate. The proliferation of in-between terms (some of which are named here for this cluster) marks the ebb and flow of such debate. The problem with the above notion of coalition politics is that, apart from presuming the existence of coherent identity-based groups that could enter into coalition, it also presumes the existence of (in Jerry Gafio Watts's words) 'political elites who can speak for and bargain on behalf of these groups'.[8] Perhaps this presumption is due to the association of coalition politics with the electoral process of multiparty parliamentary democracy. As the logic of embodiment of identity-based political positions becomes further refined, the presumption of hierarchical structures within different identity-based collectives (though usually the practical reality) seems inappropriate. The blurring of boundaries between the embodied identi(ty)fied individual member and the embodied identity-based collective that, as described above, the logic of embodiment operates sits ill with the presumption of internal hierarchies and political elites. The articulation of such hierarchies involves the suggestion that in an identity-based political position some embody better than others (even if what is meant is that it is practical to conduct a political division of labour). The relatively muted calls for coalition these days, and the superlative significance attributed to in-between terms like 'pluralism', 'diversity', 'relationality' (networking), and especially of 'difference' have, I suspect something to do with that.

The surfacing of 'difference' as a superlatively connotative term in identity politics derives largely from the efforts of Jacques Derrida, as it happens at roughly the same time as Carmichael and Hamilton's manifesto of black solidarity appeared (*De la Grammatologie* was published in 1967). In the previous chapter (in the context of assuming identity by unqualifiable performative articulation) I noted that Derrida introduced difference as a constitutive and pervasive aspect of language and the construction of ideology therein by inverting the kind of transcendental signifier of being that Heidegger used – by extension inverting all possible transcendental signifiers that different conceptual systems are centred around (different notions of philosophical essences, the centrality of faith and God in religion). It allowed an inversion of what Derrida called logocentrism (difference can be thought of as a linguistic trope that puts logocentrism into perspective), while recognizing the logocentricity in the enunciation of difference itself. The only way of displacing the logocentricity of the means of expression through which logocentricity is identified, for Derrida, consisted in giving 'difference' a distinctive turn – defamiliarizing it by playing with it, or layering it with unfamiliar significances. This complicated manoeuvre is most familiarly associated with Derrida's loading of difference in the above sense with *differance*. In the context of considering a range of theories of language and expression, Derrida's inversion of transcendent signifiers is made analogous to the inversion of writing preceding speech. This inversion depends on the discernment of a deep *differance*, barely but just about traceable, which pre-empts and underlies all expression of difference:

> On the one hand, the phonic element, the term, the plenitude that is called sensible, would not appear without the difference or opposition which gives them *form*. Such is the most evident significance of the appeal to difference as the reduction of phonic substance. Here the appearing and functioning of difference presupposes an originary synthesis not preceded by any absolute simplicity. Such would be the originary trace. Without a retention in the minimal unit of temporal existence, without a trace retaining the other as other in the same, no difference would do its work and no meaning would appear. It is not the question of a constituted difference here, but rather, before all determination of the content, of the *pure* movement which produces difference. *The (pure) trace is differance*. [...]
> Differance is therefore the formation of form. But it is *on the other hand* the being-imprinted of the imprint. [...][9]

What occurs here, it seems to me, is that Derrida gives *differance* all the weight of a transcendental signifier (along the lines of Heidegger's being, and other centres of logocentric discourses), thereby emptying the enunciation of difference of its own logocentrism, and yet makes *differance* inferable from difference. It is a subtle and oddly circular tactic that has the useful effect of both loading and emptying difference of a superlative significance.

I have dwelt briefly on Derrida's manoeuvre here because I think it helps explain the extraordinary potency of the in-between term 'difference' in identity politics. It seems to me that in identity politics difference retains the superlative and deeply embedded significance that Derrida has managed to contain in it, while dislocating it in simplistic ways from the substantive context of Derrida's formulation (in ways that Derrida himself encouraged and later embraced). In identity politics difference reductively *becomes* an in-between term, alluding to the relativized space between constantly shifting and constantly consolidated different embodied identity-based political positions. This air of relativization is, of course, quite different from the constitutive and deep significance that Derrida attributed to difference (based on *differance*) in the context of linguistic practice. The relativistic notion of difference as an in-between term in identity politics retains the weight of Derrida's use of the term, but only by displacing it from, so to say, Derrida's schema.

This displacement is most evident in the celebratory zeal that attends identity politics' promotion of difference, as a political strategy. Derrida's difference (with the implicit trace of *differance*) cannot be celebrated as something that is desirable because it is simply already, unavoidably, undisplacably, and inevitably recognized and accepted whenever speech and writing happens. Derrida's difference is not waiting for recognition and celebration; difference in identity politics *awaits* ideal recognition and *needs* celebration. And yet the superlative significance that is attributed to the in-between difference of identity politics comes with the weight of the superlative significance that Derrida attached to the term. That difference, as an in-between term, stands on its own in identity politics without need for saying 'in-between what and what', but always meaning 'in-between something and something' (different identity-based political positions) conveys a Derrida-like superlative significance to the term. This is constantly evidenced in the use of difference in identity politics as understood here. So prolific has been this kind of use that citing any number of examples would be an inadequate exercise. However, the superlativeness of the significance attributed to the in-between difference in identity politics can be gestured towards in considering some of the most sensible considerations of identity politics. Perhaps, briefly, a couple of examples would suffice to make my point here.

Steven Seidman's admirably detailed and thoughtful study of the implications of thinking through difference in its in-between relativistic sense without obstructing open critical engagements, and charting the (inherent) resistance to difference in social and political knowledge construction, concludes with a call for a 'pragmatic culture of knowledge' which is 'both friendly towards difference, indeed assumes and encourages differences, and makes possible a strong notion of socially connecting reason'.[10] This attempt to put in place a mode of thinking that incorporates apparently contrary pulls depends on the notion of pragmatism, understood thus:

> Pragmatism implies a culture which instils a deep reflexivity concerning the particular sociohistorical conditions of agents' ideas, promotes a view of the tradition-or-community- based character of 'reason,' and imagines agents willing to risk their deepest convictions in the course of communicatively negotiating interpretive, including epistemic, differences.[11]

Sympathetic as I feel to this attempt to reconcile difference with 'socially connecting reason', it is worth pausing interrogatively on the pragmatism that makes such reconciliation feasible. For one thing, it appears to me that there are internal contradictions and circularities here. The socio-historical conditions that lead Seidman to promote a pragmatic culture of knowledge are reasonably inferable from the book, but the socio-historical conditions *of* such a culture are not elaborated. And, the prescription here always begs the malaise: Is the call for a deep reflexivity about the conditions of agents' ideas itself *deeply* reflexive of the conditions that underlie this call? Is the notion that there is a tradition-or-community-based character to 'reason' (especially with those eloquent quotation marks, a gesture to distance reason from its instrumentalist Enlightenment associations) itself a tradition-or-community-based observation? At the very least there is uncertainty about the replies one can give here. More brashly, I am tempted to observe that the sentiments militate against the expression. The sentiments express a desire for a kind of conditionality on difference, which the statements, that present such conditionality as normatively universal, belie. What we have here is a pretty clear expression of the paradoxes of identity politics, of the universalization of difference (between embodied identity-based political positions). Also implicitly written into the visualization of a pragmatic culture of knowledge is precisely the kind of spreading of limitations in communication and critical engagement that I have described above, while *appearing not to*. If reason is accepted as tradition-and-community-based, then how can we be confident that it is possible to communicatively negotiate (does not that depend on some idea of rational understanding and expression?) interpretive differences? Does the tradition-or-community-based character of reason mean that agents' ideas (in their particular socio-historical conditions) actually are the ideas of different traditions-or-communities (i.e., only traditions-and-communities speak to each other through agents), and agents risking their convictions for communicative negotiations are risking tradition-or-community-convictions (*risking* is an interesting word, it implies questioning to make safe rather than, say, relegating altogether), and can these communicative negotiations achieve anything other than some kind of affirmation of tradition-and-community-based ideas (differences thereof)? The limiting of critical engagement marked by these questions is most clearly *spread out* by making communicative *negotiations* (as opposed to communication as an open process and entailing critical engagement from anywhere to anyone) between differences the only conceivable communicative acts of political moment. Behind that lies an endlessly regressed (or, perhaps, deferred) notion of difference which simply has to be accepted *a priori*. There is a whiff here of Derrida's difference (emanating from/revealing the pure trace of *différance*) – but just a whiff. If Seidman had raised and pondered the questions I have just raised, the enterprise might have slid into a deconstructive process whereby theory and enunciation themselves *occur* in the vortex of difference. But he does not; Seidman's difference is the in-between relativized difference of identity politics, which he thinks has to be *assumed* and *encouraged* as a prospective enterprise in a pragmatic fashion.

Why *pragmatic* though? This too announces a departure from the Derridean notion – despite the whiff – in giving the articulation of difference a political bent. Pragmatism is with regard to a political condition which has to be accepted, a political reality. Pragmatism has a determined affiliation with political realism: not so much with the structural neo-realism of Kenneth Waltz or the neoconservative realism of Samuel Huntingdon, but more with the political realism of Hans Morgenthau or R.N. Berki,[12] which extends certain principles of political action on the basis of what is given. Difference is the given of the political reality that Seidman (and proponents of identity politics at its best) acknowledges. Once this ineluctable reality is recognized and accepted as unavoidable, every sensible move is a pragmatic response to it.

From an almost opposite direction comes Ernesto Laclau's evocation of difference (as identity politics) in relation to democracy, and in many ways it is apparently closer to Derrida's formulation of difference. This is especially so when Laclau sees difference as something that underlies the production of empty significations which appear to be of universal moment from the particular perspectives of identity-based political positions. There is in this idea a pushing of difference as both the constructionist form and the deconstructionist base of particular identity-based political positions, which are all ultimately caught up in a temporal and insubstantial (rather than embodied and material) political flux that is the politics of difference or identity politics. But again there are problematic shifts in recruiting the Derridean sense of difference to the articulation of identity politics:

> If democracy is possible, it is because the universal has no necessary body and no necessary content; different groups, instead, compete between themselves to temporarily give to their particularisms a function of universal representation. Society generates a whole vocabulary of empty signifiers whose temporary signifieds are the result of a political competition. It is this final failure of society to constitute itself as society – which is the same thing as the failure of constituting difference as difference – which makes the difference between the universal and the particular unbridgeable and, as a result, burdens concrete social agents with the impossible task of making democratic interaction achievable.[13]

Insofar as this is an understandable statement, it seems to me interesting that democracy has been tacitly presented as the political realization of difference with much the same semi-mystical evasiveness of *différance* – only, in this instance, without exposing democracy itself to any deconstructive play. 'Democracy' operates here as a makeshift, highly abstract and normatively loaded in-between term, and lays itself open to an easy conflation (and one that Laclau does not resist) with that other conventional and practical denotation of 'democracy', as a liberal multiparty elective majoritarian political order. Apart from that potential conflation, interesting here also are the concrete (rather than empty) signifieds in that quotation: 'different groups' and 'concrete social agents'. These produce the empty signified, but are not so themselves; they capture the field by insubstantially universalizing themselves and undertaking impossible democracy. It seems to me that the entire structure of identity politics as understood here, with social groups and their concrete agents as nodes and difference/democracy as the operative in-between terms, is reiterated here against the grain of the deconstructive discourse they are sieved through – or rather, inconsistently sieved through.

The shifting of a transcendental signification of difference to a relativized in-between sense has been the mainstay, as we see in the next chapter, of the new left's embracing of social constructionist identity politics. 'Pluralism' (and in a correlated fashion, 'diversity'), recruited from theological roots and shifted from multiple ideologies to the service of identity politics, seems to me to be primarily a liberal political expression. Where *difference* comes with radical expectations of the in-between spaces of identity politics, *pluralism* comes with a staid expectation of comprehending and taming the in-between spaces in a systematic fashion. Difference is celebrated, encouraged, let loose, embraced; pluralism is managed, tolerated, comprehended, accommodated. Difference strikes a defiant attitude vis-à-vis the existing establishment; pluralism is (or should be) contained in the already emerged liberal democratic (from this perspective, read as *good*) establishment. Pluralism shuffles in uneasily, I have observed in Chapter 2, into the midst of the liberal project of individual freedom in a community setting (Kenneth Hoover, 1975) and the reluctant recognition of a need to comprehend different identity-based political positions (Peter du Preez, 1980).[14] An early, and characteristically careworn, liberal acknowledgement of pluralism (in the sense pertinent to identity politics) appears in an interview with Michel de Certeau, published in *La culture au pluriel* (1974). In response to the question (contextualized against Basque and Breton separatist movements) 'how can a real, effective political organization be drawn from a cultural demonstration?' de Certeau responded:

> I believe it can be done only by getting rid of the idea of a cultural enclave, the idea that the problem involves Bretons and Bretons alone. If Basques and Bretons have been unable to win autonomy, it is because of the global organization of the society in which they live. In this sense, the problem concerns all French citizens; at stake is the impossibility imposed on each and every person to live in a society that admits a plurality of groups.[15]

With hindsight, from the midst of the prevailing reign of identity politics, this was a prescient observation in several ways, and looked forward to liberalism's resistant engagement with pluralism. It set the tone of flinching resistance ('the impossibility imposed ...'); it expanded the question of plurality as being a part of the 'global organization of the society we live in', and acknowledged its relevance to the entire polity; and it tacitly apprehended the problem of pluralism in terms of majority and minority formations (this approach has become standard in liberal democratic political philosophy since). But nowhere is the surfacing of pluralism, in the sense relevant here, more apparent than in the liberal democratic political theorizations of John Rawls – with the resistance and inevitability of this manifestation explicitly written in. In itself, Rawls's coming to grips with pluralism is a story of failure, but it has a crucial relevance to democratic liberalism's resistant wedding with identity politics.

The failure of Rawls's consideration of pluralism has to do with the self-imposed limits within which he confines his thinking. The surfacing of pluralism occurs by the recognition that there are minority collectives which require or claim special concessions in a majoritarian democratic dispensation. In *A Theory of Justice* (1971) Rawls's theorization was confined to 'well-ordering' society within the domestic boundaries of a liberal democratic nation-state. The question of minorities was touched on only fleetingly (a sustained discussion was postponed), and only to suggest that the duty of responding reasonably to perceived injustices to minorities by the dominant group should rest with the minorities themselves.[16] Pluralism entered Rawls's theorizations by the time he published *Political Liberalism* in 1993 (bringing together his ideas of the 1980s). This was paradoxical, because he had by this time hardened the confines of the liberal democratic precincts he was contemplating to the 'closed society': 'we are to regard it as self-contained and as having no relation with other societies. Its members enter it only by birth and leave it only by death'.[17] However, this idealization did not allow him to neglect the by now powerful emergence of various identity-based political positions, which he felt called upon to acknowledge even within this 'closed society' in a regretful fashion:

> [...] the diversity of reasonable comprehensive religious, philosophical, and moral doctrines found in modern democratic societies is not a mere historical condition that may soon pass away; it is a permanent feature of the public culture of democracy. Under the political and social conditions secured by the basic rights and liberties of free institutions, a diversity of conflicting and irreconcilable – and what is more, reasonable – comprehensive doctrines will come about and persist if such diversity does not already obtain.[18]

What followed was the influential formulation on modes of achieving 'overlapping consensus'[19] to contain and accommodate plurality in the well-ordered liberal democratic closed society. But the notion of 'closed societies' is obviously not suitable for dealing with pluralism (does not allow for migration!), and Rawls naturally abandoned further consideration of this when he came to outlining a theory of international justice in *Law of Peoples* (published in 1999).[20] Here he thinks of the international order as consisting of a number of closed societies, hierarchically placed in descending moral legitimacy from liberal democratic to decent hierarchical to totalitarian regimes.

This brief excursus into Rawls's theorizations of liberal democracy demonstrates how powerful the influx of identity politics was; so powerful that Rawls was compelled to register it entirely against the grain of his theoretical proclivities (to think within increasingly impermeable borders). It also clarifies, I think, the spirit in which pluralism shoulders its way into liberal democratic thinking, in a resistant fashion, dragged in against all odds, unavoidably. The term pluralism contains the anxiety of its appearance in liberal democratic theory. This anxiety does not manifest itself any longer in an ultimate refusal *a la* Rawls, but it leaves a trace (to insert a Derridean inflection) even when the term is (has to be) embraced and made central in thinking about liberal democracy thereafter. Pluralism (and by implication diversity) has become the in-between term of identity politics which suggests that in-between spaces are fraught with anxiety, or that the entropy of in-between spaces has to be curbed. Those who have tried to theorize liberal democracy in a direction opposite to Rawls's, not closing boundaries but opening or dissolving them, have centred their efforts on pluralism in that spirit. Taking this direction of opening or dissolving boundaries is seen as an inevitability in the face of spontaneous processes of globalization (of which more later), coinciding with equally spontaneous emergences of a plethora of identity-based political positions in the form of new social movements (of which more later too). This is particularly exemplified in the work of Jürgen Habermas when he tries to conceptualize deliberative democracy in the context of transnational constellations,[21] or in the work of David Held (with Danielle Archibugi, Anthony McGrew, and others)[22] when he tries to outline a cosmopolitan democratic global order. The literature on this point is vast, and a demonstration of this in this study would be an unrealistic enterprise.

I have so far suggested that the term 'diversity' goes hand in hand with 'pluralism'. This is true in most instances: diversity is generally thought of as the disposition of a polity which has to be taken into account in the political order relevant to that polity. However, there have been some attempts to invest diversity politics with agendas that are more in line with the new left celebration of difference, and less in a liberal mould. This occurs, for instance, in Davina Cooper's attempt (2004) to reiterate the positive features of diversity politics, particularly by noting that: 'it goes beyond the conditional liberal promise bestowed upon minorities of toleration, providing their differences are kept from affecting others'.[23] It would seem that this reiteration of diversity politics is a deliberate attempt to distance some of the more familiar modes of alluding to the in-between spaces that are the substance of identity politics – such as 'identity politics' itself, or the 'politics of difference', or 'multicultural or multiethnic politics'. At the same time, an attempt is made to invest diversity politics with the aspirations and assumptions of identity politics. The thrust of Cooper's understanding of diversity politics, therefore, is not just in holding up the spaces between different identity-based political positions for open scrutiny and with political expectations, but to emphasize these as critically interrogative spaces:

> The space of diversity politics raises questions and embraces diverging opinions about the desired place of collective identities within society: are such identities oppressive or enabling? Are gender, class and race characteristics to bury or reform? And, more abstractly, is a new hegemony worth seeking or are all hegemonies, however radical they appear in theory, disastrous to the pursuit and maintenance of a freer, more enabling society?[24]

The in-between term 'relational' brings another shade to the disposition of the field of identity politics, as containing different identity-based political positions. In some sense, relational politics, seen (as I have observed already) as the way forward from identity politics (meaning different social constructionist identity-based political positions) by Kenneth Gergen, is invested with something of Cooper's understanding of the in-between spaces of identity politics as critically interrogative. For Gergen, relational politics is: 'a politics in which self/other, we/them binaries are replaced by a realization and appreciation of the significance of the relational process',[25] and involves both 'the development of relational conceptions of self and other, [and] exploration of alternative modes of talking/acting with others – and particularly those with whom we otherwise disagree'.[26] The difference from Cooper's sense of diversity is that Gergen's notion of relationality is a more overtly and determinedly celebratory one. Cooper is inclined to use the in-between spaces of identity politics to ask whether collective identities are oppressive or enabling; Gergen proposes to use those in-between spaces to develop communication between different identity-based political positions on the understanding that collective identities have proven to be enabling. To that extent, despite embracing some of the aspirations of identity politics Cooper's diversity politics contains the mechanism of self-questioning; Gergen's relational politics does not contain such a mechanism, and is geared towards celebration (words like 'realization', 'appreciation', 'significance' in the above quotations are telling) and progress within the consolidation of identity politics (in the sense pertinent to this study). The celebratory air and consolidating purpose of Gergen's relational politics (reminiscent of the celebratory approach to the politics of difference by the new left) is amply backed up by the initiatives which he identifies as exemplifying such relational politics: 'therapeutically oriented institutes' that move into community work, and 'appreciative inquiry' in organizational management wherein 'problem talk' (such as who is to blame, where are disagreements rooted) is deliberately avoided in favour of identifying ideal outcomes.[27] Gergen's observations seem to me, yet again, to give reasonably clear indications of the manner in which communication and critical inquiry is limited in identity politics.

This kind of attempt at inserting a dynamic within the in-between spaces of identity politics has proved useful, especially in the context of a perceived convergence of social movements into a 'movement of movements' or into 'collective action' (more on these phrases soon) through the 1990s. The notion that different identity-based political positions can be brought together within identity politics to provisionally oppose common enemies is now seldom thought of in terms of 'coalitions' and more usually understood in terms of 'movements', which are given shape not through the agency of 'political elites' but through the cultivation of 'networks'. The notion of relational politics as the celebratory and consolidating use of in-between spaces of identity politics, disposing those spaces to enable and mutually support exchanges and communications between different identity-based political positions, is naturally peculiarly close to contemplating how networks have been or should be formed. Those who have an interest in social movements are undertaking attempts to formulate strategic communicative practices between agents of different identity-based political positions to form networks and enable a movement of movements. This is generally done in the celebratory and consolidating spirit of relational politics. Such formulations are also usually inattentive to hierarchies in identity-based collectives, and stress the multiple and complexly entwined levels of communication and strategies of communicative adjustment between agents (a usefully neutral status-free word) of different identity-based collectives.[28]

Encompassing terms

The second cluster of terms which construct and characterize the field of identity politics are *encompassing* terms. These appear to characterize the subject or object (depending how it is posed) of identity politics, enabling a synthetic consideration of different identity-based political positions – such as 'identity', 'ethnicity', 'multiculturalism', and 'social movements'. Such terms are obviously not equivalent; they have different denotative shades and are often used in conjunction to lend greater clarity to the subject or object of identity politics (such as 'ethnic identity', 'multicultural social movements'). I bring these together insofar as these come with denotative effect, referring inclusively by their enunciation to the, so to say, nodes (different identity-based political positions) that are linked by the kind of in-between terms examined above to form the field of identity politics.

A peculiar characteristic of such denotative terms is that they seem to associate identity-based political positions with social arrangements and phenomena that are not strictly comprehended by such political positions. In other words, they appear to give identity politics an *excessive* embrace, larger than the identity-based political positions that it contains. The term 'identity' itself – the developing applications of which I have traced to some extent already – provides a characteristic and yet peculiar instance of this. 'Identity' in 'identity-based political positions' and 'identity politics', I observed above, is always with regard to collectives, and operates as an over-determination of individual identity markers. Identity construction/ attribution/ claiming/ exercising, therefore, involve a continuous relationship between individual identity and collective identity, whereby the interests of the collective appear to become synonymous and synchronous with the interests of its individual members. This is especially manifest in the logic of embodiment that attaches to different identity-based political positions: individual members become conveniently invested with embodied identity-based collective voices, identity-based collectives are concretized through individual members when they assume (through different means) identity-based political positions – and the entire problematic of unique individuality and universal commonality is side-stepped. Embodied identity-based political positions are contained in identity politics by keeping them intact, and focusing political debate and action at in-between spaces, in terms of analogues and equivalences. I repeat these points here to emphasize how central the continuous relationship between individual member and identity-based collective is in identity politics, and to draw attention to the fact that the very enunciation of the word 'identity' – the fluidity of application comprehended by that word itself – establishes this continuity. *Identity*-based political positions and *identity* politics appear to have something to do not just with certain collectives, but with every individual. The sticky etymological shifts of identity – continuously accruing nuances from and shuttling amidst shades of meaning between sameness/uniqueness, social placement/individual space, essence/ construction, identification/recognition – are never quite lost. This etymology weighs 'identity' with the excessive congruence that makes the extraordinary appeal of identity-based political positions and identity politics possible.

The excessive embrace of 'ethnicity' (multiethnic) and 'multiculturalism' in identity politics is of a different order from that of 'identity' (hence the advantages of combining these). 'Identity' effectively conflates individual apprehensions with identity-based collective interests; 'ethnicity' and 'multiculturalism' (in the prevailing political context, both these terms) associate identity politics with a democratic order of governance, democratic political organization itself. They do so because these terms emerge *as* cautious official jargon, drawn most immediately from the academic resources of social anthropology – emerge *in* majoritarian liberal democracies with markedly mixed populations (in terms of race, cultural rituals and traditions, languages, and origins), initially Canada, Australia, USA, and later Western European countries and thereafter African and Asian countries – and emerge *because* of, and *to* address, anxieties about the political stability of such contexts and to maintain majority interests in a rationalizable fashion. That, at any rate, is the context where the terms 'ethnicity' and 'multiculturalism' as currently used, within the field of identity politics, are I think located. I do not mean to say that this is the context in which the political management of heterogeneous populations had been conceived and originally implemented. The management of heterogeneous constituencies has a history far older than that of majoritarian liberal democracy, and originated well before the modern political arrangements of Canada, Australia, and USA came to exist. R.D. Grillo has examined the various modes of managing heterogeneity (or multiplicity, difference, pluralism) with a historical perspective in the patrimonial state, the patrimonial bureaucracy, the colonial state, the modern nation-state, the emerging postmodern order (for this study, the order of identity politics).[29] 'Ethnicity' and 'multiculturalism' are the official terms of identity politics as legislated and discursively aired in majoritarian liberal democracies – complementing other official terms of longer standing (like 'federation', 'association', 'secularism'), and countering other semi-official notions of long-standing (like 'assimilation', 'integration'). In this sense, they come with the distinctive baggage of the power struggles and prejudices and dispossessions of post-colonial New World contexts (particularly in terms of race,

origin, and migration), which have to be mitigated by legislative measures in favour of multiculturalism and accommodation of multiethnic
populations, and at the same time within – indeed consolidating – the
rationale of majoritarian liberal democracy. It was in this spirit that the
first official Multiculturalism Act was passed by the liberal government
of Pierre Trudeau in Canada in 1971; that a series of multiculturalist policies were adopted by parliament in Australia thereafter; and that the discourse of ethnicity and multiculturalism entered the official vocabulary
of USA after the Civil Liberties movement (and particularly in the context of education reform in schools in the 1980s). 'Ethnicity' and 'multiculturalism' came with the baggage of that history, but with the express
intention of displacing that baggage, to somehow become coeval with
majoritarian liberal democracy itself.

To put that another way, 'multicultural' and 'multiethnic' accommodation are the encompassing terms of identity politics that refer to an
official discursive space within the resistant environment of majoritarian liberal democracy (the same kind of resistant and anxiety-ridden
environment in which the in-between term 'pluralism' appears). *Inside*
majoritarian liberal democracy they represent limited measures to protect minorities *and* the majority: they have to be constantly justified
and rationalized as liberal good intentions on behalf of minorities, they
have to be constantly interrogated and restricted as liberal duty to the
majority. Normative claims (rights, duties, obligations) subsume both
sides of the argument, and the issues that are isolated in the debate on
multiculturalism and multiethnicity are *problems* on both sides (only
the liberal left defends and the liberal right attacks): what degree of
restriction on migration is necessary, what degree of affirmative action
is acceptable, what degree of toleration of minorities is justifiable, what
degree of political correctness is appropriate, how far should the celebration of majority rituals be curtailed, how far should the existence of
minorities be celebrated, etc.? The very register of the discussion of multiculturalism and multiethnicity in, and as, majoritarian liberal democracy is presumptively oriented towards the perspective of the dominant
majority collective-identity (easily conflated with the rational perspective of majoritarian liberal democracy itself), the inevitable and incon-
trovertible presence of minority collective-identities, the fragility of this
political constituency, the detail of bureaucratic resolution (how far? to
what degree?). The contemplation of loaded terms such as 'toleration'[30]
and 'political correctness'[31] themselves reveal the resistant and resigned
influx of identity politics into majoritarian liberal democracy, becoming
majoritarian liberal democracy.

The resistance which majoritarian liberal democracy presents in dealing with official multiculturalism, i.e., assuming identity politics within
its structures, is that it gets pulled into an identity-based position itself,
against its own grain, against its entire universalized normativity. This
leads, on the one hand, to the kind of compartmentalised pluralism, and
ultimately refusal of pluralism, that I noted was progressively evidenced
in Rawls's formulations. On the other hand, in Habermas's work this
takes the form of a tacit acceptance of the identity-based position of multicultural majoritarian liberal democracy as vaguely Western, or explicitly
European-American, but nevertheless also paradoxically of universal
import.[32] This paradox is not a difficult one to maintain if contextual
details under examination are confined to the so-called West, and the
generalization of the universality of difference which is identity politics
is otherwise happily received. Nevertheless, the manner in which majoritarian liberal politics finds itself metamorphosing into an identity-based
political position while seeking universal social–ethical forms and world
convergence, finds itself absorbed into and becoming identity politics,
cannot but be matter for unease and anxiety. This unease is nowhere
more explicitly acknowledged than in Charles Taylor's influential essay
on multiculturalism (1992). Here, after going through the expectations
of multiculturalism in terms of the resistant logic of majoritarian liberal
democracy, and simultaneously resisting yet again the deep individualism of modern culture,[33] he gives his qualified approval to multiculturalism in a precise way that encapsulates the official limits contained in
that term. This argument need not be repeated since it reflects (only
from *within* liberal democratic conviction) points I have made in the previous couple of paragraphs. Of greater interest here is the singular and
uneasy moment of recognition that liberal democracy may be no more
than another identity-based political position to be contained within the
identity politics that it tries to contain:

> Here is another severe problem with much of the politics of multicul-
> turalism. The peremptory demand for favorable judgements of worth is
> paradoxically – perhaps one should say tragically – homogenizing. For
> it implies that we already have the standards to make such judgements.
> The standards we have, however, are those of North Atlantic civiliza-
> tion. And so the judgements implicitly and unconsciously will cram
> the others into our categories. For instance, we will think of their
> 'artists' as creating 'works,' which we then can include in our canon. By
> implicitly invoking our standards to judge all civilizations and cultures,
> the politics of difference can end up making everyone the same.[34]

Most of the commentaries on this essay (by Susan Wolf, Steven Rockefeller, Michael Walzer, Habermas, and Anthony Appiah) in the 1994 edition introduced by Amy Gutmann, prefer not to address this particular unease at any length. It gets caught up in Habermas's dismissive observation that 'Eurocentrism and the hegemony of Western culture are in the last analysis catchwords for a struggle for recognition on the international level'.[35] Dismissive this may be, but it is perceptive: it is effectively a gesture of defiance that keeps the encroachment of identity politics at bay from liberal democratic thinking, while admitting the official efficacy of multiculturalism. In later work, Gutmann has addressed the resistance and accommodations of liberal democracy to identity politics in a more considered fashion.[36]

As I have observed, the place that the term 'ethnicity' occupies in the prevailing identity politics is akin to the term 'multiculturalism' in having the official ring that presumes the structures of liberal democracy, but in a distinctive fashion. The former term is inextricably connected to, and bounces against, race and racialism – the irreconcilable problem of traditional liberal democratic practice. By and large, the social anthropological leanings of the term (the study of differences and relations between groups that are regarded as distinct in terms of culture and origin) shift into politics as a constant interplay with the connotations of race. Most recent studies of ethnicity essentially present it as a social constructionist approach to that which has been regarded as race in an essentialist fashion.[37] But such studies also recognize that its emphatic social constructionist credentials liberate it from the binary opposition with essentialist race (and therefore from the debate on racism) – and that this liberates the term 'ethnicity' too from some of its official instrumentality. I do not think that the official instrumentality within the resistant discourse of liberal democracy is substantially affected thereby (quite the contrary, it continues to seethe), but it has been given a distinctive inflexion along the lines of the term 'difference' in a celebratory new left fashion. In the British context, this occurred most explicitly in the teasing out of a transformative future for *new ethnicities* by Stuart Hall in 1989, which effectively inflects 'ethnicity' to signify the nodes of embodied identity-based political positions with regard to which the in-between efficacy of 'difference' is best expressed. In doing so, he performs a partial dissociation from liberal democratic multiculturalism:

> We are beginning to think about how to represent a non-coercive and a more diverse conception of ethnicity, to set against the embattled

hegemonic conception of 'Englishness' [...]. This marks a real shift in the point of contestation, since it is no longer between anti-racism and multi-culturalism but *inside* the notion of ethnicity itself. What is involved is the splitting of the notion of ethnicity between, on the one hand the dominant notion which connects it to nation and 'race' and on the other hand what I think is a positive conception of the ethnicity of the margins, of the periphery. [...] We are all, in that sense, *ethnically* located and our ethnic identities are crucial to our subjective sense of who we are. But this is also a recognition that this is not an ethnicity that is doomed to survive, as Englishness was, only by marginalizing, displacing and forgetting other ethnicities. This precisely is the politics of ethnicity predicated on difference and diversity.[38]

This turn given to the term 'ethnicity' – or rather this attempt to wrench 'ethnicity' out of the liberal democratic officialese where 'multicultural-ism' continues to sit so comfortably – nevertheless continues to presume the majoritarian liberal democratic superstructure composed of majori-ties and minorities, centres and margins, and only differs in joining the resistant attitude of liberal democracy with the celebratory attitude of identity politics. Hall does here, it seems to me, precisely what Taylor and Habermas and other sympathetic discussants of multiculturalism were uneasy about: absorb liberal democracy into identity politics, mak-ing liberal democracy the field which contains and maintains different embodied identity-based political positions (my ethnicity, other ethnic-ities) into a harmonious and fluid and yet stable whole of identity poli-tics. Hall makes liberal democracy the majority of many ethnicities rather than the majority that is the dominant (tacitly ethnic) group and, more importantly, rather than a majority of simply individuals. Thereby the liberal democrat and the new left merge neatly as aspirants to one happy ethnicized world polity or body-politic. The trace of 'race' remains in new ethnicities.

The excessive embrace of the phrase 'social movements' in relation to identity politics is of yet another order, distinct from that of the terms 'identity' or 'multiculturalism/ethnicity'. When linked to identity poli-tics, the phrase 'social movements' invests identity-based political posi-tions with a direction (or rather different teleologies that may cohere in certain ways), and associates them with a range of (usually localized) emancipative struggles that are *not* undertaken as identity based. In other words, 'social movements' associates identity-based political positions with the struggles of those engaged in the protection of specific environments and habitats, opposition to the impact of multi-national corporations on local productions and economies, protests against disinvestments and relegation of responsibilities by the state, resistance to dispossession and oppression by locally powerful elites, etc. Thus identity politics appears to become connotatively linked to terms that are not ostensibly connected to it, such as *anti-globalization movement* or *anti-capitalist movement*. The trick is not to interrogate the coherence of the objectives of emancipative struggles that are not iden-tity based and of the struggles that attach to identity-based political positions (the definitive adjective *social* of 'social movements'), but to irrigate and cultivate the different senses of direction that are claimed in them (the unifying noun *movements* of 'social movements'). It is bet-ter to attach expectations and hopes to the unity of *movements* while keeping the differences in *social* simply hanging in the background (a condition to be registered, accepted, and celebrated because they can be appended to direction and activity) – this is the step in which the phrase 'new social movements' becomes the repository of aspirations. It is better to multiply the unifying possibilities of emphasizing direc-tions, as in discerning *a movement of movements*. This is a move in which metatheorizations of post-modernity, postcoloniality, globaliza-tion can acquire a kind of virtuous and constructive agency (more on this soon) rather than a deconstructive regression or alignment with dominant economic vested interests. The acquisition of a virtuous and constructive agency is itself joyously associated with the dynamic air of *movements*, so that social movements gradually become preponder-antly, even defiantly, cohesive with activism at the expense of theoret-ical sophistries (often seen as inevitably totalizing) – indeed action at the expense of thought – in turn, easily shafted in with embodied identity-based collectives being articulated/doing articulation rather than thoughts speaking. In the process, social movements can and do become identified with identity politics (just as liberal democratic theory tends to get absorbed within and become identity politics) and absorb other emancipative struggles within identity politics. In some sense thereafter other emancipative struggles become expressible as embodied identity-based political groups: in the form, for instance, of ethno-environmentalism, sustainable local production, or in the form of allocating to the working class or a nomadic group the resources of embodied identity-based authenticity and enjoining concordant limits of critical engagement.

A complicated series of manoeuvres to do with the phrase 'social movements' are rather rapidly summarized in the last paragraph. It might be useful to punctuate it with a few qualifications, and certainly it is worth clarifying the context of those moves. Again the 1980s, particularly in America and Western Europe, appears to be the decade to return to: following the ferment of different identity-based political alignments in the 1960s and 1970s, gathering reinventions of imperialistic interventions dressed up as democratizing missions, the gathering clouds of disenchantment with state communism, boom and bust time for democratic capitalist states, amidst the last agonized throes of the working-class movement in the face of state-sponsored privatizations and disinvestments helped along by increasingly better-structured international governance in favour of capitalist interests. There were numerous gestures towards registering disappointment with the working-class movement and looking for alternatives in new social movements (particularly the intellectual milieus of students, and the solidarity of women), but the time when new social movements were named in a fashion that foretold their complicity with and possible absorption into identity politics seem to me to be somewhere in 1981. This came with a sociological impulse that strove to be more than the systematization and documentation of society (however understood and approached). Indeed, this was an impulse that aspired to make sociology interventionist itself, in favour of a rejuvenation of the transformative spirit that could no longer be centred on Marxism and the working-class movement. It seems to me that this particular disposition of new social movements was announced at roughly the same time by Alain Touraine, in a sociological interventionist spirit, and by Habermas, with the potential of communicative action in mind.[39] This early announcement was primarily preoccupied with the loss of the agency of working-class alignments, and its amenability to the embrace of identity politics was yet a distant thing – but nevertheless, the ambition of sociological intervention had both. In Habermas the interventionist spirit was muted and itself the subject of academic critique; in Touraine this was suitably bold, especially when expressed in the context of an apprehension of the fading of working-class agency:

> The method of sociological intervention does not in fact lend immediacy to the research so much as put the actors in a position which encourages them to look critically at their own ideologies. In this way, it is possible to separate a multiplicity of meanings which would be inextricably entangled in normal social practice, and therefore to isolate the most important among them and produce analyses which can only enhance the participants' capacity for action. This involves

the researchers putting themselves in a position where they can offer the militants the tools they need, that is hypotheses which they can use to extend their thinking beyond the restrictions of practical categories [...].[40]

This ringing endorsement of intellectual agency as a means to political self-realization and action fell in at the time with a renewed interest in the responsibility of intellectuals generally,[41] and elsewhere in a rejuvenation of Antonio Gramsci's notion of organic intellectuals (displacing the Gramscian class-based concept of *organiçita* and subaltern history to anti-colonial movements, postcolonial subjectivity, and the feminist ideologue). The conceptual structure of identity politics lay just outside the margins of the quoted statement, in joined-up collective self-realizations beyond and at the expense of Marxist class analysis and materialism and working-class solidarity. But the naming of new social movements at this point was symptomatic: it reached towards a wide range of possibilities, and held the logic of embodiment in identity-based political positions at arm's length. Identity politics was an amenable direction, but new social movements were still much larger than identity politics in these early sociological approaches to this term (some identity-based political positions figured as a fraction of it).

The containment of new social movements within identity politics was demonstrably performed (ultimately linguistically performed) by Ernesto Laclau and Chantal Mouffe, especially Mouffe, once they were past their critique of 'totalizing', 'homogenizing' Marxism and state communism and moved towards a concretization of radical democracy (which turned out to be no more radical than 'a radical democratic interpretation of the political principles of the liberal democratic regime').[42] Radical democracy itself came with the semi-mystical normativeness that I have already noted in quoting Laclau. The demonstration of the linguistic performance of new social movements as identity politics, and sucking in of emancipative struggles that are not identity based, was most clearly revealed after the moment of *Hegemony and Socialist Strategy*,[43] in Chantal Mouffe's essays of the early 1990s. Since this was essentially a linguistic performance, it is necessary to attend closely to her language, to which end I extrapolate a couple of indicative quotations:

> The creation of political identities as radical democratic citizens depends [...] on the collective form of identification among the democratic demands found in a variety of movements; women, workers, black, gay, ecological, as well as in several other 'new social

movements'. This is a conception of citizenship which, through a common identification with a radical democratic interpretation of the principles of liberty and equality, aims at constructing a 'we', a chain of equivalence among their demands so as to articulate them through a principle of democratic equivalence. For it is not a matter of establishing a mere alliance between given interests but actually modifying the very identity of these forces.[44]

And elsewhere:

To be capable of thinking politics today, and understanding the nature of these new struggles and the diversity of social relations that the democratic revolution has yet to encompass, it is indispensable to develop a theory of the subject as a decentred, detotalized agent, a subject constructed at the point of the intersection of a multiplicity of subject positions between which there exists no a priori or neces-sary relation and whose articulation is the result of hegemonic prac-tices. Consequently, no identity is ever definitely established, there always being a certain degree of openness and ambiguity in the way different subject positions are articulated.[45]

There are boundaries of communication and critical engagement sketched in these quotations: the boundaries between a 'variety of groups' sus-tained by their memberships' sense of belonging to and advocating the cause of such groups. A couple of linguistic strategies are deployed here to render the politically determined (and with determination) holding to these boundaries consistent with the endless dispersal and scattering of 'decentred, detotalised', unhegemonic pluralism that radical democracy claims. On the one hand, the effort to bring consistency rests in the idea of a 'chain of equivalence' between a 'variety of groups' to find 'common concern' and establish 'radical democratic citizenship'. There is an unresolvable paradox here: the latter terms suggest that some sort of liberal notion of human commonality and political co-existence underlies those boundaries, but any expression of such a liberal notion is constantly deferred by asserting the hegemonic anti-pluralistic ten-dency of any such idea. On the other hand, the effort to bring consis-tency also rests in the idea of 'a subject constructed at the point of the intersection of a multiplicity of subject positions', given as something to be aspired to for radical democracy. It is difficult to discern why this is regarded as an aspiration and not as simply a description of subjectivity as commonly understood now. This can only be an aspiration insofar as

Mouffe is not passively apprehending the condition of subjectivity, but intentionally stating it to *make* it cohere with various embodied identity-based groups *as* social movements. This is an attempt not to understand subjectivity in itself, but to posit subjectivity as the link that holds the 'chain of equivalence' between different identity-based political positions *as* social movements together in radical democracy. Therein appears the unresolvable paradox mentioned, that only identity politics can contain and appear to resolve. If in the subject 'no identity is ever established' then what is the *raison d'etre* of the various groups engaged in social movements? An in-between 'chain of equivalence' passing through the unstable nodes of social movements is postulated and presented as radical democracy, precisely in the way that fluidly embodied identity-based political positions are contained in identity politics. It would not be far off the mark to maintain that radical democracy thus performed the joining of social movements to identity politics.

There is hardly any need to document the prevailing optimism attached to new social movements as *activism*, whereby the logic of embodiment operates across all kinds of protest, whether in terms of identity-based political movements or other kinds of emancipative struggles, and thus renders the conceptualization of new social movements coextensive with identity politics. Action rather than ideas, participative processes rather than analytical exercises, is an oft-mooted attitude in the sphere of new social movements, especially as these become coeval with the universalization of difference in identity politics. The celebratory literature here is voluminous,[46] and easily consulted to confirm this tendency.

Metatheoretical terms

Discussion of the third cluster, *metatheoretical* terms – in and through the interstices of which different identity-based political positions can be arraigned and identity politics may operate (primarily 'postmodernism', 'postcolonialism', 'globalization') – can only either be too long or too short. This is itself a not inconsequential observation, redolent with the anxiety of one who contemplates these terms rather than working with them or presuming their communicative efficacy. The feeling that there is no appropriate and singular way of discussing these terms, no determinable amount of space wherein such a discussion can be satisfactorily enclosed, is a constitutive aspect of such terms. What is 'postmodernism', or 'postcolonialism', or 'globalization' are questions that can neither be disregarded nor addressed with any degree of expectation of consensus or closure, because it is precisely consensus and closure that these terms resist, and it is precisely that resistance that these terms convey. So every reference to one of these terms – whether to hold it at a distance or whether from, so to say, within that term's embrace – comes either with a sense of their ambiguities being already established (the complicity with which cognoscenti speak to each other, knowing where the authorities are and where the citable texts are) or with a need to issue another definition or delimitation (which necessarily comes with new nuances and more questions).

This discussion is too short and, as the above paragraph suggests, impressionistic. The resistance to closure that emanates from these terms, the transience of the limits with which they are evoked, are written into their associations. The post-predicable form of 'postmodernism' and 'postcolonialism' allows for an oft-noted conflation between providing closure to something past (as say, "post-war" might) and postponing or regressing closure at the same time. It is so difficult to say when modernism ended or whether that has happened at all, and similarly when and where colonialism ended and whether that has happened either, that the appendage of *post-* is taken as a sophisticated play on ideas of closure rather than an attribution of closure. When these terms were joyously received in critical and academic vocabularies in the late 1970s they appeared to come as declarations of closure, the closure of certain discourses: grand narratives, instrumental (Enlightenment) reason, construction of the Orient as other, imperial (colonial) discourses, indeed hegemonic discourses generally. These terms therefore present themselves as, in some sense, an already realized – by their utterance and exposition – *posterior* to the discourses that they close. But, at the same time, they seek to critique the continuity and prevalence of the discourses that they have not quite closed, so that they come to represent *prospective* aspirations too, of which no more than glimmerings could be said to exist in the present, glimmerings emerging from the utterance and exposition of these terms themselves. And yet, again at the same time, these terms base their critique on an apprehension of their superior application or deeper legitimacy – so, in some sense, *anterior* to that which they place their closure in terms of. The complexity of being posterior, prospective, and anterior at the same time is compounded by the investment in (as much as disinvestment from) that which such terms connote their posteriority, prospective place, and anteriority to, and this too is contained in the play on *post-*. The performance of postmodern understanding is as much a departure from the grand narratives (in Lyotard's terms), the instrumentalist rationality (with different inflexions through Adorno, Baudrillard, Giddens, and others), the uniform ideological dispositions (with different emphases, Althusser and Foucault) of modernity, as made possible by modernity. Similarly, postcolonial departures from the Orientalist construction that Said so persuasively presented, or the mutually polarized and yet locked bind that Fanon so presciently analysed, is seen at the same time to emerge from and develop upon those conditions. Metatheoretical terms like 'postmodernism' and 'postcolonialism' manage a dispersal of implicature and relevance[47] that is extraordinarily suggestive.

Something similar occurs with 'globalization' too. When 'globalization' entered academic parlance, mainly by thrusting aside 'internationalization', in the late 1970s and early 1980s it came clearly from a specific location, the USA, and from specific interests. It connoted the desire to develop the study of sociology in America as a world-embracing enterprise or track such study as expanding into domains outside the USA;[48] more importantly it expressed the desire of US business leaders representing multinational corporate interests to seize the moment[49] and academic management gurus of the time to reconceptualize business studies accordingly.[50] Since then the history of the term has been one that gradually eschews the specific contexts from and interests with which it emerged and moves towards its assumption of metatheoretical status. And again, in this its associations help. 'Globalization' suggests a process, like 'internationalization', but of what? In wilfully rising above the specific context and interests of its emergence, and by becoming a term that replaces and does not coincide with the erstwhile 'internationalization', the content of the process is emptied out. It becomes a process that applies in various possible ways across the whole world; not so much a description of the content of the process as of its field of application (everything). And in distinguishing itself from 'internationalization', it also suggests that the process that it encapsulates is indifferent to nation-state boundaries and the prerogatives usually attached to that (the relationship of globalization to nation-states is understandably one of the most prolifically discussed areas in recent years). By such shifts and accretions of connotation the term 'globalization' exercises, like 'postmodernism' and 'postcolonialism', an extraordinary dispersal of evocations.

What ultimately gives these terms their metatheoretical character is their almost absolute refusal of containment: these terms simply refuse to be put into perspective or thrown into relief (while constantly seeking to throw every other consideration into relief by containing them), they absorb their apparent opposites into themselves, they metamorphose to formulate every social and political phenomenon as manifestations of themselves, they disperse themselves (just as I have metaphorically understood identity politics as spreading itself) into various layers of apprehension and formulation with slightly different and yet seemingly coherent nuances. These terms do not admit of alternatives (they merge into each other when pressed together), and they do not admit of oppositional positions outside themselves. By a little twist these terms expand beyond any formal application into abstractions that can be dispersed anywhere.

Thus, postcolonialism registers and analyses colonialism and anticolonialism and neo-colonialism, but thereby rises above and beyond every specific experience of any of these to become constitutionally that which, in Robert Young's words, 'focuses on forces of oppression and coercive domination that operate in the contemporary world [...] to develop new forms of engaged theoretical work that contributes to the creation of dynamic ideological and social transformation'.[51] Postcolonialism seems to be regarded as the optimism of progress itself (and therefore the despair of regress), however cast and understood. In contemplating postcolonial studies/ literature/ criticism, Graham Huggan's attempt to distinguish the field of critical attention to cultural and political conditions after colonialism from the field of branding/ marketing/consuming – or exoticizing – practices with regard to former colonies, rests significantly upon a syntactical inflection: he marks the former as 'postcolonialism' ('an anti-colonial intellectualism') and the latter as 'postcoloniality' ('a value-regulating mechanism within the global late-capitalist system of commodity exchange').[52] The discernment of the exotic within postcolonial studies/ literature/ criticism – within postcolonialism – obviously undermines the emancipative thrust of the term (exemplified by Young). However, by using that obviously connected syntactical inflection to convey the distinction, Huggan acknowledges the containment of his resistant argument within the field it interrogates – the postcoloniality within postcolonialism. Ultimately, the product of this argument itself, Huggan's text, inevitably comes as both a contribution to the institutional field of postcolonialism and a product that is appropriable in the value-form of postcoloniality. 'The postmodern', Lyotard had observed in an unusual but succinct vein at the time (most do not grapple with the term, just define and qualify and assume), 'would be that which, in the modern, puts forward the unpresentable in presentation itself; that which denies itself the solace of good forms, the consensus of a taste which would make it possible to share collectively the nostalgia for the unattainable; that which searches for new presentations, not in order to enjoy them but in order to impart a stronger sense of the unpresentable'.[53] Lyotard's is a particular apprehension of what the postmodern condition entails, but this description captures something of the kind of abstraction through which the embrace of the term expands. Lyotard's characterization is one that admits for postmodernism nothing other than recognition – it can be regarded and withheld – since to do more, to describe its connotations, for instance, would be to present the presentable. Similarly, globalization is in the process of constantly expanding to contain its ostensible opposites. By dint of attempting to oppose not just globalization's specificities and interests but also its dispersals and expansions, the so-called anti-globalization movement itself becomes a strand of that term's connotations (*globalization* from below, the *globalization* of protest). This allows David Held and Anthony McGrew to extend a project of cosmopolitan democracy which provides a: 'common ground in global politics [that] contains clear possibilities of dialogue and accommodation between different segments of the "globalization/anti-globalization" political spectrum'.[54] In brief, it becomes impossible for an anti- or post- postcolonial position, or anti- or post- postmodern position, or an anti- or post- globalization position to be assumed that is not at the selfsame moment no more than a postcolonial, postmodern, or globalizating gesture itself.

In discussing this cluster of terms here, it is not my intention to suggest that the terms – 'postmodernism', 'postcolonialism', 'globalization' – are in themselves responsible for the pervasiveness of identity politics as understood in this study. A great deal of the work done as postmodernist theory, postcolonial critique, and globalization studies has little or nothing to do with identity politics. Such work often undertakes, for instance, explorations of specific social, cultural, and political discourses and contexts without presuming that an embodied identity-based political position is inevitably entailed or that concordant limitations of communication and critical engagement should be held together. Equally though, precisely the latter presumptions are often – almost unthinkingly – promoted too through such work. These metatheoretical terms allude, I feel, to modes of conceptualization and formulation that are not necessarily akin to identity politics, but that nevertheless are amenable to enabling identity politics to extend through their interstices. This amenability derives precisely from their metatheoretical status. Such is the metatheoretical compass of these terms, such is the reach from their loci, that an overwhelming interest develops in the factors which are, so to say, within grip: who is speaking them and from where. These terms are therefore obsessively concerned with notions of location/locality, place, movement (migrations and diaspora), on the one hand, and of subjectivity and actors (in the sense of those having or not having political agency, such as activists, intellectuals, migrants), on the other. It is not difficult to see how identity-based embodiments can attach themselves to these concerns, and why identity politics as described above seeps through such metatheoretical terms, is constructed upon their scaffolding, and spreads its universalization of difference through the interstices of metatheory.

The amenability of such metatheoretical terms to association with identity politics is particularly strong in postcolonialism. The kind of abstraction from formal colonizations/anti-colonial struggles/ decolonizations that is performed in postcolonialism is necessarily conducted in accordance with identity-based claims and attributions – understandably, particularly of nationhood, race, and gender. The embodied identity-based political positions of nationalism, feminism, and race, and their containment in identity politics, have therefore come to become inextricably entwined with postcolonial theory and critique. This works in various ways. It works at some level in the Western academy (in Northern America, Europe, and Australia) as bearing an embodied racial trace. Sara Suleri's revealing analysis of the manner in which the 'postcolonial woman' becomes an icon of virtue at the juncture of race and gender in academia, comes to mind[55] (and such observations are legion). It occurs through the extension of the biogenetic notion of hybridity to a postcolonial cultural constructionist sphere, most familiarly by Homi Bhabha and Robert Young. That in turn leads to different kinds of identity-based political embodiments again, remarkably of – as Aijaz Ahmad robustly argued in his controversial and, for postcolonial academics, intensely discomfiting book[56] – so-called Third World immigrant academics in Western metropolitan universities. Despite the many careful theoretical refutations of Ahmad's arguments, the particular advantages that immigrant or diasporic writers and intellectuals enjoy in postcolonized (or decolonized) pockets of the Western academy inevitably smacks of a relatively new kind of embodied identity-based political position: that of the migrant from a former colony in the colonizer's domain, who is happy to look favourably at other embodied positions, and subscribes cheerfully to identity politics. Not far behind that rests an arena of postcolonial academic contests, where newly re-embodied native postcolonials articulate their claims and attributions, often bitterly, in competition with diasporic and migrant postcolonials, or where the latter offer collaboration and enlightenment to the former.

As I have observed already, all these are prodigiously discussed matters; the consideration of this cluster of terms can either carry on in a prolonged fashion, or, as here, simply inadequately finish.

The above discussion of three clusters of terms – in-between terms, encompassing terms, and metatheoretical terms – and their connotations and significances convey in a cursory fashion the field through which identity politics constructs and spreads itself. The dynamic spaces demarcated by in-between terms allow the fragile containment of embodied identity-based political positions to be contained within identity politics, by spreading limitations of communication and critical engagement. The excessive reach of the encompassing terms facilitates the spreading of identity politics by extending the logic of embodiment where it does not strictly belong, even against the grain of universalist and individualist formulations. The abstractions involved in and ineffable ambits of the metatheoretical terms are amenable to the dispersal and generalization of identity politics through the interstices of research and conceptualization surrounding those terms.

The construction and pervasiveness of identity politics conveyed through the above consideration of these terms, however, still does not complete the elaboration of the definition of social constructionist identity politics relevant to this study. Identity politics, and the limitations of communication and critical engagement it entails, is characteristic of the current ethos mainly because of the *evidence* of its prevalence – because of its concretizations. The elaborated definition of identity politics cannot be complete without containing the mechanism of how and why identity politics works and the modes of the institutionalization of identity politics.

5
Identity Politics at Work

Institutionalization and historicization

One knows identity politics is at work because it becomes institutional-ized, because it comes with potential structures of institutionalization constituted within it, and expands by confirmation within institution-alized practice.

I use institutionalization here in the sense used by Berger and Luckmann, that is, more as a habitual disposition of social organization rather than the processes pertaining to a closed area of social control (closure as the organization or institution):

> Institutionalization occurs whenever there is a reciprocal typification of habitualized actions by types of actors. Put differently, any such typification is an institution. What must be stressed is the reciprocity of institutional typifications and the typicality of not only the actions but also the actors in institutions. The typifications of habit-uated actions that constitute institutions are always shared ones.[1]

For Berger and Luckmann the boundaries of institutions are determined by their habitualized disposition, rather than the habitualized disposition being enjoined by the closure of institutional boundaries. The latter is more the emphasis of Weber's notion of organization (*Verband*): 'A social relationship which is either closed or limits the admission of outsiders [...] when its regulations are enforced by specific individuals: a chief and, possibly, an administrative staff, which normally also has representative powers.'[2] Placing the emphasis on habitual social disposition rather than boundaries and control gives institutionalization a somewhat different inflection from simply regarding it as something that pertains to specific and bounded organizations or institutions. Eventually, this study is addressed to a range of such bounded institutions in relation to each other – educational and research institutions and their various divisions and subdivisions, the publishing and mass media industries, to do with literary studies – but that is, as I have already said, no more than a convenience. In this study, referring to the institutionalization of identity politics does not mean referring to matters pertinent to particular kinds of institutions or organizations, but to a prevailing habitualized social disposition which can become concretized or manifest in a range of institutions, or simply apparent in a wide variety of ways within a wide variety of institutional boundaries. The emphasis on institutional boundaries in my use of 'institutionalization' is even more dilute than Berger and Luckmann's.

The description of identity politics given above could be said to be at work insofar as it is institutionalized, i.e., it is manifested in a range of habitualized actions and practices with effect on a range of formal and informal institutions, and broadly across (particularly the so-called Western, but also many other strands of) contemporary society itself. This is a big claim, and no more than indicative demonstration of this is possible, which is attempted with regard to literary studies in Part II of this study. Even the attempt to undertake such a limited demonstration requires some sense of the environment in which identity politics has come to be institutionalized. It is not enough to simply register what identity politics is and what the mechanisms are through which it conceptualizes and consolidates itself (the substance of the previous three chapters), but also to acknowledge the conditions under and environment within which identity politics has, so to say, risen to its present pervasive eminence. What is required, in other words, is a historicization of identity politics as understood here.

To recapitulate briefly, as understood here, identity politics embraces different embodied identity-based political positions through analogues and equivalences while maintaining the centrality of difference as its main organizing principle – operating what I have called a universalization of difference. This process is a social constructionist one. This kind of identity politics is powerfully opposed to former essentialist identity-based political positions, and arises out of struggles against essentialism. In this process, both the fluidity of identity and the potential for consolidating (however temporarily) specific identity-based political positions through a logic of embodiment are recognized. The consequence of this fluidity and consolidation, I have argued, entails a spreading of limitations on communication and critical engagement, rather than

accepting the exclusions of essentialist identity-based political positions. I have observed that this form of identity politics is not only
closely associated with the new left, and has close connections with liberal thinking, but also gradually enjoys a wide if grudging prevalence
among a range of other ideological alignments – increasingly within
conservative folds too (hence its institutionalization). I have also
observed that it is primarily since the late 1970s, and especially through
the decade of the 1980s, that this form of identity politics has been formulated, debated, and developed, deriving from a number of specific
identity-based political positions of longer standing and their efferves-
cences. Historicizing identity politics would necessarily entail a particular focus on the last three decades of the 20th century.

As it happens, attempts to historicize identity politics in the above
sense are yet to be undertaken. There exist a large number of histories of
different identity-based political positions (of feminist movements, of
gay and lesbian politics, of race politics, of modern forms of ethnicity
and nationalism, etc.) and a large number of histories of the struggles of
specific identity-based political positions seen in juxtaposition against
each other in particular national contexts (notably with reference to
USA and France). All of these note the expansion and impact of identity
politics as described above within their particular frames of reference,
but these do not amount to a historicization of that expansion and
impact, only a noting thereof. Sociologists and political theorists have
often given a historicist character to their formulations/championing of
identity politics, usually in terms of metatheoretical formulations of
modernity/postmodernity, postcoloniality, and particularly globalization. But, in these, history is generally instrumental to the sociological
metatheorization in question, the sketchy and selective sequence or the
illuminated moment that justifies the metatheoretical formulation.
Indeed, it seems to me that a history of the rise and prevalence of social
constructionist identity politics remains as yet a project for the future –
and there it must, at present, be left. It is possible however, even within
the sweeping remit of this study, to register some directions that such a
project might interrogate and illuminate and clarify.

Crisis of the left movement

Historicizing the rise of identity politics, along the lines delineated
above, occurs understandably in attempts to historicize the (ongoing)
crisis of the left movement (or the resolution of a new left on identity
politics). The new left's taking up and championing of identity politics,

to align a wide variety of emancipative struggles, is usually understood as resulting from the delegitimization of the working class as the focus of socialist politics. Of course other more familiar factors are numerously mooted here. These include naturally political economic considerations such as the stagnancy of centralized economies in a large number of former communist states; the success of late or advanced capitalism in terms of fiscal expansion, temporary accommodations with welfare economics, compromise with workers' prerogatives by enabling bargaining structures, widening the ambit of corporate and governmental stakeholding, etc.; and the demonstrability of this success by de-linking private and public interests – enabling devolution of economic responsibility from states and accountability from corporations – with some immediate evidence of economic growth and market-led vitality. Normative factors play with these: the association of liberal capitalist states with democracy and freedom, on the one hand, and the dissenting movements in former communist countries against totalitarian regimes, on the other. These are constantly iconized in the fall of the Berlin Wall in 1989. And, in connection with the above, certain theoretical considerations are also aired to understand the crisis of the left: primarily by pitting marginal utilities against the Marxist labour theory of value, and proposing the spontaneous freedom and justice of the market mechanism against the determination of centralized planning. Though all of these considerations are important to historicize the growing crisis of the left movement in the late 20th century, none leads as directly to the new left's embracing of identity politics as the interrogation and (some would say) discrediting of the working-class movement as the scaffolding on which left politics was constructed. The vacuum left behind by withdrawing workers as primary agents of change, was filled in by accepting marginal embodied identity-based actors as principal political agents. Behind that lies a critique of Marxist class analysis: it was not just that the working class was displaced by marginal identities, but that the entire frame of social-class analysis was overtaken by identity-based theorization.

   Historicization of identity politics within the frame of historicization of the left's crisis follows, therefore, the interrogation of Marxist class analysis closely. This is usually done most cogently and passionately by those within the left (new or old). As observed above, those who have questioned the new left's embracing of identity-based political positions and identity politics from within the left – Todd Gitlin, Eric Hobsbawm, Aijaz Ahmad (especially addressing Third Worldism in postcolonial theory) – have maintained the continuing efficacy of class analysis to make their point. Equally, those who have accepted this as a matter of historical necessity within the left too – such as Alain Touraine and Stanley Aronowitz – have done so primarily in terms of doubts about the continuing efficacy of Marxist class analysis. Self-critique within the left as a historicist enterprise, whereby the identity politics of the new left is positioned, has too many instances to chart out here.[3] A concise and indicative example could serve to clarify the situation here; such an example is available in Andrei Markovits's essay on the periods of development in the left in post-war Europe and America.[4] Markovits presents post-war developments in the left as divisible into four periods. The first period he calls the orthodox period, 1945–1968, where the lines along which the left was delineated were ideological ones: externally, against liberals, fascists, conservatives, etc.; and internally, between communists and social democrats. The second period is dubbed the heterodox period, 1968–1979, wherein some of the basic presumptions of the left were challenged, and primarily from the USA (in the context of anti-Vietnam war and Civil Rights movements) rather than Europe. In Europe, left politics centred powerfully on trade unions and in the relationships between parties and unions. Several factions emerged, including those who continued along orthodox Marxist lines, those who felt that the focus should be on Western workers, those who believed that the recently decolonized Third World should absorb left aspirations, and those in or from the developing world who exercised a sort of neo-nationalist perspective. The third period, 1980–1989, is understood as one of paradigm shifts, especially the, 'weakening of – perhaps even severing – of an alliance that once had defined the left, with the working class as subject of history and driving force of progressive politics'.[5] New social movements and Green parties emerged in this period as aligned to the left. The fourth and ongoing period, 1989/1990–present, is seen as one of fragmentation and polarization – with new left identity politics at centre-stage.

This broad periodization accords well with the development of identity politics in relation to the left observed above. The precise negotiations and debates through which identity politics crept up to compete with and ultimately overturn the centrality of class analysis for the left needs a great deal more documentation than is feasible in an essay; and though the emphasis on Europe and the USA is useful, for that is where new left identity politics has emanated from, its spread and pervasiveness also calls for a wider contextual scope. The shifts marked by the advent of the decolonized developing world in identity politics terms and the alignments sought among so-called new social movements, naturally makes a wider scope imperative. This, as I said, remains a project of the future. There is a wealth of documentation that can be called upon: records of conferences and meetings, of critical analysis of current events and concordant theorizations in a range of left journals and magazines, of the self-definitions of the left during the gradual dissolving of trade unions and in relation to changing paradigms of democratic or centralist party politics, of the alignments within which the left operated with regard to issue-based protest or activism.

To briefly touch upon an example of the documentation that characterizes the rise of new left identity politics (still with the USA and European focus), records of three evenly spaced out conferences can be usefully cited here. The first, organized by the Kansas *Telos* group on 'The Crisis of the Left' in 4–6 December 1980, is recorded in summary and with some contributions (by Paul Breines, Paul Piccone, Tim Luke, Robert D'Amico, and Russell Jacoby) in the subsequent edition of *Telos*.[6] In this the various reasons for the collapse of the left are examined and theorized, the rise of the post-1968 new left is sceptically noted but the conservatism of the Leninist left is more severely castigated, and some of the influential identity-based political positions (feminism and black liberation) registered in a doubtful fashion. The debate as a whole was characterized by a sort of despairing grasping at straws: the old left is unsustainable but the new left seems already to have run out of energy, and aligned identity-based political positions are caught up in their confused particularities. The second event I have in mind was one organized by Lawrence & Wishart in May 1989 to address the new political agenda of the left, entitled 'Changing Identities', papers and an interview from which were subsequently published as an edited volume.[7] The contributions here (by Jonathan Rutherford, Andrea Stuart, Kobena Mercer, Jeffrey Weeks, Pratibha Parmar, Stuart Hall, and Homi Bhabha) came from prominent left thinkers and, more importantly, those who regard themselves as representing specific identity-based political positions. These are bright and optimistic, and announce an alignment in identity politics (in terms of a universalization of difference and logic of embodiment exactly as characterized above) as the new left. The consensus on difference is given a ringing and future-looking endorsement in the opening paper by Rutherford:

> Such a politics [of difference] wouldn't need to subsume identities into an underlying totality that assumes their ultimately homogeneous nature. Rather it is a critique of essentialism and mono-culturalism, asserting the unfixed and 'overdetermined' character of identities. The

cultural politics of difference recognises both the interdependent and
relational nature of identities, their elements of incommensurability
and their political right of autonomy.[8]

The third event I would like to recall was held in October 1996 and
entitled 'Liberalism and the Left: Rethinking the Relationship', organized by *Radical History Review* in collaboration with the Graduate
Program in History of the City University of New York and recorded in
the following volume of *Radical History Review*[9] (publishing papers
from Blanche Cook, Eric Forner, Amber Hollibaugh, Manning Marable,
Sara Evans, Gerald Horne, and Robert Westbrooke). This displays a
partly satisfied and partly resigned acceptance of identity politics as
defining the agenda of the left; that left politics is now identity politics
is taken as a foregone conclusion. More interestingly, this registers not
just an attempt to find accommodation between liberal and left politics, but a recognition that such a convergence is already underway
through identity politics. The tone of faint nostalgia for the old left
mixed with hope in new left identity politics is best given in Amber
Hollibaugh's paper (undertaking to convey – embody – a 'progressive
lesbian activist's' perspective):

> The question of organizing and building a left has, for the last ten
> years, seemed as though it were a kind of ironic fantasy that some of
> us had clung to from the sixties or earlier, and was never going to
> come again. The best we could do was identity politics. Many of us
> have been part of those movements, pushing from the left, but feel-
> ing that there was never again going to be a movement that said
> words like 'class', and built the ideas of organizing across lines of gen-
> der and race and sexualities; but with a social definition that chal-
> lenged the very core of what this country has come to represent.[10]

Arguably, subsequent discussions have hardened the convergence of liberal and left politics through identity politics, even as anti-globalization
protest and activism for peace, particularly after 11 September 2001,
have gathered momentum in the early 21st century.

Such historicizing of identity politics as an aspect of historicizing the
crisis of the left in the last decades of the 20th century, however, wilfully conflates identity politics with the new left in a way that I feel
overendows the new left's claim to identity politics – and ultimately
does it a disservice. Though much of the new left (increasingly con-
verging towards normative liberalism) appears to be determined to

claim identity politics as its exclusive domain and possession, it would be disingenuous to simply accept that. The pervasiveness of identity politics in our world; legislation and practice that is increasingly heedful of identity politics in liberal and conservative establishments; the evidence of habitualization of thinking and action, therefore institutionalization of identity politics – all these could be understood in two ways. Either these could be seen as hard-won concessions won by struggles (from mainly identity-based political positions) aligned now in the new left (as identity politics) – and so, to some extent, of course they are. Or these could be seen as concessions given by what is thought of as a dominant liberal democratic capitalist establishment, because identity politics suits the environment of capitalism and of establishment liberal politics – indubitably, to a significant extent, this is also true. Perhaps the latter is more the case: the line between what is won by demand and struggle from the establishment and what is given by the establishment on its own terms and for its own consolidation and advantage, seems to me very thin indeed. It seems to me very likely that identity politics is a field of entanglements where establishment and oppositional politics intersect with each other so that the conflict between the two sides becomes part of a larger game and a larger direction – often gestured towards in the pluralistically univocal mystique of postmodernism, postcolonialism, and globalization.

Liberalism and contemporary capitalism

In 1994, Todd Gitlin observed in his critique of the left's turn towards identity politics a current 'curious reversal [... it is] the aspiring aristocrats of the Academic Right [that] tend to speak the language of universals – canon, merit, reason, individual rights, transpolitical virtue'.[11] There was a reversal, but somewhat more than that has come to pass. In many ways identity politics emerged from, as observed above, the resistant and universalistic cogitations of liberal democratic philosophy and sociology, as a painful but unavoidable coming to grips with plurality and the institutionalization of necessary multiculturalism. The relegation of class analysis in favour of identity theorization was not something that was of defining interest to the new left alone; it was of great interest to liberals. It was partly of interest as marking the end of an adversarial relationship with the orthodox left, but also more than that. For many, it was an indication of a change in the social order that had made the left both possible and potent: the idea is that the left had sustained itself by focusing on working-class agency because Marxist class analysis was realistic; and the fact that the left was in a crisis was because the social disposition had changed and Marxist class analysis no longer applied. The crisis of the left was therefore not so much due to a loss of conviction in the efficacy of class analysis and the agency of the working class, but because society itself has changed to dilute class differences. Robert Nesbit has mooted the idea of the changing character of society with regard to social classes as early as 1959,[12] and this seemed to come to the fore after the declared period of the left's embracing of identity politics. A 1993 special issue of *International Sociology* on 'Are Social Classes Dying?'[13] saw views divided between those who felt that social classes continue to exist but that their political effectiveness has diminished because of the mess the left was in, and those who felt that social classes as distinguishable strata were ceasing to exist. Of the latter view was Jan Pakulski,[14] who thereafter produced a co-authored book on the subject[15] and generated a lively debate in the pages of *Theory and Society.*[16] The stir that the contemplation of a social condition that makes class analysis redundant in liberal (across the spectrum from left-leaning to centre-right to conservative) circles, indicated a sort of liberation from adversarial reckonings with the left. Liberalism had already registered the possibilities of pluralist principles and multiculturalist legislation within its resistant discourse. By the 1990s it was comfortably assimilating the new left and identity politics within its broad fold – playing on the blur between universality and difference where identity politics expands.

The historicization of identity politics could be an aspect of the historicization of liberal politics since the mid-1970s. There has been even less of this than in the case of the left. A sense of crisis draws attention and leads to historicist soul searching; triumphal paternalism crows, but is less attractive as a historical object. That also could be looked forward to as a project for the future. Something that seeps through these and indeed all ideological sieves whereby identity politics expands itself and entrenches institutionalized tentacles is, as is often observed, contemporary or advanced capitalism. Contemporary capitalism is what we are in the midst of, without limits and without boundaries any longer. In economic terms the condition of contemporary capitalism was last seen from *outside*, it seems to me, in Ernest Mandel's Marxist analysis – in terms of the shift of production from consumables to the means of production themselves, and a steady intensification of the social contradictions of capital.[17] In metaphoric terms, Henri Lefebvre's (and others') characterization of the ever-expanding *space* of contemporary capitalism can be kept in mind alongside that.[18] And so can Foucault's final attempt to characterize the *content* of marginal discourses, of 'discourses from below', without the limitations of communication and critical engagement that mark embodied identity politics.[19] Then there is a flip into the late 1970s and the 1980s, and that theory and politics fall into the midst of and are constituted by capitalism, become only speakable within and – however tortuously – under the conditions and structures of late capitalism. Contemporary capitalism's one-dimensionality no longer allows even for a great refusal along Marcusean lines;[20] it becomes every dimension by itself. And along with that identity politics comes into its own, contains different identity-based political positions, and spreads limitations of communication and critical engagement. However vehemently the new left tries to possess identity politics *against* advanced global capitalism, the mutually sustaining relationship between contemporary capitalism and identity politics can hardly be disavowed.

The historicization of identity politics as an aspect of the historicization of contemporary capitalism is not a task that should be relegated too far into the prospect. It is urgently needed, but it is a task that poses almost insuperable difficulties. That is why such an attempt does not yet exist; there are plenty of recognitions of the need, and acknowledgements of the relationship, and theoretical formulations of and empirical observations *apropos* the relationship,[21] but there are not even honourable defeats of historical scholarship to point to. This has to be undertaken from within (cannot but be) and has to be documented with a sense of the ubiquity of contemporary capitalism. The present study is obviously not the place to undertake such a very challenging project; to draw this chapter and part to an end I make a few gestural observations in that direction, still confining myself to a USA/Western Europe frame.

Let me return to the latter part of the 1970s and the 1980s. In May 1979 Margaret Thatcher came to office as prime minister of the UK, and in January 1981 Ronald Reagan took office as president of the USA. They popularized the most far-reaching free-market principles and instituted economic programmes of deregulation of markets and privatization of the public sector in their countries. These reforms also, it is widely agreed, set in motion the processes that now characterize state and world capitalism. At the same time, it is prolifically documented that both the Thatcher and Reagan governments, by active legislation or inaction, exacerbated racial tensions and polarization in their respective countries and hardened patriarchy and conservative sexual morality. At least one observation that emerges from this conjunction of policies is that resisting deregulation and privatization became inextricably connected to

resisting racialization and sexual/gender marginalization. It was no accident that Stuart Hall's influential critique of Thatcherite ideology[22] was
also a project that let loose the UK new left's embracing of identity
politics – or new ethnicities. Or perhaps, the economic neoliberalism of
Thatcher and Reagan powered through while oppositional attention was
ghettoized, by a concatenation of designs and accidents, within newly
embodied identity-defined margins. The burden of interpretation rests,
it seems to me, with history (without end).

The unleashing of late capitalism has another, and wider, association
with that period. The largest overhaul of North–South economic relations since the establishment of the Breton Woods agreement of July
1944 and the formation of the World Bank was also underway. World
Bank, and later International Monetary Fund (IMF), lending for international development along ideological lines had been primarily a matter of propping up capital-friendly states or creating state-controlled
Third World dependencies till the 1970s. In January 1977, at World
Bank President McNamara's call, an Independent Commission on
International Development Issues under the chairmanship of former
German Chancellor Willy Brandt was set up to examine the impasse
between poor and rich nations on terms of loans and assistance.
Eighteen countries (none from the communist block) were represented
in this. The report that followed in 1980 proposed among other recom-
mendations the removal of protectionist measures by developed countries against developing countries, and particularly modifications in the
existing adjustment policy:

> There should be agreement on the adjustment process which will not
> increase contractionist pressures in world economy. The adjustment
> process of developing countries should be placed in the context of
> maintaining long-term economic and social development. The IMF
> should avoid inappropriate or excessive regulation of their
> economies, and should not impose highly deflationary measures as
> standard adjustment policy. It should also improve and greatly
> extend the scope of its compensatory financing facility, for example
> by relaxing quota limits, measuring shortfalls in real terms and mak-
> ing repayment terms more flexible.[23]

What occurred, however, was the devising of the infamous Structural
Adjustment Loan (or Structural Adjustment Facility [SAF]) – the first of
which was given to Turkey by the World Bank in March 1980. These made
the administration of loans conditional to extensive infrastructural

changes within poor countries taking loans, especially by instituting greater dependency on market forces and reducing direct state intervention and control, encouraging export and mobilization of domestic resources, and making state enterprise self-reliant. From 1986 to 1999 the IMF administered over 90 SAFs and ESAFs (Enhanced SAFs were introduced in December 1987) to 56 poor countries. Widespread and disastrous disinvestments by states in these poor countries followed, often without the hoped-for growth and sustainable development and only falling deeper into a spiral of debt and sanctions. The effects of IMF and World Bank conditionality, the evolution of an international capitalist regulatory system in the 1980s and 1990s, and the imperialist agenda of developed capitalist interests that operated through these have been extensively studied – popularly, for instance, by Joseph Stiglitz.[24] Between the mid-1980s and -1990s protests against SAF/ESAF-impelled state disinvestments and deteriorating economic conditions were evidenced in Algeria, Benin, Bolivia, Ecuador, Jamaica, Jordan, Mexico, Niger, Nigeria, Russia, Sudan, Trinidad, Uganda, Venezuela, Zaire (Congo), and Zambia, among other countries. While these localized actions were gradually given some coherence in the course of the 1990s within the fold of 'new social movements', and through anti-globalization protests directed against the international economic regulatory bodies (and demanding the cancellation of Third World debt), they remained no more than a particular factor in the maelstrom of the politics of difference. It probably would not be too much of an exaggeration to say that the world capitalist regime that was imposed from above through such programmes as the SAFs/ESAFs could not be opposed in their unabashedly totalitarian and holistic ambition by new social movements working indistinguishably from identity politics. The latter simply disperses concentration away from the economic logic of world capitalism and across the universalization of embodied differences and locations. By recognizing identity-based claims, by allowing this loosely formed opposition certain victories in identity-based matters, by encouraging the absolute absorption of opposition into identity politics and propelling an incremental convergence in itself towards identity politics, the establishment that drives the world capitalist regime does no more than oil its wheels and keep effective obstructions outside its path.

The historicization of identity politics as an aspect of the historicization of contemporary capitalism may well complicate some of the patterns that even these very cursory observations bring up in the domestic and international development of capitalism. But I doubt whether such historicization can obviate the discernment of such patterns. Simply, identity politics is pervasive and becoming institutionalized because it is to the advantage of contemporary capitalism, and within the environment of contemporary capitalism. It is to the advantage of contemporary capitalism because it allows the economic logic to unravel in an autonomous and untrammelled fashion, and locates the problems of contemporary capitalism in the margins of cultural identities. The rousing and the quelling of passions in identity politics mark both another moment in the institutionalization of identity politics and another step in the consolidation of corporate capitalism. At bottom, identity politics is *designed* not to be able to come to grips with the totality of corporate capitalism and its economic coherence, to always miss corporate capitalism as an object to oppose and vanquish. This is not the design of a deep conspiracy; it is the structural design that has always been discernible within the operations of capitalism, even in the early Marxist critique of 19th-century capitalism.

Finally, part of the project of historicizing contemporary capitalism and identity politics therein would also have to be devoted to clarifying how the productions of/for/through the latter are at the behest of the former. It is here that Fredric Jameson's ponderings on the manner in which the production of postmodern culture marks a phase of late capitalism could provide a useful analogue.[25] If identity politics thrives and becomes institutionalized in the environment of and under the conditions of contemporary capitalism that must be because it is itself produced and reproduced in the circulation of capital. Arguably identity politics maps the global market in a convenient way that is either indifferent to traditional boundaries (such as of nation-states) or instrumentalizes such boundaries (such as of ethnic identities). Identities are endlessly commodifiable, especially when embodied, and all the more intensely when politicized. And so on. The almost impossible project of historicizing contemporary capitalism may ultimately be the only way to historicize identity politics as it works – in all its pervasiveness – in our world.

The position taken in this study

To conclude this part, the social constructionist position that is espoused in this study against the kinds of limitations of communication and critical engagement that are spread through social constructionist identity politics could be briefly stated. This position seems so obvious to me that my presentation of this can only take the form of a series of concise, quaint, platitudinous, prescription-like statements.

Nevertheless, in the face of the prevailing habitualization and gradual institutionalization of the logic of embodiment in identity-based political positions and their containment in identity politics, it is probably useful to state this position. The position taken in this study consists in the following avowals:

1. Any expression of a political position, however contextualized and particular or however general and acontextualized, is open to critical engagement and debate by anyone anywhere who is exposed to it, in terms of the relevances and associations that are available to him or her. If the expression of a political position is available within one's horizon of communication and critical engagement it becomes open to his or her scrutiny, evaluation, interrogation, and criticism.

2. No greater or lesser authenticity or authority attaches to whomever chooses to critically engage with a political position; the only issue is what measure of information, understanding, and integrity is being brought to such critical engagement and debate. This is a crucial point which needs to be distinguished carefully against the logic of embodiment. To be (placed and constructed as) a woman in a patriarchal society with a history of gender discrimination and prejudice might give easier access to understanding gender marginalization, and therefore an informed and passionate conviction in the politics that struggles against the entire social order of which such discrimination and prejudice are a necessary symptom. It might be difficult for (one placed and constructed as) a man to have the same ease of access to understanding such marginalization and adhering to oppositional politics, but there is no reason to believe that it is not possible for him to understand the implications of that experience and its political consequences. It is perfectly possible that a man with sufficient curiosity in the issue and integrity in his enquiry into the issue will come to substantially the same kind of understanding and emotional investment in his consequent political response. Indeed, that men and women will respond critically from all sorts of positions is inevitable as soon as the politics of the struggle against gender discrimination is formulated and expressed. As soon as that happens, the politics of this struggle becomes a site to which anyone anywhere (however gendered or ungendered) can be drawn, without limits on his or her ability to question, debate, and communicate therein. It does not matter *who* (as a gendered body) is articulating or acting in this political arena; all that matters is what basis of integrity, knowledge, understanding, and emotional investment (by a critical and communicative agent) is

being brought to the arena. It may happen that there is a great deal of coincidence between the identity and the critical investments of a political actor, but to make the former a condition of political authenticity and authority in the latter (as happens in the logic of embodiment) is, simply, an unwholesome spreading of limits and polarities. This applies to any political position in which the construction and attribution of any kind of identity is a focal issue, and the evidence of discrimination and prejudice is a central concern.

3. There is a very great need to continue to address the evidence of prejudice and discrimination along various lines through critical political thought and open debate and action. This entails addressing the existing institutions and prevailing social attitudes and ideas that are relevant to these – including the current vogue for embodied identity-based political positions and their containment in identity politics. This entails an ever-expanding and interrogative form of social constructionist thinking, which is not just endlessly open to differences but also endlessly open to similarities and the (however contingent or potential) erasure of differences.

Such prescription-like avowals bear an unfortunate similarity to the prescriptions that are made by theorists of deliberative democracy and rational communicative action like Jürgen Habermas and Joshua Cohen[26] (as the normative basis of what they think of as Western liberal democracy). This is more a stylistic matter than a matter of coherence in ideological perspectives. A few immediate distinctions are relevant. One, unlike deliberative democratic prescriptions, these avowals are not meant as prescriptions at all, to be instituted in a programmatic and institutional way. These avowals delineate the salutary situation that I think already largely obtains in our time and contexts, though often forcibly distorted and remoulded to suit particular ideological interests. The latter are, increasingly, the limited interests of alignments invested in embodied identity-based political positions or invested in containing them in identity politics, and the interests of the elites of contemporary capitalism, who sustain and grudgingly encourage these from, as it were, without and in-between while colonizing and exercising universal economic arrangements. Two, contrary to deliberative democratic prescriptions, the above avowals are not meant as universal norms emanating from the West outwards to ultimately end history by their universal establishment; these avowals are strictly of the historical moment and condition wherein identity politics prevails. They are as immutable or historically contingent as identity politics is.

Part II   Literary Studies

6
Theory, Institutional Matters, Identity Politics

Institutional reckonings

At the end of Gerald Graff's 'institutional history' of the development of literary studies in the USA, *Professing Literature* (1987), and in view of the impact of Theory on the discipline, he speculated on the following institutional outcome:

> If history runs true to form once more, then we can expect literary theory to be defused not by being repressed but by being accepted and quietly assimilated or relegated to the margin where it ceases to be a bother. Something of the sort seems already to be happening, as forward-looking departments rush to hire theorists, who form a new ghetto alongside those occupied by the black studies person hired several years ago and the women's studies person hired yesterday. (Marginalization may affect women's studies and black studies less, however, since they have outside political ties.)[1]

This presents an interesting conjunction of anxieties and negotiations that characterized debates in the literary academy of the time (the 1980s). The institutional history which informed this observation was a fleshing out of an intervention in the Theory debate which Graff had made earlier, in *Literature against Itself* (1979).[2] The latter book effectively provided historical evidence for Graff's view that the ostensibly anti-humanist political turn that post-New Critical and poststructuralist literary theorists in the 1960s and 1970s had converged on was in many ways a continuation of traditional literary humanism, though Graff acknowledged the distinctiveness and efficacy of Theory. This statement appeared therefore as another intervention in a debate which was (and sometimes continues to be) crudely, and misleadingly neatly, thought of as Theory vs. anti-Theory. Indeed Graff's balanced and theoretically nuanced approach to the matter itself undermines the reckless polarization of that 'versus'. More than an intervention though, this statement, and the larger project it derives from, were part of an ongoing reckoning with the institutional and political fallout of Theory. The 1980s has often been regarded as a period when the Theory debate became entwined with institutional stocktaking, and almost assumed a post-Theory character in places. Looking back from the vantage point of a couple of decades, Terry Eagleton was to observe that, 'The halcyon days of cultural theory [by which he meant what passed then as Theory] lasted until about 1980',[3] whereafter some development of existing ideas took place and, in his view, more political regression. The quoted sentiment from Graff was therefore a reflexive one – true, it was an intervention in discussions on the claims of Theory, but more pertinently it was a reflection on what institutional response should or could follow given that the claims of Theory are out there and known to all. Grounding this within an institutional history was a strategy that others followed in this stocktaking phase of Theory (I come back to this later in this chapter). Presenting this as a matter of how institutional structures would be organized (also addressed further below) was no more than registering a widely debated matter in the 1980s, i.e., how should institutional literary practice respond to Theory: in terms of the manner in which academic research is disposed, curricula are organized, students are taught, relationships with other departments and disciplines are perceived and conducted, etc.

Establishing a link between traditional humanistic theory and the politics of Theory announced Graff's liberal convictions loudly. Graff was avowedly sceptical of the radical pretensions of Theory: in *Literature against Itself* he had bemoaned Theory's unthinking bid to get rid of every association with 'bourgeois culture'.[4] Not much later, he was to welcome an institutional reconfiguration of literary studies in programmes which 'integrate literary theory and history in an interdisciplinary framework, often under such rubrics as "cultural studies" and "cultural history"'[5] – interdisciplinarity was another Theory-related bee in the bonnet of the literary academy. But there is a gap in Graff's awareness here, which only the above statement seems to fill – but fill *as a gap*. With the enormous investment of Theory in black studies, feminist studies, gay studies, postcolonial studies, and vice versa already well in view it was not likely that Graff was unaware of the complicities of Theory and identity-based political positions. However, the envisaged institutional disposition of literary

studies in the above statement suggests no more than an analogous institutional space for Theory to black studies or women's studies in the
future. Graff did not see any crossover between these; he simply saw separate and therefore duly tamed academic ghettos of the future, Theory
alongside black studies, women's studies, and presumably so on. He did
not perceive any possibility of the extrinsic political interests of the latter rubbing off on Theory and therefore literary studies, or of the latter's
attempt to capture some of those political interests within itself. One
may say, Graff noted a connection in this statement, and refused to note
it at the same time.

In this too, Graff's statement is indicatively symptomatic of (though
not common or usual in) its time. The ambiguous recognition which is
nevertheless immediately withdrawn in this statement is perfectly
poised in the mid-1980s – a decade in the course of which stocktaking
and reflection on the institutional impact of Theory, and the political
underpinnings thereof, gave rise to social constructionist identity politics (as delineated in Part I) as the institutional organizing principle of
literary studies and the ideological cohort of Theory. Graff's statement is
merely a way into this matter; this chapter is devoted to quickly tracing
how social constructionist identity politics emerged through and from
and at odds with the Theory debate in the 1980s and thereafter. This
chapter in turn leads to a coming to grips with the institutionalization
of identity politics in contemporary literary studies. Literary studies is
the case in point within the more general field covered in Part I.

Whether there really was a schism, neatly dovetailing into the beginning of the 1980s, between the efflorescence of Theory and a stocktaking of and retrospection on its institutional and political effects – as
Eagleton and others, and I above, have suggested – is a moot point.
Eagleton has posited an emphatic shift at some such time, the end of a
golden age of cultural theory associated with certain star theorists, a roll
call of whose names convey not just a set of distinct concepts or formulations but also a mesh of exchanges that aspired to break and make
anew, an ideological spirit: Jacques Lacan, Claude Lévi-Strauss, Louis
Althusser, Roland Barthes, Michele Foucault, Raymond Williams, Luce
Irigaray, Pierre Bourdieu, Julia Kristeva, Jacques Derrida, Hélène Cixous,
Jürgen Habermas, Fredric Jameson, and Edward Said. The convenience of
iconic thought-biographies or signed-concepts mapped on to the convenience of demarcated periods and phases has, however, only a tenu-
ous connection to literary critical reading and writing. The perception
that reading (and therefore writing, certainly critical writing) always
begins *in medias res, a la* Stanley Fish for instance ('one doesn't choose

one's readings; one is *persuaded* to them [...] by coming up with answers to questions that are constitutive of the present practice of producing readings'[6]), appeals I think more to how things *are*, just as convenient iconic figures and discernment of periods appeals more to how things *were*. The experience of the ongoing present and of a retrospective past, I suspect, constitute their own discontinuity in indeterminate and fluid ways that leave both the Fish-like sense of flowing continuities and the Eagleton-like penchant for beginnings and endings open to valid scepticism. What does it mean then to begin with the 1980s as a decade of stocktaking of Theory? To do so is inevitably to begin *in medias res* as well as to make an overneat periodic demarcation, but in this context it appears to me to be something more. The question really is when was Theory, as a literary matter, constructed? I have, not without precedent, given it the capital T, but its singular form and air of denoting something new (different from, for instance, Wimsatt and Brooks's notion of literary theory, or debates about the prerogatives of theory between Derrida and Foucault, or even from theory with small t as understood in Said's 'travelling theory' for instance) is a familiar shared signification. When was it constructed as something to be reckoned with, bringing together ideas and formulations and activities which simply *were* theoretical practice rather than being held up as that discrete thing Theory? This construction itself made stocktaking, retrospection, institutional effect, and political formalization – as I see it, the alignment with identity politics – possible. This question is not posed here as it might be in a quiz show. I am not interested in an instance of originative usage, but in the context of Theory's consolidation as such. The 1980s, loosely, was thick with usage of Theory with this construction, so to say, accepted and behind it. From 1978 ... 1980 ... or thereabouts, there appears a certain density of literary critical texts in which Theory is understood as meaningful, which immediately makes its institutional possibilities and political effects not just imminent but a matter of urgency, very self-consciously so. From this consensus on Theory, as something meaningful and already there, a series of manoeuvres and developments can be traced, leading pertinently in this study to the institutional embedding of identity politics in literary studies. Hence I focus on the 1980s and thereafter.

Tracing the manoeuvres and developments in question entails certain linked conceptual steps: one, attention to the nuances with which Theory was constructed (how was 'What is Theory?' engaged with) vis-à-vis literary studies, and therefore, two, consideration of how those constructions gave rise to (perhaps constituted within themselves) certain deliberately institutional and therefore implicitly or explicitly political and politicized responses and outcomes, and finally, three, discernment of the growing dominance of identity politics among those responses and outcomes (i.e., its institutionalization within literary studies).

The construction of Theory

There were, it seems to me, two influential directions which merged in the construction of Theory *apropos* literary studies. Unsurprisingly, the construction of Theory as a tendentious field-in-itself (that emerges from and alludes to engagements with theoreticians, the practices of theorization, reflections on theorizations) was conducted by some of those who were most closely associated with the latter, were representative of the latter, *were* in some sense products of the latter – those who might figure in Eagleton's star list of the golden age of cultural theory of the 1960s and 1970s. The two directions which I feel can be discerned are amenably presented in the clarifications of Theory vis-à-vis literary studies by Paul de Man (who does not figure in Eagleton's list) and Edward Said. Both directions of the construction of Theory thus presented were resistant of Theory – constitutionally within Theory for de Man, and simply in ideological opposition for Said – while in some sense laying before readers the process of the construction. Both approaches to this construction were also responsive to an already emerged discourse of Theory and so were interventions in that process of construction. The process of constructing Theory thus both precedes and proceeds from these interventions. For de Man it appears through the retrospection demanded by an institutional reckoning which he could not accede to – so his essay on 'The Resistance to Theory' (1980–1981), which I begin with here, was an MLA commissioned piece, the rejection of which was anticipated by de Man in its arguments. For Said, the collection *The World, the Text and the Critic* (1983) was a responsive retrospection (essays written between 1969 and 1981) and elaboration of a response to such emergent and divergent constructions of Theory as Gerald Graff's *Literature against Itself* (1979) and Geoffrey Hartman's *Criticism in the Wilderness* (1980).

The 'Resistance to Theory' in de Man's essay is, as often noted, constitutive of Theory as he constructs it, and is charted in the two definitions of literary theory (I distinguish these as theory and Theory) that are offered there. The first – theory – comes as a charting of the usual considerations that appear to attach to that term:

> A general statement about literary theory should not, in theory, start from pragmatic considerations. It should address such questions as

the definition of literature (what is literature?) and discuss the difference between literary and non-verbal forms of art. It should then proceed to the descriptive taxonomy of the various aspects and species of the literary genus and to the normative rules that are bound to follow from such classification. Or, if one rejects a scholastic for a phenomenological model, one should attempt a phenomenology of literary activity as writing, reading or both, or of the literary work as the product, the correlative of such an activity.[7]

This statement of what might be expected of literary theory is obviously an ingenious bringing together of conventional academic notions of theory (associated with the methodology of definition, elaboration, classification, evidence, etc.) or phenomenological modelling as theory, with extant attempts at theorizing literature (drawing in as much I.A. Richards's as Leavis's theories, Ingarden's as Lukács's, Northrope Frye's as Kenneth Burke's). At the same time, it is also obviously an emptying of both the conventional academic notion and the entire set of extant associations from theory – to construct Theory. This strategy of emptying out theory in this fashion before filling it again as Theory was integral to constructing Theory elsewhere too, but usually took cruder forms. It usually assumed a narrowly focussed synecdochical method: so that emptying theory became coeval with overcoming New Criticism (as in Hartman's or Lentricchia's works) or literary humanism (Graff) or expressive realism (Belsey). De Man's was both a more economical and a less immediately suspect mode of going about this important process, and achieved a larger encapsulation of what was emptied, and therefore also a larger embrace of what the relationship of Theory to the stuff of the now emptied theory could be. Theory did, for de Man as indeed for others who tried to construct Theory, derive from the struggles and failures of the would-be aspirations of theory – the emptied vessel of theory was refilled with the same stuff but with a distinctly different flavour, a Theory flavour – and accordingly the second definition was presented in the following words:

Literary theory can be said to come into being when the approach to literary texts is no longer based on non-linguistic, that is to say historical and aesthetic, considerations, or, to put it somewhat less crudely, when the object of discussion is no longer the meaning or the value but the modalities of production and of reception of meaning and of value prior to their establishment – the implication being that the establishment is problematic enough to consider its possibility and its status.[8]

Or, as de Man summarized it, Theory 'occurs with the introduction of linguistic terminology in the metalanguage about literature'.[9] This definition naturally had its own emphases, or more precisely allegiances (to the incorporation of first structuralist linguistics and more recently deconstructionist linguistic philosophy in literary theory), but it also returned the theory that had, so to say, been emptied – with a different orientation. The theory that was emptied returned as Theory here by having always had a linguistic attention or aspect, necessarily so given the linguistic opacities and performances of literary studies. The resistance to Theory, then, became a constant element of attempts at theorizing literature at a metatheoretical level, yet also operated for de Man as a gesture of allegiance to something new (deconstruction) and the rejection of something foregone (non-linguistic aesthetist and historist reading). The resistance to theory, in brief, became that which enabled Theory to be constructed.

As a matter of consistency with the practice of criticism and theorization that de Man himself had performed and was then still performing, Theory, thus constructed, gave a name and sense of containment to the deconstructionist literary project. For de Man this consisted in an ongoing attention to and excavation of the philological and rhetorical devices of literature, and therefore of a carefully self-reflexive folding-in-upon-itself of literary studies. 'Actual perception' in literary studies, as de Man qualified, would consist in 'analytical rigour [among students and teachers of literature] of their discourse about literature'.[10] In its metatheoretical address, therefore, this construction of Theory was a confirmation of the practice of literary criticism that de Man undertook; redolent with the 'real' insights of the collection *Blindness and Insight* (1971),[11] for instance. And thus constructed, Theory seemed to suggest that the deconstructionist critical project could be a perpetual exercise of rhetorical and philological archaeology, departing from the theory of aesthetist and historist concerns that is perpetually retrospective positioned (which would make the future of Theory a perpetually new thing). Or to put it another way, de Man did not seem to realize that by naming Theory as such, by constructing it as such, a step had been taken which could not but limit the practice of deconstruction in literature as he presented it, and open up institutional accommodations and protestations. Nevertheless, the influence of deconstruction in de Man's sense, and the influence of de Man himself, was powerful enough not to make the paradoxical presence of Theory immediately self-defeating. Theory, thus understood, was not only kept alive by those who partook of his project, such as Hillis Miller, but also by those who were attentive to the institutional locations of (and not just the doing of) Theory – an attentiveness which was enabled by such a construction. This construction of Theory, therefore, chimed in with Hartman's celebratory welcome of Theory in *Criticism in the Wilderness* (1980): as a new, but not New, criticism – a 'criticism without a name' whose 'only programme is a revaluation of criticism itself';[12] and which was re-enlightened and liberated by its incorporation of linguistic awareness:

> The issue of language has now reached criticism itself, which becomes aware how much it has given up or repressed. Criticism is haunted by an archaic debt, by the eccentric riches of allegorical exegesis in all its curiously learned or enthusiastic and insubordinate modes. [...] Criticism is freed from a neoclassical decorum that, over the space of three centuries, created an enlightened but also over-accommodated prose.[13]

It chimed also, but curiously, for reasons that I soon go into, with Frank Lentricchia's characterization of Theory 'as a kind of rhetoric' in *Criticism and Social Change* (1983),[14] which was echoed and extended thus by Susan Horton in 'The Institution of Literature and the Cultural Community' (1989): Theory is 'a type of rhetoric, neither true nor false, imposing or forcing nothing at all, but simply offering certain ways for us to see what it is we do, and to be judged well or ill depending on the extent to which that rhetoric does or does not contribute to the formation of society'.[15] It echoed clearly in Ralph Cohen's introduction to a collection of essays revolving, with an air of having Theory well *behind* it, *The Future of Literary Theory* (1989):

> It is as though the concept of 'theory' as model-building, as hypotheses about meaning, as governed by 'evidence,' 'observation,' and tested by 'validity' was being converted to new concepts of the self, of evidence, of meaning of model building, of validity. It is as though one were watching the transformation of a caterpillar into a butterfly. Each form of theory writing has its own shape and function and yet is related to earlier forms.[16]

Cohen really seemed to briefly go through the construction of Theory here in the same terms as de Man almost a decade earlier. A ring of de Man is available in every exhortation (by Fish, Eagleton, and others) of the theoretical need to attend to rhetoric in literary studies, what was known then as the 'rhetorical turn'. But each of these chimes and rings and echoes of de Man's construction of Theory were also ironic given their particular intentions and locations[17] – the irony of bringing up the de Manian construction to deliberately undermine the purity of the project it derived from – to get to which I turn to the second direction of constructing Theory.

Said's contribution to the construction of Theory in *The World, the Text, and the Critic* was in the form of an objection to the de Manian construction of Theory, or more broadly the post-structuralist deconstructionist project-based construction of Theory. But this emphasized an explicit political orientation to the de Manian construction that was still, indeed now particularly, Theory – a sort of continuation of the de Manian construction that came to be Theory thereafter, with some of the smell of de Man in it but much of his austere and insistent presence removed, or more precisely, undermined and disregarded. There appeared, thus, in this collection of essays a construction of Theory that enabled Said to formulate his scepticism about it, particularly in the first, 'Introduction: Secular Criticism', and the last, 'Conclusion: Religious Criticism', of these. The construction of Theory here occurred in taking stock of and discerning a direction in recent and ongoing criticism and theorizing:

> From being a bold interventionary movement across the lines of specialization, American literary theory of the late seventies has retreated into the labyrinth on 'textuality,' dragging along with it the most recent apostles of European revolutionary textuality – Derrida and Foucault – whose trans-Atlantic canonization and domestication they themselves seemed sadly enough to be encouraging. It is not too much to say that American or even European literary theory now explicitly accepts the principle of non-interference, and that its peculiar mode of appropriating its subject matter (to use Althusser's formula) is *not* to appropriate anything that is worldly, circumstantial, or socially contaminated. 'Textuality' is the somewhat mystical and disinfected subject matter of literary theory.[18]

That this construction of, and attack on, Theory was sieved through religious metaphors – referred to as 'apostolic' virtues and 'canonizing' bids – was not merely to pack a stylistic punch; it was to gesture towards a serious complicity that Said suspected Theory of. In the conclusion he decried a perceivably religious or metaphysical shade in Theory, inherited from rather than departing from New Criticism, and infecting the discourse of Orientalism that he had himself opened to critique: 'Folding back upon itself, criticism has therefore refused to see its affiliations with the political world it serves, perhaps unwittingly, perhaps not. Once an intellectual, the modern critic has become a cleric in the worst sense of the word'.[19] The totalizing cleric-like voice of Theory was referred not only to the explicitly neoconservative religious criticism of Harold Bloom or Thomas Altizer that Said cited, but also to: the rhetorical appeal to religious tropes to understand Theory such as Hartman's (e.g., in seeing deconstructionist criticism's break from representational values as akin to theology's abandonment of allegorical commentary);[20] to de Man's sense of the 'impossibility of political and social responsibility'[21] in the practice of Theory; and even to the later theorizations of Foucault (obviously a powerful influence in Said's own theorizations) in whose theory of power a 'form of theoretical overtotalization'[22] could increasingly be discerned that undermined the possibility of resistance.

This construction and rejection of Theory was presented, superficially like de Man, with reference to an apprehension of theory. Entirely unlike de Man though, Said's sceptical construction of Theory was not based on an emptying out and reoriented readmission of theory, but on an embracing of theory – travelling theory – in a spirit of opposition to Theory. Said's theory – distinguished here by a small t – was not the allusive emptying out of historicism and aestheticism, of phenomenological models and of contextualized and accommodative understandings, but a rereading of all those in all their worldliness. The worldliness of theory was expatiated on in various ways: by elaborating on filiations and affiliations in literature and criticism, by reflecting on the oppositional responsibilities of intellectuals (a theme he was to extend soon after in his Reith lectures[23]), by observing the absences within and hegemonic reifications in canonical texts of literary and cultural studies (the recognized thrust of *Orientalism* (1978) and his writings on Palestine[24]), by reiterating the necessity of challenging totalizing closures and maintaining open and socially/politically aware interrogation in theory. But most importantly it rested in the construction of theory against Theory, as a matter of continuities that demonstrate worldliness, flowing through worldly contexts and becoming revitalized or muted through worldly imperatives. In the essay on 'Traveling Theory' this trace of self-consciously worldly theorists was drawn from Georg Lukács's concept of reification through Lucien Goldmann and Raymond Williams to Michel Foucault and Noam Chomsky; in 'Criticism between Culture and Society' the worldly possibilities of both Derrida and Foucault were teased out, despite their oppositions, by dwelling on their similar subversion of accepted norms and conventions of criticism; in 'Reflections on American "Left" Literary Criticism' the worldly concerns that push towards unworldliness (wherein the fiercely polarized polemics of a new left and right appear to converge) were reviewed with worldly concern. About a decade later, in 'Traveling Theory Reconsidered' (1994), he was to qualify the construction of theory by balancing what he felt had been a bias in his examples in the earlier essay 'Traveling Theory' – considering not only the 'reconciliatory and resolvable aspects' of theory's travel, but also transgressive and resistant travels that move '*away* from its original formulation'.[25] In referring to Said's construction of theory (small t) below I bring together both the earlier construction in its context in the collection and the later qualification. As such, Said's sceptical construction of Theory was also, of course, an approbatory construction of theory – a call for politically effective, socially aware, contextually located, historically informed, intellectually responsible criticism – which could and should by that construction both disable the institutional colonization of Theory that that construction portended, and enable the institutional effervescence of theory of the travelling sort.

As it happened, the exhortation of political responsibility that went with Said's construction and embracing of theory, and his construction and rejection of Theory, somehow transposed itself on the de Manian construction of Theory – thus dislocating both de Man and Said, with insufficient recognition of their opposition, from Theory. The construction of Theory emerged from them and their reflections on such emergent constructions, and despite them. Theory (not travelling theory) – that new, innovative, subversive, difficult, deconstructive, self-reflexive, textually and linguistically exploratory de Manian sort of enterprise that has a kind of closure while appearing to be a perpetual quest – became not only a thing out there that urged an institutional response by this construction, but also urged in this institutional response a desire for the kind of oppositional or resistant political responsibility and worldliness that Said had associated with the continuities of travelling theory (increasingly associated with the loaded connotations of the 'radicalism' of Theory). Definitions of Theory that I have cited above as possessing an ironic ring or echo of de Man were ironic because they subsumed in that definition some of the desire for worldliness that Said expressed, thereby acquiring also an ironic ring or echo of Said's construction of Theory/theory. Thus, Hartman's celebration of the self-revaluing pursuit of Theory which folds in on itself was couched in a language reminiscent of political revolution and emancipative resistance:

> The relation of creative and critical must always be reenvisioned; and while the revisionists may overturn this or that orthodoxy, this or that fixed ideal, and while they specifically expose the falsification, even repression, of Romantic origins in Arnoldian and much New Critical thought, their reversal does not fix, once again, the relation of creative and critical. The variety and indeterminacy of that relation are disclosed in a radical way.[26]

'Reenvisioning', 'revisionists', 'overturning orthodoxy' and 'ideals', 'radical way' gave the celebration of the ahistoricist unaesthetist project a political force; the discourse of revolution imbued Theory with a political location. This juxtaposition, familiar already and predating *The World, the Text and the Critic*, expressed the paradoxical desire perhaps of worldliness that Said could not construct into Theory and could only find in theory. But the juxtaposition had already put it into Theory, and seemed to extend sympathies in the radicalism of variety and indeterminacy of criticism towards the new left turn – towards, for instance, radical democracy. Thus too, Lentricchia's understanding of Theory as 'a type of rhetoric' was only to open it to political fashioning (already clear in Horton's echoing of that definition to relate to the 'formation of society'):

> I conceive of theory as a type of rhetoric whose persuasive force will not be augmented in our time by metaphysical appeals to the laws of history, [...] and the kind of Marxist theory that I am urging is itself a kind of rhetoric whose value may be measured by its persuasive means and by its ultimate goal: the formation of genuine community.[27]

This positioned Theory at an institutional moment, within the academy, as amenable to politically effective placement: 'our potentially most powerful political work as university humanists must be carried out in what we do, what we are trained for'.[28] And thus also, the de Man-like emptying of theory and reconstituting of Theory by Ralph Cohen that I quoted above appeared at the onset of a collection of essays on *The Future of Literary Theory* (a fumbling, already in 1990, against the passing of Theory), which concerned itself with the political paradox of the academic institutional confines within which Theory has become enclosed rather than flowing out into a heady tide of world revolution.[29]

Said's resistant construction of Theory against the approbatory construction of (worldly, travelling) theory was quietly but indicatively and
firmly displaced in the placement of Theory by a theorist who was
regarded as travelling along the line Said envisioned for theory. Terry
Eagleton's Marxist method, sieved through Lukács, Goldmann,
Williams, Jameson (among others, of course) placed Theory (against its
grain) firmly within the world, but neither as an embracing of theory
and nor as a rejection of Theory – rather as a collapsing of theory and
Theory, so that they become the selfsame expression of an oppositional
political recognition. So, in *The Significance of Theory* (1990), Eagleton
observed:

> Theory on a dramatic scale happens when it is both possible and
> necessary for it to do so – when the traditional rationales which have
> silently underpinned our daily practices stand in danger of being dis-
> credited, and need either to be revised or discredited. [...] Like small
> lumps on the neck, it is a symptom that all is not well.[30]

This was an intelligent manoeuvre, reminiscent of Plekhanov's reading
of 19th century Russian art-for-art's-sake writers as a symptom of a
social malaise.[31] It was also a manoeuvre that indicated that Said's sceptical construction of Theory and assertive construction of travelling theory had turned into a politically meaningful construction of Theory.

But these rings and echoes of de Man's and Said's construction of
Theory in the later 1980s were already way ahead of those constructions, already implicated in the institutional imperative that was written into and released by those constructions, already less innocent than
the institutional imperatives of those constructions. By this time Theory
was in its reckonings and institutional implantations already embroiled
with identity politics as understood in Part I. The institutional turn of
Theory released by constructions such as de Man's and Said's, indeed
released before that by the constructions these were derived from, and
the seeping in of identity politics within that turn, form a distinctive
thematic thread.

The institutional turn of Theory

By the time the above-mentioned constructions of Theory were being
offered it had become abundantly clear that literary theorizations had
again infringed the conventional disciplinary boundaries of literary
studies in irreversible ways. The cross-currents from structuralist and

post-structuralist linguistics, Derridean deconstructionist philosophy, Lacanian psychoanalysis, Foucauldian social history, Althusserian political theory had updated earlier accruals (despite New Criticism and textual formalism and reader-centred criticism) of modernist cross-currents from history, politics, philosophy, psychoanalysis, anthropology, sociology, even biology, and physics. In critical practice the travels of theory across institutionally constituted academic disciplines was nothing new, but the institutional urge that underlies and derives from the construction of Theory came as a need to reconstitute the academic discipline, to revisit and if necessary replace the distinctive space of literary studies. The latter was understood as concretized through curricula and canons and pedagogy, given form in department memberships and recognition of academic status, transmitted in categorizations of booklists and libraries, reiterated in funding practices, ensconced in the discourse of academia at large. The political desire that was constructed into literary Theory in the early 1980s was expressed in the hope that the interrogation/ reconceptualization/ displacement of the institutional space of literary studies would itself become a fruition of the politics of Theory, or at the least a step in the process of fulfilling Theory's political potential.

What should be done with Theory, constructed as such, vis-à-vis the institutional space of literary studies was a question that appeared as soon as the construction of Theory was available – even as soon as it became imminent. Indeed the construction of Theory, all too neatly presented above through de Man and Said, contained the consideration of its institutional possibilities. Both de Man's and Said's work cited above were replete with self-reflexive observations on the practices of teaching literature, the literary academic profession, the institutional disposition of literary studies, and its history. Since Theory was perceived as having been and continuing as a radical oppositional force to the institutional ideology of literary studies in place, the contemplation of its incorporation in literary studies was necessarily a political step. This was complicated by the larger political aspirations of Theory, or by the transposition of worldly responsibilities (*a la* Said) on the deconstructionist impetus of Theory. This was also complicated by the confusion that followed that transposition: it was not immediately evident in what fashion the alteration of the institutional space of literary studies by Theory would relate to (perhaps serve) the larger political aspirations of Theory in the world. In fact, this problem has never been quite resolved. At best the politics of Theory could be regarded as a political self-fashioning for theorists and academics, but its reach seemed to be closed within the institutional locations (within academia) where they were already placed. That the political pretensions of Theory were excessive in terms of institutional realities was noted often: Graff felt that Theory's effect on the humanities was 'mirroring the very society [theorists] seek to oppose';[32] Goodheart saw in it an 'inability to deal with the question of values and, in particular, of its own values' (in liberal political terms values are political);[33] Cain found that 'The political debates in contemporary theory are intense, even frenzied, but not very productive or precise';[34] Felperin was doubtful about '*whose* politics it serves or advances';[35] Berman pondered 'the social powerlessness of the literary critic';[36] Cohen observed that the institutional base of Theorists 'delimits both their vocabulary and their contribution to the larger non-academic audience they wish to change';[37] Donoghue saw in Theory 'the confusion of theories with principles and ideologies';[38] and so on. That a political, a worldly, desire for change was constituted within Theory and demanded institutional impact was affirmed as, if not more, often: Belsey called for a 'new critical practice [that] requires us to come to terms with concepts of ideology and subjectivity' from outside literary criticism;[39] Spivak was looking forward to a literary study which could 'slide without a sense of rupture into an active and involved reading of the social text';[40] Lentricchia hoped that Theory would lead to 'the formation of genuine community' through academic work;[41] and increasingly thereafter in the voices of feminist, black, gay, postcolonial literary critics – but that capture of the political desire in Theory is the point of this chapter, and should be approached more gradually.

The advent and construction of Theory in literary studies initiated several sorts of institutional responses, not all of which were (or became) implicated with the institutionalization of identity politics, though the latter occurred through the interstices of the Theory-and-institutionalization discussions. One of the powerful responses in the 1980s and 1990s was a bid to maintain the academic space of literary studies as a distinctive one but with a renewed awareness (while conserving what had passed in criticism already), more or less in line with de Man's construction of Theory, of the textualist project – close attention to philology and rhetoric, a phenomenology of reading and criticism – despite the worldly political desire of Theory. At most this awareness could recognize the political desire by expanding the range and scope of texts for attention, thereby stretching or interrogating canons, but within the remits of literariness and as a textually engaging strategy of self-questioning and institutional-interrogation itself. Hillis Miller's work through the 1980s and 1990s marks a somewhat unhappy engagement in this direction – unhappy because of his sense of being overtaken by an irresistible worldliness in the politics of Theory vis-à-vis literary studies. Thus, his *The Ethics of Reading* (1987) was conceived as a project in which a distinctively literary ethics, which *precedes* political and social considerations, can be teased out from the very encounter of reading. This was clearly a response to what he perceived as an institutional embracing of the political desire of Theory, and in the direction of a conservation of literature with de Man's sense of Theory:

> If there is to be such a thing as an ethical moment in the act of reading, teaching, or writing about literature, it must be sui generic, something individual and particular, itself a source of political or cognitive acts, not subordinated to them. The flow of power must not be all in one direction. There must be an influx of performative power from the linguistic transactions involved in the act of reading into the realms of knowledge, politics, and history. Literature must be in some way a cause and not merely an effect, if the study of literature is to be other than the relatively trivial study of one of the epiphenomena of society, part of the technological assimilation or assertion of mastery over all features of human life which is called 'the human sciences'.[42]

The will to maintain the importance of literature, not to see it as 'relatively trivial study', is of course an institutional battle. To Hillis Miller thereafter it seemed this institutional battle was on the path to being lost: by 1989 he was wondering whether Theory as he accepted it (in de Man's construction) was not already a thing of the past – at any rate, he maintained, 'The era of "deconstruction" is over'[43] and that what remained was both the task of 'preservation, conservation, the keeping of the archives, the whole work of memory, remembering, and memorialization' along with the recognition that these things happen now in a different fashion, 'remembered differently'.[44] And by 2002, with an odd mixture of ruefulness and defiance, he averred that: 'The end of literature is at hand. Literature's time is almost up. [...] Literature, in spite of its approaching end, is nevertheless perennial and universal'.[45] But Hillis Miller's mournful tune was not the only kind that sought to maintain a distinctive academic space for literary studies against the aggression of the political desire of Theory. Arguments regarding the professional integrity of the achieved (through a complex socio-historical process) institutional space of literature and its justified immunity from the larger political pretensions of Theory, except within itself and in terms of what it addresses (literature, literary texts), was a constant strain through the 1980s and 1990s too. That was the vein in which Graff's *Professing Literature*, with which I began this chapter, was presented. And the argument was made with admirable clarity and verve by Stanley Fish in *Professional Correctness*:

> Changing the mode of literary analysis or changing the object of literary analysis or changing the name of literary analysis will not change the material effectiveness of literary analysis and make it into an instrument of political action. That kind of change, if it is ever to occur, will require wholesale *structural* changes of which literary analysts might take advantage, but which they could never initiate.[46]

Neither Hillis Miller's mournfulness nor Fish's pugilistic stance need be considered much more than polemical attitudes however, for it seems to me that they were not really resisting sweeping change but speaking from within a well-established and little endangered institutional space. Despite the advent and emergence and (as we shall see) alleged demise of Theory, and the institutionalization of identity politics, in its *institutional arrangements* – in the presence of departments and faculties and schools, in the prerogatives of membership, in the organization of teaching, in the conduct of research and publishing, etc. – the academic space of literary studies (in the guise of English or Comparative Literature, for instance) was then and is still very far from being under serious threat. And, indeed, very far from being unrecognizable in terms of that space half a century back.

Another kind of institutional response entailed proposals for developing a new disciplinary space of cultural studies as a mode of absorbing the political aspirations of literary Theory to effectively transcend literary studies and become something quite different, something expressive of and attune with and effective outwards from the worldliness of Theory. Such an enterprise could be assured of institutional success, since it could both derive from literary studies and absolve itself of literature. And it could align itself with (therefore also deriving from) other relatively new institutional spaces – in sociology and political studies for instance – that emerged with similar political desires as Theory: such as the post-second war construction of area studies, the rapidly developing sector of mass media and new communication technology studies, and studies of minorities and movements such as women's studies and black studies (Graff's academic ghettos). Indeed in the course of the 1980s and 1990s numerous literary studies departments in the USA and UK developed cultural studies sections within but at odds with it, in some instances cultural studies so to say 'broke away' from literary studies, in others were simply constituted as new programmes or departments or centres within faculties and schools of humanities enjoying a symbiotic relationship with literary studies and other disciplines and faculties. As a derivation from Theory and from, and yet in opposition to and at the expense of, literary studies, the responsive construction of cultural studies was perhaps most lucidly presented in Anthony Easthope's *Literary into Cultural Studies* (1991). Inserting an institutional imperative that is cognizant of such sociological, political, and literary critical analyses of culture and mass media as were collected in the 14 volumes of *Literary Taste, Culture and Mass Communications* (1978),[47] for instance, and uniting such conceptual exchanges with the rather expanded connotations of text in the poststructuralist work of Barthes and Derrida, Easthope was able to derive from and undermine literary studies – and anticipate a paradigm-shift, constitute cultural studies as the institutional corollary/alternative – by interrogating the notion of the literary text (ensconced in a high cultural or canonical tradition), or by questioning the disciplinary convention of 'literariness' with regard to texts. The latter Easthope regarded as the repository of the hegemonic ideology that literary studies perpetuates and that Theory resists, against which cultural studies could engage with the texts of mass or popular culture, broadly understood, wherein Theory may be realized. As an institutional formation, in pedagogy, for instance, Easthope saw such cultural studies as a mode of emancipating students through an engagement with popular and worldly cultural texts – pedagogy would become implicitly political action both in its institutional form and in its worldly effect:

> Cultural studies should situate its pedagogic subject not primarily in relation to truth but rather to the textual structures within which he or she is actually constituted [...] Confronting textuality not just cognitively – as generalisable meaning – but experiencing the work/play of the signifier and to move secondarily to criticism and analysis may disclose for the subject something of his or her own actual determinacy and situatedness.[48]

The ambition was obviously worthy of Theory's political desire, and answered some of the quibbles within literary studies' confined reach. That the institutional composition of cultural studies came to be regarded in many quarters as the offspring of the collision and bouncing away of Theory and literary studies, has been evidenced numerously: much recent ponderings on the end of the Theory enterprise, or the failure of Theory, is presented as a fading away of cultural studies (in Eagleton's *After Theory*, 2003, for instance). At the same time though, for Hillis Miller the impending demise of literature was because of the ascendancy of cultural studies.

Yet another kind of institutional response to Theory, in many ways coincidental with cultural studies but not 'breaking away' as self-consciously from literary studies, sought an interdisciplinary dimension within the disciplinary space of literary studies, or between and criss-crossing that space and other disciplinary spaces. This was so variously and consistently expressed in the 1980s that the trend is conveyed by simply citing some instances. Catherine Belsey concluded from her survey of Theory in *Critical Practice* (1980) that 'criticism can no longer be isolated from other areas of knowledge'.[49] As an institutional response to Theory, Jonathan Culler, at the end of *The Pursuit of Signs* (1981) recommended the development of collaborative arrangements between literary studies departments and departments such as philosophy, linguistics, anthropology, sociology, and (his words) perhaps even psychology and history to develop courses in theory for literature students. 'The kind of course I envision', he remarked, 'is impossible so long as "theory" is assumed to mean method; it becomes conceivable and practicable, if theory is treated as a series of substantive topics, such as the nature of narrative, myth, symbolic exchange, and speech acts'.[50] Other disciplines, in brief, could be expected to feed into the academic work of literary studies from outside, so to say. William Cain's sceptical approach to the politics of Theory, in *The Crisis in Criticism* (1984), took the institutional response of recommending a broadening of the literary studies curriculum and directing of attention towards history, society, and culture.[51] And so on and so forth. Towards the end of the 1980s, a collection of essays indicatively entitled *Literary Theory's Future(s)* (1989), edited by Joseph Natoli, brought together opinions which more or less unanimously decided, in the editor's introductory words, that: 'The future of an emerging cultural critique captures more than literary theory, extends to a number of heterogeneous discourses that, like literary theory, trespass across disciplines and departments'.[52] Another in the same year entitled *The Future of Literary Theory*, edited by Ralph Cohen, included an essay by Gerald Graff applauding the promise of 'numerous programs now being planned and implemented which integrate literary theory and history in an interdisciplinary framework, often under such rubrics as "cultural studies" and "cultural history"'[53] – but I have quoted this already. Interdisciplinarity was a much touted institutional response to Theory *apropos* literary studies. It was not necessarily well received by all theorists. In *Deconstruction and the Interests of Theory* (1988) Christopher Norris regarded the 'move to colonize other disciplines in the name of an all-embracing literary theory' as a reductive one,[54] for instance. Others were sceptical of Theory's assumption of centrality within critical thinking itself: in *The Failure of Theory* (1987) Patrick Parrinder worried that 'Theory is all-devouring, consuming theories, anti-theories, and non-theories alike',[55] while Howard Felperin was sceptical of the status of Theory as 'guiding light' for 'legitimate literary-critical activity'[56] in *Beyond Deconstruction* (1985). But an institutional response to Theory in literary studies with an interdisciplinary direction was favoured by many at the end of the 1980s and indeed has been thereafter.

Going back a couple of sentences to that interesting juxtaposition of Cohen's *The Future of Literary Theory* and Natoli's *Literary Theory's Future(s)*, the former collection indicated something else that was not particularly registered in the latter. Apart from Graff's welcoming of interdisciplinary programs and Hillis Miller's and Hartman's expressions of discomfort about the passing of deconstruction, this collection gave voice to a number of other literary theorists. These were not concerned especially with the institution of literary studies and the impact of Theory in the generalized and agonized manner of Graff or Hillis Miller or Hartman, and these came with a confidence of possessing the future of literary theory in their hands. These were by, among others, Catherine Stimpson on the building of feminist criticism, Henry Louis Gates, Jr. on the particularities of being a black critic, Elaine Showalter on the parallels between Afro-American and feminist literary criticism. In this context, I point to these as an indication of the place identity politics had already found in the Theory debate of literary studies. This is indicative not because of their discrete and separate interventions – each identity-based political position had already enabled highly sophisticated interventions in literary studies and Theory – but because of their simultaneous and parallel placement in a book of this nature. It is that placement which tells us something about the already achieved entrenching of identity politics, as understood in Part I, in literary studies.

The entrenchment of identity politics

It is of course not in the least surprising that, through the construction of Theory and its impact on the institution of literary studies, identity politics would gradually rise as a defining political motif and organizing principle of that discipline's political self-positioning. The theory – especially the travelling theory (in Said's sense) – that had been constructed/transposed into Theory vis-à-vis literary studies came with an extraordinarily energizing and refreshing investment from different identity-based political positions, especially in terms of feminist politics. No roll call of theorists of what Eagleton thought of as the golden age of theory before the 1980s could disregard the work of Simone de Beauvoir, Betty Friedan, Kate Millett, Elaine Showalter, Sandra Gilbert and Susan Gubar, Julia Kristeva, Luce Irigaray, and Hélène Cixous – all explicitly or implicitly melding identity-based political theorization with literary criticism. The trace of travelling theory that Said drew up to his own work on Orientalism shows, among other things, the extent to which left political theorization in concert with literary criticism had constantly explored the modalities of hegemonic silencing and repression. Marxist class analysis had constantly dug into the roots of discrimination of minorities on the grounds of gender, sexuality, race, ethnicity, and nationality. Every key ideologue of what was constructed as Theory – Althusser, Foucault, Lacan, and Derrida – had explored the significations and resonances of identity-based prejudice, discrimination, silencing, neglecting, repression, and released resistant possibilities into literary criticism.

Theorization which contested disciplinary boundaries and questioned the institutional politics of such boundaries (Derrida's 1980 paper 'Mochlos: or, the Conflict of Faculties'[57] is now well recognized as an *event* in Theory) was naturally embedded in the worldly political desire that was constructed in Theory. Theory-aware literary scholars (and which was not so in the 1980s and 1990s?) were not just necessarily but wilfully engaged in worldly politics, for or against Theory, because its institutional response was regarded as a matter of some urgency. And the political and social contexts of the 1980s and 1990s, as observed in Chapter 5 above, were disposed towards a convergence on identity politics – the particular kind of anti-essentialist social constructionist identity politics that we are concerned with here – through both the celebratory discourse of difference of the post-Marxist new left as well as through the resistant multiculturalist discourse of liberals (which even neoconservatives could not dismiss out of hand). Post-Civil Liberties movements of the 1960s, in the midst of a series of perceivable new social movements, especially in the so-called decolonized Third World (Fredric Jameson turned to these with interest as the inheritors of the 1960s in 1984,[58] only to be greeted soon by Aijaz Ahmad's objections to Third Worldism[59]); amidst growing recognition of the evolving

post-Bretton Woods economic order and the consequent encouragement to global capitalism; with the critique of orthodox Marxist total-
ization and totalitarianism not only in vogue but becoming concretized
in the stirrings of mass protest beyond the Iron Curtain; in the midst of
an apparently endless hold of neoconservative neoliberal capitalist
regimes (Reagan–Bush in the USA; Thatcher–Major in the UK) where
much of the Theory debate was unfolding alongside the identity-based
political resistance that grew out of this establishment's racism and
sexism – in these contexts, as I have observed, identity politics was the
repository of both radicalism and liberal good will (or neo-conservative
concession or altruism), and simply amenable to seepage and assimilation into every kind of institutional arrangement. Few areas could have
been more receptive of this environment than literary studies in the
academy; the urge for an institutional response to Theory, in concert or
discord with its desire for political efficacy, met this environment half-
way (or responded to it, or devolved from it – does not really matter
how it is seen). The result was inevitable.

By the 1990s the institutional entrenchment of identity politics was
not simply a matter of positioning the academy within the world, but a
matter of resisting the manifestation of the hegemonic establishment,
the iniquities of the world, *within* the academy. In the USA and UK this
was manifested in a series of neoconservative attacks on Theory and
moves to reconstitute academic work at odds with Theory and its constantly sceptical, destabilizing, perceivably radically oppositional
impact on the discipline. In his introductory essay in *The Culture of
Literacy* (1994), Wlad Godzich conducted a searching analysis of recently
initiated literacy programmes in the USA, discovering in them a 'new
vocationalism' that seemed designed to undermine the interrogative
and oppositional spirit of Theory.[60] Through the 1990s there appeared
a series of works that declared themselves 'against Theory' (I discuss
these below, they are relevant to the place of identity politics in literary
studies). The serious and necessarily complex political desires and constraints of the Theory debate and institutional responses in literary studies descended into a mire of invective and propaganda, culminating in
2000 with the publication of *Losing the Big Picture* by the US National
Association of Scholars (NAS).[61] It notoriously reduced and fragmented
Theory, not through any substantive argument, but literally by presenting a list of 115 so-called Theory terms which students should beware
of when they appear in university course catalogues. The list was glee-
fully reproduced in the *Times Literary Supplement* in UK on 6 October
2000. By the early 1990s it already seemed as if the politics within the

academy would stifle Theory and any institutional response to it other than that of neglect. The response of literary theorists was now not only to construct Theory with its worldly political desire constituted within it, but also to defend Theory in some sense by going beyond it, by turning the political desire into some semblance of political agency and action. This defence of Theory in the literary academy could not be in terms of Theory itself. The construction of Theory had accepted the de Manian folding-in of literary studies and transposed Said's worldly desire upon it in a fashion that would always defer agency and action, always maintain politics at the self-interrogative pulse of desire. The defence of Theory had to be in some sense after Theory, and involved an embracing of the agency and action of different identity-based political positions that had invested so effectively in the practice of and responsive institutional deliberations about Theory vis-à-vis literary studies. It meant, briefly, embracing identity politics and thereby going beyond Theory to defend it. As it happened this embracing was already intricately enmeshed, as observed above, in the very construction of Theory. In some sense, in the beginnings of the construction of Theory was also its end (but not, as sometimes averred at the time, in the sense of being defeated by its own plenitude[62]).

This transition was admirably theorized in the early 1990s in Thomas Docherty's *After Theory* (1990) and Paul Bové's *In the Wake of Theory* (1992). The shift is clear even between Docherty and Bové. Where for Docherty the turn to an 'after Theory' to bring to fruition Theory's political desire was because the

> successful institutionalisation of theory, modernism and marxism, has stymied the radical pretensions of their movements and philosophies; and, what is worse, theory and marxism have become complicit with the institutional imposition of limits upon their revolutionary potential;[63]

for Bové this occurred due to a deep resentment about the checking of Theory's political desire *within* the academy by reactionary forces:

> Even though we live in an age that increasingly exercises both hegemony and domination in and through sign-based structures, the literary academy not only failed to reorganize itself to address the new social and intellectual problems created by these structures, but it has returned to 'core curricula' and tried to minimize the influence of 'radicals' within the academy.[64]

For Docherty this meant giving Theory a necessary post-Marxist 'after Theory' character, i.e., stopping Theory from being hegemonic itself, and laying out a set of post-Marxist principles for 'after Theory' reminiscent of Laclau and Mouffe's work (see Chapter 4) for the critic. In the latter the only agency that has a concrete presence is that offered by identity-based political positions captured under the umbrella of identity politics:

> Postmarxism accepts the necessary historicity of political and ethical practices, the historicity of truth itself. In its respect for heterogeneity it must reject all systems of Grand Theory, all systems which make a claim upon the ability to totalize knowledges and synthesize them in one consciousness or identity. Knowledge is nothing unless shared by the Other, and unless oriented towards difference rather than the construction of the identity of an individualizable consciousness or Subject. The political point of this is to open the Subject to the availability of her or his own historicity and mutability. The mere opposition advanced by Marxism is not enough for a radical criticism; it must be fully implicated in the much more radical pursuit of the unknown rather than the always-ready-known-but-merely-forgotten; and it must be fully implicated in the ethics of alterity.[65]

In Docherty's characterization of 'after Theory' there was obvious confusion arising from both defending Theory and in some sense opposing or going beyond Theory. He seemed to present the enemy as not 'against Theory', not the reactionary forces quelling the political desire of Theory, but the potential of Theory itself to become hegemonic and institutionalized. Here we have the contradiction of advocating a knowledge which does not construct a Subject, but is at the behest of the Subject which recognizes its historicity and mutability; a demand for detotalized knowledge which endorses a totalizing exclusion of 'the always-ready-known-but-merely-forgotten'. For Bové there was no doubt about what his 'after Theory' was directed against: the reactionism and conservatism of 'against Theory'. And the demands he made were, therefore, not so much in a contradictory post-Marxist rhetoric but in an almost spiritualist manner – demanding purgation and renewal in the critic's work:

> [About] the composite aim in critical work today: Critical intelligence involves a demystification of intellectuals' sense of their independence, a constant genealogical self-criticism, and research into

specific discourses and institutions as part of the struggle against forms of oppressive power, forms of surplus-value extraction – if one talks about the international question in those terms. [...] Critical research should operate in this complex of problems and because they are some of the issues that demand attention in our culture. They are increasingly linguistic-based problems of ideology and representation. They touch more and more the ability of intellectuals marginal to the dominant group and of subaltern groups to speak, to be heard, and to understand the discursive relation of the psyche or 'internal nature' to society. If literary study affiliates itself with these other modes of critical work, not only will the profession and institution be modified, but perhaps it will also help ease the shortage of critical intelligence in a society now so easily manipulated by image-producing agencies of politics and corporations.[66]

Bové's 'after Theory', unlike Docherty's, did not wish a withering away of the institution of literary studies or Theory but a modification thereof. Most interesting in that quotation is the possessive in '*our* culture'. Whether that 'our', obviously a reference to the Western intellectuals he referred to earlier, includes voices of subaltern groups or looks for a remedy from those voices outside their fold remains an open question.

What slipped through in the early 1990s construction of 'after Theory', which I have presented here as occurring with and between Docherty and Bové, was an opening of and invitation to and taking within of social constructionist identity politics, encapsulating the political agencies of different identity-based political positions through the perception of analogues and equivalences, in the institution of literary studies. Docherty's impassioned call for the Other in the Subject, the ethics of alterity and difference, but not 'individualized', merged into Bové's call to Western intellectuals to enable marginalized and subaltern voices to speak and be heard. The concrete political agency that will defeat the reactionary forces 'against Theory' is, by implication and in fact, an agglomeration of those contained in identity politics. There was a familiar air about these calls, particularly Bové's – it was faintly reminiscent of the Marxist bourgeois intellectual's desire to cultivate a proletarian consciousness that Kaustky and Lenin pondered without any satisfactory solution, and Gramsci could not really resolve. The entrenchment of identity politics, as understood here, in the institution of literary studies slipped through such deliberations and gradually thickened, so to say, or sedimented itself within the institutional discourse of literary studies. As the 1990s progressed the Theory debate took on a peculiar character of not occurring between those crudely polarized between 'for Theory' and 'against Theory', but those necessarily grimly locked in a slippery opposition of being 'after Theory' critics and 'against Theory' critics. That identity politics was institutionalized as this debate progressed is abundantly clear from the terms in which it was conducted. To a great extent the acrimonious exchanges between 'after Theory' and 'against Theory' were and are *about* identity politics. It is not necessarily clear whether either of the camps can be clearly labelled for or against identity politics. In fact that is not the ground of battle here and there is a great deal of cross-over and ambiguity about identity politics on both sides. But it was clear to all sides that engaging in this debate entails talking about and in terms of identity politics. That is the point of institutionalization.

Increasingly it has been the 'against Theory' critics from the 1990s onwards, at least those who have formulated their positions at any length, who have, implicitly or explicitly, understood Theory as incorporating identity politics. More often than not such incorporation has been understood cautiously, leading to a questioning not of the logic of identity politics but of the rationale of Theory's pretensions when it seems to serve identity politics or identity-based political positions. Thus, in *The Pure Good of Theory* (1992) Denis Donoghue was anxious to clarify that: 'I hope you understand that I am not, in the vulgar phrase, "against theory". [...] What I am against is the confusion of theory with principles – or rather, the confusion of theories with principles and ideologies – and the prosecution of principles and ideologies under the pseudonym of theory'.[67] He went on to suggest that 'we regard the work of theory as prolegomena toward the establishing of a concept – whatever the concept may be – and regard principles as finding their destiny in application of that concept and in the consequence of that application'.[68] Donoghue's notion of 'concept' (which he regarded as the proper province of Theory) was similar to the first definition of literary theory given by de Man in 'The Resistance to Theory', and he seemed oblivious to the emptying of that approach to literary theory (small t) to enable the construction of Theory which had occurred. That Donoghue found an ambiguity about concepts in Theory is therefore hardly surprising, since Theory was constructed through an interrogation of just such a notion of concepts. More substantively, what Donoghue was complaining about really was not so much the ambiguity about concepts, as the insertion of 'principles and ideologies' therein – which I have presented above as occurring with the transposition of Said's politics of travelling theory into Theory. But it was precisely what Donoghue meant by 'ideology' that is of interest here. The kinds of ideologies that he went on to name later as playing confusingly with concepts in Theory were principally the ideologies of identity-based political positions. In *The Practice of Reading* (1998) Donoghue clarified:

> An ideology, in my sense of it, is a system of ideas, vocabularies, and practices that has become second nature to its adherents and is deployed as an instrument of power. It is the structure of attitudes that is taken for granted in a particular group. In the classroom, an ideologue tries to transform students as social subjects that the ideologue represents. Women's studies, Feminism, Gender Studies, Gay and Lesbian Studies, African American Studies, Marxist Criticism, Psychoanalytic Criticism, Deconstruction, New Historicism, Cultural Studies, Postcolonial Studies: the list is incomplete, if only because it omits the Bourgeois Liberalism that many societies still take for granted. Each of these is taught as an independent set of interests: the motto for such studies might be Caliban's, 'This island's mine'.[69]

It is difficult to see how Psychoanalytic Studies, Deconstruction, and (strictly speaking) New Historicism and Cultural Studies could be regarded as ideologies. These are more concept-oriented, in Donoghue's sense, and methodology-based; though these have all proved useful for the development of the other kinds of Theory courses that are mentioned – and *those* are obviously associated with identity-based political positions (even Marxism in the guise of post-Marxism, and, for that matter, Bourgeois Liberalism). The pointed comment on the exclusion of Bourgeois Liberalism, the reference to Caliban (much traversed in postcolonial criticism in Shakespeare studies), were all indicative of Donoghue's unease about *identity-based political ideologies* masquerading as literary Theory, or his misgivings about the entrenchment of identity politics through Theory.

Donoghue's qualified and carefully formulated position 'against Theory' – by which he meant against (mainly) identity-based ideological agendas being presented as literary concepts – was reiterated, but with a quite different emphasis, in Stanley Fish's *Political Correctness* (1995). The play on 'political correctness' in the title is indicative in itself. In attempting to purge the Theory-led political aspirations of literary studies (and for that matter cultural studies), and reiterate the professional integrity and essentially hermeneutic aims of the discipline as it has developed, so to say, 'against Theory', Fish too identified the complicity of identity politics and Theory as a particular indication of misplacement:

> The conclusion (resisted by many) is that the effects of one's actions will be largely confined to their disciplinary settings even when those settings receive grandiose new names like cultural studies. Even as I draw this conclusion I can think of at least three forms of academic study that would seem to constitute a challenge to it: feminism, black studies, and gay and lesbian studies. [...] No one can deny this evidence, but one can ask what is it evidence of. It is not, I would contend, evidence that academic work can ripple out to effect changes in the larger society, but that, rather, when changes in the larger society are already occurring, academic work can be linked up to them by agents who find the formulations of that work politically useful. It is a question of direction of force. Unlike the new historicism and cultural studies, feminism, gay rights activism, and the civil rights movement did not originate in the academy, and academic versions of them acquire whatever extra academic influence they may have by virtue of something already in place in public life; academic feminism, academic gay rights studies, and academic black studies do not cause something but piggy-back on its prior existence.[70]

Fish's and Donoghue's 'against Theory' positions were not against theory (with a small t) but against the political aspirations and desire of Theory as it became institutionalized. For both this was associated primarily with the incorporation of identity-based political positions (the construction of identity politics) in the institutional response in literary studies – cultural studies – to Theory; but neither were against (quite the contrary probably) such political positions, or against identity politics. They both recognized, however, that the institutional response to Theory that they worried about was to a great degree *about* identity politics. They discerned a problem in that preoccupation, some sort of methodological or conceptual problem rather than an ideological problem.

Less sophisticated 'against Theory' critics since the 1990s not only recognized that Theory and identity politics are increasingly closely related in their institutional forms, they assumed that Theory *is* identity politics, and usually presented their 'against Theory' polemics as an 'against identity politics' argument. This disregard for the variety and depth of Theory and its genesis, coupled with their incomprehension of both the ideology of identity-based political positions and identity politics, often derived from a kind of blanket conservatism that seemed to not have registered any kind of theory/Theory at all – that seemed to be bogged in a mindset which justifies identity-based political positions and renders them efficacious. Only marginally more aware than the mass media centred attacks on Theory that Bové, for instance, reacted to, John Ellis's *Literature Lost* (1997) and Valentine Cunningham's *Reading after Theory* (2002) – the title should not take us in – are good examples. John Ellis's was simply the crudest form of 'against Theory'-means-'against identity politics' kind of criticism.[71] It was directed against what he regarded and constantly dubbed as 'race-gender-class scholars'/'race-gender-class programs'/'race-gender-class studies'/'race-gender-class orthodoxy' (that smooth elision of different identity-based political positions is, nevertheless, a clear apprehension of the embrace of identity politics), and came with an announcement of the need to celebrate Western society's superiority against evidence of the reprobate record of Asian and African countries, and to reinstate conviction in 'great' literature. The institutionalization of identity politics through Theory was regarded as a dangerous fad or fashion. Cunningham's iden-tification of the embedding of identity politics in literary studies after Theory was less ham-handed; it came as a masterful demonstration of how to say the opposite of what one means:

> 'Is there a woman in this text?' we ask now as normally, and very properly, as once we asked whether there was an irony or an ending, a moral-revelation or a Christ-figure. By the same token, we wonder without any sense of forcing about the presence, or indeed the sig-nificant absence of, or silence about, blacks and gays, and 'signifying monkeys', and subalterns, and bodies of all kinds and types. Our tex-tual communities and cities and lands are so much more vividly peopled, so much more amply presenced, now than before Theory.[72]

That this is not an especially different stance from Ellis's becomes apparent when the recognition of an achievement that is at the self-same moment a dismissal of that achievement is disposed off in favour of Cunningham's view of what literary reading and interpretation should be:

> The Judeo-Christian tradition dwells constantly on the sweetness of the Word of God. The words of Jehovah in the Psalms are frequently sweet ones, like honey in the mouth. [...] the point is that for read-ing on this model there is always something to taste, something def-inite and defining to take in. [...] The Word of God, the body of

Christ, become you: to your emotional, spiritual benefit. And so it is with all reading where this model of reading as a selving, a self-making has prevailed. [...] These are traditional notions and assumptions which Theory deliberately – at least in theory – estranged itself from.[73]

The paradox here is that Cunningham's appeal to a Judeo-Christian model and Ellis's celebration of Western society were, of course, themselves reassertions of dominant identity-based political positions as *universal* precisely as if interrogations of such assumptions in Theory, extending a political desire in Theory, do not need to be registered or argued against – as if Theory could simply be wiped away. It would seem that this brand of clumsy 'against Theory' attitude particularly recognized the institutionalization of identity politics within literary studies through Theory, and argued so vehemently against it, because the identity-based political positions of the authorial voices were under threat. In that sense, such 'against Theory' criticism could be regarded as part of the process of the entrenchment of identity politics in literary studies through the impact of Theory.

Meanwhile the kind of early 1990s 'after Theory' theorization described above in the terms given by Docherty and Bové, defending Theory 'after Theory' by activating its political desire, proliferated over this period: *Post-Theory* (1996) edited by Bordwell and Carroll; *Post-Theory* (1999) edited by Martin McQuillan; *What's Left of Theory?* (2000) edited by Butler, Guillory, and Thomas; *Beyond Literary Theory* (2001) by Eduard Strauch; *After Theory* (2003) by Terry Eagleton; *Life after Theory* (2003) edited by Payne and Schad; *Post-Theory, Culture, Criticism* (2004) edited by Callus and Herbrechter; *After Criticism* (2004) edited by Gavin Butt; and *After Theory* (2005) by Vincent Leitch and Jeffrey Williams.[74] These books on the general theme are supplemented by numerous scholarly papers in journals along these lines, and even more numerous books and papers on specific issues in literary and cultural studies in the context of 'after Theory' theorizations. Some of these simply revisit and assess the golden age of theory in the 1960s and 1970s, some ponder the construction of Theory and its institutionalization in various forms, and in different ways most are cognizant of the central place of identity politics in these developments – either by charting how different identity-based literary criticism has been affected and continues to be conducted, or by exploring the allegiances that become possible 'after Theory' in an environment of an overarching identity politics. It would be simplistic to seek a consistent and uniform *endorsement* of identity politics in the 'after Theory' field; in fact much of the 'after Theory' field specifically withdraws from identity politics, but usually as expressions of identity politics' ubiquity and presence in the academic institution 'after Theory'.

Terry Eagleton's *After Theory* (2003) is particularly worth noting in this context. This offered a critique of identity politics in current cultural studies, which he saw as the result of the institutional impact of literary studies and Theory (specifically after the theory of the 1970s). But unlike Donoghue's or Fish's critiques, this was not presented as an attempt to depoliticize literary studies in favour of conceptual rather than ideological development or in favour of maintaining the integrity of the literary profession; for Eagleton the turn to identity politics was a *depoliticization* of Theory, a misplacement of Theory's political desire, and his recommendation was for a more rigorous and broad-based political engagement in 'after Theory' literary and cultural studies. The entrenchment of identity politics in the institutionalization of literary and cultural studies 'after Theory' was regarded, following the tactic of his *The Significance of Theory*, as a symptom of the political contexts through which they developed. So, with regard to postcolonial criticism's turn to ethnically based identity politics he observed:

> Most post-colonial theory shifted from the focus on class and nation to ethnicity. This meant among other things that the distinctive problems of post-colonial culture were often falsely assimilated to the very different question of Western 'identity politics'. Since ethnicity is largely a cultural affair, this shift of focus was also one from politics to culture. In some ways, this reflected real changes in the world. But it also helped to depoliticize the question of post-colonialism, and inflate the case of culture within it, in ways which chimed with the new, post-revolutionary climate in the West itself.[75]

Broadening the argument, Eagleton then conducted a survey of the development of global capitalism since the 1970s to contextualize the turn of 'after Theory' literary and (to) cultural studies towards identity politics, and concluded:

> Culture had always been about signs and representations; but now we had a whole society which performed permanently before the looking-glass, weaving everything it did into one vast mega-text, fashioning at every moment a ghostly mirror-image of its world which doubled it at every point. It was known as computerization.

> At the same time, culture in the form of identity had grown even more pressing. The more the system unfolded a drearily uniform culture across the planet, the more men and women aggressively championed the culture of their nation, region, neighbourhood or religion. [...] Blandness found its response in bigotry.[76]

This of course is itself a particular kind of *political* response against the ideology of identity politics – and therefore firmly 'after Theory' (in Docherty's or Bové's sense, and yet against them), not 'against Theory'. Eagleton's attempt to elaborate the methodological and philosophical underpinnings of this politics by exploring notions of truth, objectivity, and ethics are open to debate. But, for this study, the important thing is that it registers the wide range of 'after Theory' entrenchments of identity politics, and recognizes the pervasiveness of identity politics in the institutions of literary and cultural studies now.

Disciplinary histories

Reasonably careful attention to the development of the Theory debates from the early 1980s onwards reveals, it seems to me, the ways in and means through which identity politics has come to become institutionalized in literary studies. The above cursory observations on this are necessarily programmatic (selecting and disposing material with a somewhat predetermined agenda); however, a deeper consideration of all the complexities of the Theory debate will not, I am confident, undermine the main argument above. A more studied approach to this important issue awaits us despite the prodigious amount of scholarly attention this area has been given already, and with it will come a more nuanced understanding of the ways in which identity politics, as it is understood here, shifts, adjusts, and ensconces itself through the interstices of the Theory debate in the literary academy.

There are other intertwined ways in which the entrenchment of identity politics in the institution of literary studies can be traced. These are not separate from the Theory debate, but are part of a sort of distinctive thread which is sutured around that debate. Reconsiderations of the institutional history and status of English as the pre-eminent arena of literary studies in the USA and UK, for instance, also throw up relevant observations here. To look to the history of the academic discipline of English as a way of coming to grips with its present constitution and practice entails several argumentative possibilities: the enterprise could look to that history to discern continuities within the current institutional disposition

and warn of radical deviations from those proven continuities (the conservative argument); or the enterprise could look to that history to discern
the marginalizations and misrepresentations (owing to larger social pressures) that have occurred in institutional practice and seek to rectify them
by recommending an overhaul of the institutional space (the radical argument); or the enterprise could identify certain territorial imperatives in
that history and seek to make them clear in the institutional space (which
could work in favour of both the radical and the conservative arguments).
On the whole, such a reckoning with the history, and therefore current
status, of English as an academic discipline is largely a matter of delineat-
ing the modes of professionalization in literary studies and the responsibilities that devolve upon professionals (teachers, critics) in the present.

In the USA, attempts at coming to grips with the institutional history
of English (not American studies) along those lines turned towards the
radical argument in Richard Ohmann's *English in America* (1976): 'The
humanities are not an agent, but an instrument. [...] There is no sense in
pondering the function of literature without relating it to the actual society that uses it, to the centers of power within that society, and to the
institutions that mediate between literature and the people'.[77] This
involved a critique of the post-Second War bourgeois culture within
which the profession was then described (echoing something of sociological perceptions of intellectuals in Bourdieu's, Gouldner's, or Debray's
works), and which enabled a superficial discourse of freedom to contain
the study of English within a carefully confined elite and carefully
depoliticized space. The humanism that was instrumentalized for this
manoeuvre was beginning to, Ohmann observed, turn upon the profession itself to discern its politics. Taking some of this argument forward,
but disinvesting it from radical outcomes, Gerald Graff's *Professing
Literature* (1987) – as observed already – looked to the humanistic tradition in the academic disciplines of English (and American) literature as
a matter of continuities which are more replicated in the present than
radically inverted or subverted by itself. Somewhat belatedly by 1998,
Robert Scholes's *The Rise and Fall of English* drew on that history to propose a return 'to the roots of our liberal arts tradition, and reinstate
grammar, dialectics and rhetoric at the core of college education'[78] – a
conclusion reached through tortuous earlier considerations of the
impact of Theory on English studies, and the need therefore to 'stop
"teaching literature" and start "studying texts"' but without accepting a
political desire or responsibility.[79] If the path from Ohmann to Scholes
seems to be one of retrogression in instrumentalizing the history of the
discipline for releasing political desires, it was not because that was the

dominant trend, but because each of these steps resists the dominant trends of their times. For Ohmann the radical argument was the oppositional position vis-à-vis the academy; for Graff, and more so for Scholes, the different degrees of conservative arguments were their oppositional positions. The latter were arguably designed to resist the drift of the radical argument, or in the broader picture resist the shift of English's institutional response to Theory's political desire.

To continue with histories of the academic disciplines of English, in post-war UK this normally recalls the early work of D.J. Palmer. His history of the profession of English literature in *The Rise of English Studies* (1965) came from what was then the left of the ideological spectrum. His exploration of the working class affiliations of the discipline's origins in the 19th century were no doubt directed against the bourgeois establishment the discipline seemed ensconced within since the Second World War. Looking back on English literature's institutional history was effectively an act of retrieving an early investment in working class interests:

> However inadequately it was articulated, there was a widespread feeling [in the 19th century] that the spiritual and physical conditions of the industrial revolution impoverished the cultural lives of a large class of people, that they had been cut off from their traditional past, and that therefore they needed to be given new means of establishing connections with a national cultural heritage. Thus it was the historical attitude to literature which eventually emerged, and the missionaries of adult education were particularly concerned with the working classes.[80]

For Palmer, therefore, English studies emerged as a utilitarian and evangelistic alternative from the elite education in classics and rhetoric, and was firmly associated with an early institutional space in Mechanics' Institutes and Working Men's Colleges. English's subsequent rise into academia was also a move away from those marginal origins, ending in the stronghold of the academic establishment with the establishment of, as far as Palmer went, the Oxford English School. This mode of rediscovering and perhaps reinvigorating the marginal affiliations of the beginnings of English literature was arguably more prolonged in the context of the UK and former colonies than in the USA. In the USA the political desire of Theory merged with contingent and of-the-moment battles about canons (expanding the canon, opening the canon, creating alternative canons) and struggles over alignments with relatively new institutional spaces (area studies, race/gender/ ethnicity studies, cultural studies, media studies) and assertions of ideological claims through the institutional practice of English (just *doing* or *opposing* radical politics through teaching and criticism) – and left the possibilities of institutional histories as the recourse of the conservative argument. In the UK and elsewhere, however, the radical potential for delving into English's institutional history remained open and active alongside – though usually in a responsive fashion to the USA – all those corollaries of Theory's political desire. Thus Chris Baldick's *The Social Mission of English Criticism* (1983) affirmed the marginal factors that originally brought English literature into higher education:

> These are first, the specific needs of the British empire expressed in the regulations for admission to the India Civil Service; second, the various movements for adult education including Mechanic's Institutes and Working Men's Colleges, and extension lecturing; third, within this general movement, the special provisions made for women's education,[81]

and proceeded to examine English's institutional embracing of conservative values closely, through such canonized representatives of 'Englishness' as Arnold, Eliot, Richards, and the Leavises. Brian Doyle's *English and Englishness* (1989)[82] offered a more sustained examination of those marginal origins, emphasizing particularly the initial amateur feminine character of the area and the gradual masculinization of the discipline as it became professionalized. Gauri Vishwanathan's *Masks of Conquest* (1989)[83] went back to the debate between Orientalist educationists and Anglicist educationists in India to discern the placement of English literature as caught between the contrary logics of colonial assimilation and imperial cultural hegemony. This fed into influential reflections on the place of English in the contemporary Indian academy, notably in Svati Joshi's edited collection *Rethinking English* (1991), Rajeshwari Sunder Rajan's edited collection *The Lie of the Land* (1992), and Harish Trivedi's *Colonial Transactions* (1993).[84] Meanwhile careful institutional historicizing with implicitly radical intent continued into the early 1990s in UK. John Dixon's *A Schooling in 'English'* (1991)[85] revisited the particularities of English's emergence through extension lectures. Robert Crawford's *Devolving English Literature* (1992) set out to 'force 'English' to take account of other cultures which are in part responsible for the initial construction of 'English literature' as a subject',[86] and made the case for the Scottish and provincial English invention of English literature and

then the Scottish invention of Scottish literature. David Johnson's
Shakespeare and South Africa (1996) charted the development of English
studies in South Africa in the 19th and 20th centuries, using the teaching
and reception of Shakespeare therein to exemplify different phases.[87]

Conservative arguments along the lines of Scholes made their appearance against the increasingly dominant mode of instrumentalizing the
institutional history of English with radical intent in the UK too. Guy
and Small's *Politics and Value in English Studies* (1993)[88] is a case in point,
attempting a defence of the academic discipline and institutional practice of English against Theory-inspired interdisciplinarity and politiciza-
tion through a historical awareness of the disciplinary place of English
in relation to other academic disciplines. But by this time it was clear
that the project of institutional historicization of English with radical
intent had fulfilled its purpose. More interestingly, something else apart
from radical intending and conservative recuperating had emerged in
that line of institutional historicizing of English from Palmer and
Ohmann through Baldick, Graff, Doyle, Vishwanathan, Crawford,
Scholes, and others. What emerged was a sort of territorial imperative,
which was not simply broadly located in ideological domains of left and
right, radical and conservative, but increasingly sieved through narrower
ideological domains of ethnicity, geopolitics, gender, and race. Whereas
for Palmer and Ohmann the territorial placements of English were
coeval with the expansive lines of class critique and analysis of bourgeois
society, for most others mentioned above the historicizing project
became a ground of territorial investments and claims from specific margins and centres. These were assessments of the discipline's history, and
therefore its current institutional possibilities, conducted through the
standpoints of Western liberalism and a Western humanist tradition,
colonial and post-colonial environments, provincial and marginalized
peripheries, gendered spaces and exclusions. Whether these were ideologically necessary or historically objective are not questions that
I intend to address here; my intention is no more than to note the emergence of this trend, however justified or unjustified it may have been.
Noting this trend is tantamount to noting that this line of critical
engagement also merges with the concerns of the Theory debate and the
institutional response to that in literary studies, the quarrels over canons
and counter-canons and alternative canons, the struggle over alignments with emerging academic spaces, the institutional playing out of
political desires ... to the entrenchment of identity politics in literary
studies. That the historicizing project *apropos* English seemed completed
in the 1990s does not mean that its tendency was dissolved; it meant

that the current ponderings on the institutional space of English absorbed them in the grid where social constructionist identity politics had emerged as the dominant arrangement. The demonstration of that would have to be a prolonged and, in this context, separate project. There are a host of books which charts the travels and travails of the profession of English studies which can be recruited to that project: Patrick Hogan's *The Politics of Interpretation* (1990), Carl Woodring's *Literature* (1990), Harold Fromm's *Academic Capitalism and Literary Value* (1991), Gubar and Kamholtz's edited volume *English Inside and Out* (1993), Robert Heilman's *The Professor and the Profession* (1999), Donald Hall's edited volume *Professions* (2001), and Jeffrey Williams's edited volume *The Institution of Literature* (2002)[89] come to mind. But that is a distinct track to follow.

Indeed there are plenty of other tracks that could be followed to demonstrate in what manner and to what degree social constructionist identity politics as understood in Part I has inserted itself and became institutionalized in literary studies. A tempting line of enquiry in this context might follow the trace of literary study's association with a particular identity-based political position (e.g., feminism or ethnicity) and the incorporation of that into the identity politics (that embraces different identity-based political positions) that gradually becomes institutionalized in literary studies. But all these possible lines of enquiry are openings in a similar direction: the demonstration of *how* identity politics becomes institutionalized in literary studies. And there it stays, I feel, institutionalized – though Theory, according to Tilottama Rajan in 2001, 'has migrated out of English into continental philosophy departments and book series',[90] literary studies arguably still shares its political energy with cultural studies, which has become,

> the epitome of this [transnational global civil] society: a paradigmatic use of the humanities within a modular structure that appears to promote dissidence. Its tiered architecture accommodates what has long been a point of contention in Marxist theory between agency and a more pessimistic sense of the social as the epiphenomenon of decentred (super)structures. [...] Seeming to resolve the aporia, Cultural Studies interpellates minority identities and localisms into a disciplinary complex which, in its upper reaches (a refurbished New Historicism, hypertext theory, globalization studies) does not criticize structure and reification but rather reprojects the affect of identity onto a specular identification – either ascetic or jubilant – with technology and economics.[91]

The point of this part is, however, not merely to show *how* identity politics comes to be reified in institutional academic pursuits (in the case
of literary studies); an engagement with the *effects* of such institution-
alisation is also my objective. The idea is to demonstrate how the
abstract critique of social constructivist identity politics offered in Part I
may be concretized through the institutionalization of identity politics
in literary studies. In other words, the idea is to see how the institutionalization of identity politics in literary studies extends the logic of
embodiment and spreads a series of identity-based constraints (rather
than exclusions) along the lines delineated in Part I. This entails a necessarily impressionistic calling to account for some of the assumptions
and principles of institutional practice in literary studies now: in teaching, in critical practice, in the institutionally moderated disseminations
and transmissions that constitute the field. The following two chapters
are devoted to these. Chapter 7 attends primarily to the institutional
self-locations that literary critics announce in undertaking critical reading and writing, with close attention to some examples. Chapter 8
addresses pedagogical presumptions by examining literary theory textbooks and revolves the implications of theorizing, questioning, and
constructing literary canons. The final Chapter 9 briefly speculates on
the everyday institutional life of literary studies now in the context of
social constructionist identity politics.

7
Self-Announcements and Institutional Realignments

Self-awareness

The travel of theory to the construction of Theory, and then to the constructions of 'after Theory' and 'against Theory', instilled an increased demand for self-awareness in literary studies. Self-awareness in literary studies has two directions which usefully obtrude upon and refine each other. *On the one hand*, there is the self-awareness that applies within the discipline itself (the self of the discipline), or the awareness of disciplinary prerogatives and presumptions while, so to say, doing the discipline. This is the stuff of Theory textbooks for literature students (an area of some moment to this study, to which Chapter 8 is devoted); many begin by explaining to students that to engage with Theory is to become aware, as Steven Lynn puts it, 'of a variety of different assumptions about texts, and [of] how to use those assumptions to explore and understand literature',[1] or to realize that reading is not, in Raman Selden's words (echoing Terry Eagleton), 'an *innocent* activity'.[2] These exhortations to disciplinary self-awareness are addressed to students, couched in a register appropriate to exchanges between master and novice, where the master's voice represents the discipline itself for the novice, becomes the discipline's self. Such explanations have, for this study, the great advantage of making explicit the shared disciplinary knowledge that is so obvious that it is seldom expressed among peers. Such statements have the added advantage of being designed to consolidate the institutional character of the discipline, to be pitched for institutional transmission. But along with this level of institutional consolidation, there are others that locate disciplinary peers in relation to each other within their discipline, in the register appropriate to peers in conversation (or masters talking among themselves). This is a rather

more closely studied area. Significant research has been conducted on
how academic narratives follow certain ritual or standardized practices
(in using hedges, passive constructions, footnotes, etc.[3]), and how academic discourses sustain different academic tribes and territories (from
ethnographic, sociological, and educationist perspectives).[4] Of interest
here is one limited strategy that has become characteristic (though not
exclusively) of the academic discourse of literary studies: announcements of *self*-awareness, or awareness of individuality, or of being a
subject (not being subjective), or of having an identity, within the institutional academic forum. So, *on the other hand*, there is this kind of *self*-
awareness, one that is often found in the marginalia of monographs
and papers in literary studies (prefaces, introductory remarks), in passing comments, shouldering text that cultivates the more impersonal
strategies of academic discourse. This aspect of *self*-awareness is particularly germane to the place of identity politics in question here. The bent
of literary theory (Theory to 'after Theory') has, as the previous chapter
argues, been inclined to the excavation of subjectivity and identity; and
a declaration of identity claims (such as, in the terms of Chapter 3,
unqualifiable performative articulations) is now powerfully associated
with the desire to embody identity-based political positions and thereby assume social constructionist identity politics. Such announcement
of *self*-awareness therefore appears at the crux of the entrenchment of
identity politics through the travel of Theory within the institutional
practice of literary studies.

These two directions of self-awareness in the context of Theory col-
lide with and refine each other because both are complicit with the
institutional disposition of literary studies. The understanding of institutionalization that I subscribe to, drawn from Berger and Luckmann, is
worth recalling here: 'Institutionalization occurs whenever there is a
reciprocal typification of habitualized actions by types of actors. Put differently, any such typification is an institution'.[5] In revolving this in
Chapter 5, I had noted that this approach to institutionalization
emphasizes habitual practice rather than closed spaces of practice (the
specificity of organizations or institutions). *Self*-aware announcements
at the margins of scholarly narratives and self-aware disciplinarity
voiced in literary theory textbooks mediate the process through which
identity politics come to be institutionalized in literary studies. Both of
these are at the same time habitualized performances in themselves as
well as modes of transmitting such habitual performances. An attempt
to trace these two directions of self-awareness can therefore be recruited
here to effectively chart the evolving patterns of habitualization that *are*

the institutionalization of identity politics in literary studies. This is attempted, necessarily impressionistically and with reference to symptomatic texts, in this and the next chapter: this chapter attends to self-announcements in literary studies narratives, and the next to literary theory textbooks and notions of canonicity.

In addressing in this chapter the *self*-aware announcements of literary scholarship, there are further specific advantages that present themselves. It is in the nature of such announcements that they interrogate the institutional habit which is instantiated in their enunciation. Thus, such announcements are not merely manifestations of habitualization (demonstrative of the structure of institutional practice in literary studies), they are also explorations of that institutional practice and critiques of the centrality of identity politics therein. *Self*-awareness can naturally be expected to deconstruct the self – or the subject in the institutional arena – to the point where the subject disappears and lays bare the ideology of its and others' institutionalized projection. It is because of this penchant for a broader exposure in trying to expose *self*-awareness in literary studies that focusing on such announcements may amount to a delineation of identity politics in action within – in practice within – its pervasive capture of literary studies. I have specifically chosen for attention here a few passages, textual statements of such announcement of *self*-awareness, which specifically both perform and unpick the institutional prerogatives of embodying identity-based political positions and of subscribing to social constructionist identity politics. These passages seem to me to capture the institutional moment/momentum of identity politics in literary studies. By making this selection I do not assume that these are singular instances; on the contrary, I assume that these are representative of many such announcements, and moreover reveal now recognizably habitual patterns of identity politics in literary studies at large. My assumption here may be excessive (I said this would be impressionistic). Three of these passages particularly register the institutional moment of embodying identity-based political positions, and three register the embrace of social constructionist identity politics in a wider sense. In Part I, I had argued that embodying identity-based political positions and espousing social constructionist identity politics are often coeval endeavours – or rather, that identity politics is my theme insofar as these are coeval. The social constructionist identity politics that is unembodied, I have already maintained (this is a prudent reminder), is where this study emerges and is itself located; that remains the frame from which this study emanates and not its object of investigation.

A couple of incidental thoughts about attempting to address such select *self*-aware announcements from the textualized margins of literary scholarship come to mind. It occurs to me that this is by way of turning a well-honed practice of close textual reading that has sustained a great deal of critical theory *upon* texts of critical theory themselves – a ploy that has interesting, albeit only tangentially relevant, theoretical nuances in this context. This is not in any way an original enterprise; quite otherwise really, for it resonates with the early moves of the construction of Theory. Much of Derrida's writing, for instance, did not merely devote close, indeed disembowelling, critical attention to theoretical texts but also to the process of their own textualizations. But when this occurs within the discourse of institutionally self-aware literary studies there is an added resonance to this turn: a sort of turning inward of New Criticism or literary critical attention to rhetoric seems to occur which both echoes that heritage and pushes that heritage into posteriority. Another way of thinking about this may be to consider this as analogous to Jean Michel Rabaté's attempt to (via Proust and Joyce) get at 'a "theory of the novel" provided by novels themselves, the search for a theory of literature immanent to literature'[6] in *The Future of Theory* (2002). The attention that is given to specific passages here is in the spirit of looking for the theory of literary criticism that is immanent to literary criticism. The theoretical dilemma that Rabaté comes to from his quest applies to a large extent to the following too:

> Theory aims at the most general questions, at a philosophical questioning of 'totalities' positing, as Broch thought, a 'Platonic logos,' but it cannot avoid being enmeshed in the letter of the text in partly untranslatable signifiers, in the intractably entangled network of private and historical allusions without which literature would not open to *mathesis singularis*, in other words, to theorizing in particular.[7]

More significantly, the examination of such *self*-aware announcements could be regarded as a sort of ethnographic exercise, where self-announcements are taken as 'autoethnographic expressions'. In literary studies the term is most familiarly referred to Mary Louise Pratt's *Imperial Eyes* (1992), a study of travel writing in 18th and 19th century colonies:

> I use ['autoethnography' and 'autoethnographic expression'] to refer to instances in which colonized subjects undertake to represent themselves in ways which engage with the *colonizer's own* terms. If

ethnographic texts are a means by which Europeans represent to themselves their (usually subjugated) others, autoethnographic texts are those the others construct in response to or in dialogue with those metropolitan representations.[8] [Pratt's emphasis]

Pratt largely regards such autoethnographic expression to be salutary interruptions in imperial ethnographic discourses, questioning their assumptions while assuming their terminology, through an authenticity and authority which derives from the ethnographer's *belonging within* the ethnographic field that the colonizer occupies, explores, and exploits. At the same time, this added authority of belonging within, and ability thereby to interrogate and possibly subvert, is accentuated by the disciplinary ground that the autoethnographer encroaches upon alongside the colonial ethnographer – that of ethnography itself. The autoethnographer, therefore, wrests a space within that disciplinary ground which the colonial ethnographer also occupies and instrumentalizes for exploitation. That this sort of autoethnographic expression would be of peculiar interest to identity-based political positions within the embrace of social constructionist identity politics is easily apprehended. The optimistic expectations of autoethnography, the desire to recognize the authority of belonging *within* evidenced there, are obviously akin to recognizing the authenticity of embodiments of identity-based political positions. In many ways such expectations are an encouragement to making ethnography consonant with the embodiment of ethnic-identity-based political positions. By thus maintaining in the discipline of ethnography a meeting ground between dominant ethnos and other ethnicities, however much at odds with each other, that discipline is itself prospectively disposed as a field of social constructionist identity polities. Prospectively, it is expected, the discipline would become a field in which different ethnically identified autoethnographers agree upon and accept the centrality of difference, respect each others' authorities of belonging within, communicate with each other accordingly, and defer to certain limits of and prerogatives of disciplinary exchange.

What renders Pratt's understanding of autoethnographic expression of particular interest here is the implicit disciplinary self-awareness that is written into it. In an important sense, autoethnographic expression does not merely attend to ethnicity and its manifestations in demarcated zones, but attends also to the culture of the discipline of ethnography – it is, tangentially, ethnography of ethnography. This aspect of autoethographic expression is both worth deconstructing within the discipline of ethnography, and in terms of its extensions in other humanistic disciplines (particularly in concert with the institutionalization of identity politics). This has been attempted in a splendid essay, 'On Auto-Ethnographic Authority' (2003), by James Buzard,[9] with a scope of reference that far precedes Pratt, and in a manner that registers its extension in a range of humanities and social sciences disciplines. The critique of autoethnography that Buzard offers is effectively a reckoning with the institutional orientation of the ethnographic discipline, and is similar to the critique of embodying identity-based political positions, and of social constructionist identity politics in Part I here. Buzard wonders what checks are there for autoethnographers as ethnographers, and what registering of unevenness and silences and power-play in an ethnographic field is possible in autoethnographic expression. Various sceptical questions can be raised in this regard: Are not the expectations of autoethnographers too uncritical of their place and status within the field? Is it perhaps too eagerly inferred that belonging within the ethnographic field gives autoethnographers authority over the *whole* field, somehow transcending schisms within that field even though they are inevitably invested in such schisms by belonging? Are the autoethnographer's and the outside ethnographer's insertion of a disciplinary quest within the observed field greatly different insofar as the discipline is not itself the field? Buzard also makes the connection between autoethnography and autobiography (of which, as we see below, *self*-aware announcements are restricted and institutionally typified instances) that postcolonial, feminist, and other identity-invested literary critics make.

Coming back to the significance of the notion of autoethnographic expression here: it has, I observed, something to do with disciplinary self-reckonings, with exploring the institutions and cultures of academic work themselves. The spirit in which ethnography can thus turn inwards is still most cogently expressed by Clifford Geertz in his essay 'The Way We Think Now' (1983):

> [...] the various disciplines (or disciplinary matrices), humanistic, natural scientific, social scientific alike, that make up the scattered discourse of modern scholarship are more than just intellectual coigns of vantage but are ways of being in the world, to invoke a Heideggerian formula, forms of life, to use a Wittgensteinian, or varieties of noetic experience, to adapt a Jamesian. In the same way that Papuans or Amazonians inhabit the world they imagine, so do high energy physicists or historians of the Mediterranean in the age of Phillip II – or so, at least, the anthropologist imagines. It is when we begin to see this,

to see that to set out to deconstruct Yeats's imagery, absorb oneself in black holes, or measure the effect of schooling on economic achievement is not just to take up a technical task but to take on a cultural frame that defines a great part of one's life, that an ethnography of modern thought begins to seem an important project.[10]

Something of this spirit is manifest in the *self*-aware announcements that I briefly propose to look at in this chapter, as symptoms of the institutional disposition of literary studies.[11] These are all autoethnographic expressions in two overlapping ways: one, in exposing the identity-position of the critic (as a woman, as an immigrant, as gay, as black, etc., in some sense representing the social collectives of women, immigrants, gays, blacks, etc.); two, in critically acknowledging an institutional status and affiliation in literary studies (being in and performing and reflecting on the institutional arena, that is, literary studies). These statements are, therefore, *self*-aware with regard to identity-based political positions or social constructionist identity politics, and with regard to the institution of literary studies as a field of practice, in ways that inextricably link both. Insofar as these are the latter, they may be regarded as autoethnographic sources for 'the way we think now', in Geertz's terms – these announcements (along with textbooks, literary canon formations, etc.) may be regarded, continuing with Geertz's terms, as a variety of 'convergent data':

> [...] descriptions, measures, observations, what you will, which are at once diverse, even rather miscellaneous, both as to type and degree of precision and generality, unstandardized facts, opportunistically collected and variously portrayed, which yet turn out to shed light on one another for the simple reason that the individuals they are descriptions, measures or observations of are directly involved in one another's lives [...][12]

Attention to the autoethnographic character of *self*-aware announcements in literary studies narratives, which conflate identity-claims and institutional reflections, reveal something, I hope, about the institutionalization of identity politics in literary studies. The consideration of other such convergent data (such as textbooks) in the next chapter brings further clarification of this theme.

As I have said already: three of the passages discussed below particularly register the institutional moment of embodying identity-based political positions, and three register the embrace of social constructionist identity politics in a wider sense.

Castle's apparitional lesbian

When Terry Castle of Stanford University, already a noted authority on 18th century English literature and culture and author of such books as *Clarissa's Ciphers* (1982) and *Masquerade and Civilization* (1986),[13] published her first collection of essays addressing explicitly the cultural representation, experience, and theorization of lesbians ('apparitional' but not 'veiled' here) – *The Apparitional Lesbian: Female Homosexuality and Modern Culture* (1993) – she chose to begin with a 'Polemical Introduction'. A couple of interesting paragraphs in this explained the process through which she came to write this book, on the assumption that it might surprise readers accustomed to her institutionally defined specialist writings.

> It wasn't easy for me to begin this book; only a kind of spectral visitation prompted me to do it at all. As late as 1989, I was still entrenched in my 'official' academic speciality – eighteenth century English literature – and trying feverishly to get on with what I invariably referred to (without irony) as my 'big book'. The subject of the big book, interestingly, was to have been ghosts – and, in particular, the waning of belief in apparitions in Western culture after the Enlightenment. To this end, I had spent almost two years doing research and writing outlines, and my study overflowed with books and piles of notes [...]. Before I could get very far with this grandiose scheme, however, a ghost of my own came back to haunt me. For weeks I struggled to find a way to begin, only to discover that the more I thought about 'the apparitional', the more vaporous and elusive and impossible the subject became. One evening, after a particularly dispiriting session at the computer, I found myself – in a Garbo-like fugue of my own – jotting down the first words of the autobiographical essay that appears here under the title 'First Ed' [...]. Casting my old notes aside with strange exhilaration, I proceeded to plan out the first essays included in this volume.[14]

She continues:

> In retrospect everything made more sense than it did at the time. Lesbianism has always been a 'phantom' in my scholarly work – a theme that I often yearned to write about (and sometimes did in carefully veiled ways) yet for a variety of reasons felt unable to address directly. The big book, I realize now, was a last ditch attempt

to avoid the issue. Yet even so I was constantly torn. [...] By arriving so suddenly and unaccountably, the eponymous 'Ed' released me from my inhibitions. And, in turn, in conjuring up this spectral visitor from my own lesbian past, I had unwittingly turned toward – or let myself be captured by – my real subject.[15]

Several interesting manoeuvres are performed in the language of these passages, in the use of synecdoche and metaphor, which are relevant to my theme.

One, it announces succinctly the conceptual thread that holds this book together, the idea that there has been something ghostly or apparitional in the figuring of lesbianism in literary and other cultural forms. By the time the reader comes to Chapter 3 and the elaboration of this thread, the central metaphor of ghostliness is already in place, already (so to say) connected and simply in need of repetition and evidence: 'To try to write the literary history of lesbianism is to confront, from the start, something ghostly: an impalpability, a misting over, an evaporation, or "whiting out" of possibility'[16] ... 'at least until around 1900 lesbianism manifests itself in the Western literary imagination primarily as an absence, as chimera or *amor impossibilia* – a kind of love that, by definition, cannot exist. [...] It cannot be perceived, except apparitionally'[17] ... 'in nearly all of the art of the eighteenth and nineteenth centuries, lesbianism, or its possibility, can only be represented to the degree that it is simultaneously 'derealized,' through a blanching authorial infusion of spectral metaphors'[18] ... and so on. Unravelling apparitional metaphors and *leitmotivs* in the expression of lesbianism in literary history is, it is conveyed briefly, the theme that this book addresses itself to.

Two, the above-quoted passages *assume* (in the sense of seeking to embody) a particular kind of aptitude for this undertaking on the part of the author. In fact, two kinds of aptitudes that the author could embrace are raised, and the author embraces one *against* the other in this instance. The rejected aptitude is the institutionally defined scholarly one – that of the diligent researcher with piles of notes, the officially acknowledged specialist, the writer of a 'big book'. That would have led, it is averred, to a different book addressing 'the waning of belief in apparitions in Western culture after the Enlightenment'. The assumed aptitude is that of the author's own lesbian identity, the aptitude that derives from the author's own 'lesbian past'. What is interesting in this moment of embodying the identity-based position that makes this book necessary is that it is performed at the level of metaphorical consonances. The author is apt for this undertaking because the theme of apparitional lesbianism that she addresses is invested with the author's own lesbian apparitions – in the 'Ed' who is delineated in the autobiographical Chapter 2, in the 'phantom' of her past scholarly work. Nothing as simplistic as a material interest in representations of lesbianism arising from the author's own experience of lesbianism is announced. That would have been an understandable but not necessary causality; it might have implied that this book was undertaken because of this fact, but may well have been undertaken even if she had not been a lesbian but somehow acquired an interest in this topic (however). Indeed, that might have diluted the eschewal of the scholarly aptitude: researchers may acquire research interests in themes and concepts with or without any personal investment. That the author embraces her theme in this book because of an affinity between the apparitional nature of literary representations of lesbianism and the apparitions in her own lesbian past – because the metaphor of apparition/spectrality/ghostliness unite theme and authorial sexual identity in a unique bind – gives this book a weighty and necessary character. It is, in many ways, a most suggestive metaphorical confluence of author and theme: the apparitional cannot be rationalized or argued with in material terms. It is the 'spirit' of the identity-based position that subsumes this authorial enterprise, not the institutional materiality of scholarly production. The authorial embodiment of a sexual identity-based position that is this book is as final and outside debate as, say, a performative articulation of religious identity.

Three, in the process of performing these manoeuvres the nature of institutional literary studies is negotiated in a complex and revealing fashion. The 'big book' operates in the quoted passage as a synecdoche for institutional literary studies at large. As such it is a suggestive phrase, associated with the circulation of cultural capital that determines academic status and hierarchies, and with the meshing of research and educational and productive (publication and dissemination of knowledge) activities that lie at the heart of the academy. The abandonment of the 'big book' project in favour of a project with a powerful investment of embodied sexual identity effectively sounds like the abandonment of institutional constraints in favour of a liberating identity-based political position. But this apparently anti-establishment announcement is somewhat belied by the performance that *is* this book itself. To begin with, there is the complicated matter of understanding the difference between the 'veiled' expression of the author's investment in lesbianism in former institutionally apt productions, and the more explicit treatment of

the 'apparitional lesbian' in this book. That institutionally acknowledged productions forced a 'veiled' treatment of lesbianism upon the
author is analogous to the 'apparitional' lesbianism that is discerned in
18th and 19th century literary history in this book. Institutional expectations (whether in 18th and 19th century literary production or in the
20th century academia of Castle's time) could not quite suppress the
expression of lesbian experience; it enforced subterfuges like the 'apparitional' and the 'veiled'. Tracing the career of lesbian identities to reach a
politically effective identity-based position cannot, by implication, actually result in an abandonment of institutionally acknowledged production (despite the author's announcement); this process rests in *addressing*
the 'apparitional' and the 'veiled' of institutional practice explicitly
rather than *doing* the 'apparitional' and the 'veiled' implicitly in institutional practice. Further, though the author claims to have abandoned
one kind of 'big book' (and thus reneged from conservative institutional
literary studies) it is evident that *The Apparitional Lesbian* itself is a 'big
book' too, in an institutionally acknowledgeable form – only not conceptually conservative. It conforms to the habitual practices of academic
production that mark institutional currency: it comes with the weight of
an institutionally located authorial signature (the 'apparition' of the
Professor of English at Stanford University, author of other 'big books',
academic specialist in 18th century English literature is everywhere evident though blanched in this book); its register belongs to literary and
cultural history and criticism; it is replete with the scholarly apparatus
that signifies a 'big book' (references, citations, bibliography, index, etc.);
its dissemination is as a scholarly work (first published by a university
press, allocated space in scholarly productions and categories of book
shops and libraries, introduced in scholarly reviews and curricula, etc.).
Arguably, the author's claim of liberating herself from institutional constraints to a liberating embodied identity-based expression in this book
is belied by the appearance and content and circulation of the book
itself. That claim then is a rhetorical ploy. *What this book represents, and
what I think is tacitly inferable from the above-quoted passage, is a realignment of the institutional practice of literary studies with embodied identity-
based expression and politics (in this instance, lesbian identity-based).*
I emphasize this observation because it is this understanding that guided my selection of this passage – this particular autoethnographic
expression – for examination here.

To repeat, *The Apparitional Lesbian*, especially as discerned through
the above-quoted passage in its 'polemical introduction', is a representative instance of the realignment of embodied identity-based political

position with a particular kind of habitual institutional practice in literary studies – the production, status, and impact of 'big books'. The metaphoric investment of the author's lesbian apparitions in the critical enquiry into apparitional lesbianism in literary and cultural history introduces the logic of embodiment in critical practice: the rhetorical ploy of ostensibly abandoning a 'big book' (that compromises with subterfuges) while effectively performing/producing a 'big book' (that addresses such subterfuges) gives this critical practice an institutional turn. A couple of other autoethnographic self-announcing passages are used below to illustrate other modes of realignment of institutional practice in literary studies with embodied identity-based positions.

A final observation on *The Apparitional Lesbian* before moving onwards: by an interesting coincidence the year of the publication of this was also the year of publication of another influential deployment of apparitional concerns, Derrida's *Specters of Marx* (published in French in 1993 and in English translation the year after).[19] This coincidence, while fortuitous as coincidences are, is suggestive of a certain coherence arising from the socio-historical environment – the ethos – in which the two books appeared. At any rate, when brought together by this shared rhetorical penchant they seem to capture and contain a period-characterizing shift in political sensibilities. Derrida's much awaited statement on Marxism underlined the necessity of keeping the spirit of Marxism alive, in the midst of increasing convergence on principles of liberal democracy and capitalist production. He hoped that the radical potential of the deconstructive process, the undeconstructible universality of justice (oddly contradictory positions), and a renewal of the spirit of Marxism would enable that. Derrida took the *spirit* of Marxism seriously: a revitalised *spirit* of Marxism would have to be coeval with the plurality and shifting nature of 'realities' and the discourses they are approached by, and not the totalizing affair that Marxism had become. With characteristic sensitivity to rhetoric, Derrida both contributed to the new left critique of Marxist materialism/economic determinism and reiterated the new left's attempt to co-opt Marxism's emancipative ambitions by deliberately deploying the slippages of terms like spirit/spectre/haunting – terms evocative of both death and continuity, death of the material and continuity of the spiritual. Necessarily this was akin to ringing the death knell of Marxism while appearing not to, because removing Marxism's materialistic critique is precisely what goes comprehensively against the spirit of Marxism. Derrida could be said to have decidedly shelved Marxism into spectral continuity, just as the *Communist Manifesto* had decidedly shoved a revolutionary spectre towards fleshly existence. That the years in which Derrida was making this all-too potently symbolic statement are also the years in which Terry Castle traversed a like rhetorical ground to wed the logic of embodiment with institutional practice in literary studies is, it must be retrospectively admitted, a peculiarly meaningful circumstance. In the theatre of the apparitional Derrida and Castle independently and yet jointly seem to enact the moves that led to the entrenchment of identity politics in the new left (discussed in Chapter 5), and cohesively to the entrenchment of identity politics in the travels of Theory (discussed in Chapter 6), of the 1980s and early 1990s.

Felman on what women want

Let me stay with 1993, and another self-announcing passage which aligns the embodiment of an identity-based political position to the institutional practice of literary studies. This is drawn from the intro-ductory remarks in Shoshanna Felman's *What Does a Woman Want? Reading and Sexual Difference* (1993), and comes from a distinct and yet like direction. The book presents, in its own words:

> close readings by a woman reader, on the one hand, of some women writers' autobiographical attempts [...], and, on the other hand, of three texts by male writers who dramatize, each in his own way, a male encounter with femininity as difference, a male experience, that is, of femininity as precisely the emergence of the [...] question: 'What does a woman want?'[20]

To some extent the likeness to Castle's project in *The Apparitional Lesbian* is evident: just as Castle's own assumption (as author) of a les-bian sexual identity gave her access to the unravelling of lesbianism in literary history, so Felman's gender identity ('a woman reader') gives her access to the play of gender in the works of gender-identified authors ('women writers'/'male writers'). The modality of access is held in a nec-essary bind in both: what they professedly *are* allows them to critically address their themes. Both expose this bind by considering how they happened to write these books (a phase in their own autobiographies) in their self-announcements. However, the necessity of this connection between author's autobiography and theme addressed are approached quite differently. For Castle this is established by the deployment of a metaphorical field of consonances, the field of the 'apparitional' (ghostly, spectral, evanescent), whereas for Felman this rests in a series of negations and assertions. Commenting on the difficulty she faced in completing this book or giving it closure, the author observes:

> But it has thus exemplified ironically and vitally, in practice, at once the desire and the difficulty, or the *self-resistance*, not simply of reading as a woman (since what that means is not immediately graspable outside of the prescriptions and beliefs of patriarchal structure) but of *assuming* one's own sexual difference in the very act of reading; of assuming, that *is*, not the false security of an 'identity' or a substantial definition (however nonconformist or divergent) but the very insecurity of a differential movement, which no ideology can fix and of which no institutional affiliation can redeem the radical anxiety, in the performance of an act that constantly – deliberately or unwittingly – *enacts* our difference yet finally escapes our own control.[21] [Author's emphases]

With this explanation of the investment of the gender-embodied reader in the presented readings in place, Felman goes on to describe the institutional academic entry of her book as follows:

> At the outset of the writing process of the book, my current feminist positions were not a given. They were neither altogether conscious nor truly owned by me with their full critical potential: I arrived at them through reading, acquired them in writing. The impact of these insights on the audiences that first heard them presented in lectures, the knowledge that early published versions of them found resonance and repercussions in female colleagues who were discussing them in conferences and assigning them in classrooms, and the letters I received from women readers in turn deepened their own *impact* on me and rendered more compelling and more articulate the critical significance of the feminist convictions to which the readings and the writing led me.[22]

Reading for and writing and transmitting this book to an audience and thereby to institutionally defined fora (lecture halls, conference venues, classrooms), in this instance, is thus understood not only as a realignment of that institutional space with her identity-based political position but simultaneously a realization of her investment in that identity-based political position. It is the selfsame process of reading-writing-transmitting-institutionalizing that brings the author, her audience and the academic spaces they occupy to a joint confirmation of

feminist politics. There is a caveat here though, an interesting limitation of address and reach: 'I should hasten to explain that by adopting
the generic 'we' in what I have just written [...], I am not proposing to
speak in the name of women: the 'we' is a rhetorical structure of
address, not a claim for epistemological authority. I am speaking not *for*
women, but *to* women.'[23] In brief, the author clarifies that this is a work
that both *is* autobiography (or the absence of autobiography) and *about*
autobiography, where it is understood that the autobiographical subject is female.

At both ends of this explanation there are certain silences or a certain implied deafness. The anterior placement of gender in the consideration of reading and writing enables both the embodiment of an
identity-based position and the investment of this in the institutional
practice of literary criticism. That writers and readers are gender-
identified *before* the texts, the processes of reading and writing, are
approached is the key strategy of embodiment here. Since this gender-
framing is taken as given, it coalesces into the gender-framing of
the reading–writing subject of the author. The advantages of the anteriority of gender are most clearly expressed in the enunciation of the
reading–writing subject of the author. Each step of the second quotation from Felman above, a single breathless sentence, is both an assertion of the primacy of gender location and a withdrawal of that location
from qualification, so that it appears *before* qualification, *anterior* to all
attempts to grasp it. It cannot be stated in terms of 'prescriptions and
beliefs' because those are all-consumingly patriarchal, it cannot be
reduced to 'the false security of an 'identity' or a substantial definition',
it cannot be fixed by 'ideology' or by 'institutional affiliation'. The
gender-identification of the reading–writing subject is anterior to all
those clarifying possibilities. All that can be said is that it is (the three
emphasised words) *self-resistant* (even anterior to the apprehension of
self), it is *assumed* (as an office or responsibility can be performatively
assumed), it is *enacted* (is done or, perhaps, simply happens) – the gender-
identification of the reading–writing subject of the author simply,
uninterrogably, unqualifiably, *is*. This precedent *is*-ness of the gender
identification of the reading–writing subject is as effective a strategy of
embodying an identity-based political position as Castle's apparitional
desires are. There is no saying anything about this characterization of
the female reading-writing subject and no debating with it; anything
that can be said is either a patriarchal prescription or false security
or ideological reduction or institutional formulation. Analogous
to Adorno's perception of existentialists voicing existence itself, the

reading–writing subject – the author – here voices the female itself, from a point of pristine gender-identification in the midst of an absolute silence.

Given that the author thus embodies an identity-based political position, so that every gesture of reading-writing that composes this book becomes complicit with that embodiment, the institutional realignment involved in disseminating this book becomes an exercise in extending that unarguability, that immunity to debate and discussion. Only those who can embody a similar sort of unapproachable gender-identification, who can accept it within themselves *a priori*, can respond to this book. The logic of embodiment spreads into the consolidation of this identity-based political position, and the consequent silences and exclusions are smeared across the institutional practice of literary studies insofar as this book engages in that. It appears that the lectures delivered by the author from this book were not heard by, found no resonance or repercussions among, any but female-identified colleagues. Only women were entitled to assign these in curricula and classrooms. Male colleagues, or those who are uncertain of their gender-identifications, in those lecture halls and classrooms and conference centres are simply *not there* – it does not matter whether they were trying to listen and understand, they are wilfully *made* deaf. This is not an exclusiveness which can be thought of as even political, because there is ultimately no space for advocacy and agency in the dispersal of this embodied communication within the institutional sphere. As Felman puts it, 'I am speaking not *for* women, but *to* women.' If a few men, a few souls uncertain of their gender-assignments and -identifications, happened to have overheard the author or cast their eyes unwittingly on this book, they did not have to be engaged, rejected, recognized, cold-shouldered, or anything. They are, as far as Felman goes, outside the circulation of these exchanges, deaf as lampposts.

Leaving aside the arguments raised about the logic of embodiment, exemplified so well here, there is an immediate kind of resistance that runs through this explanation even while it is given. This has to do with the institutional realignment (dispersal) which is described here, and read-written into this book and its transmissions. Like Castle's *The Apparitional Lesbian* this book itself is self-evidently an institutionally framed object. As for Castle's book, we can say Felman's book too comes with the weight of an institutionally located authorial signature (the reading–writing subjectivity of the Professor of French and Comparative Literature at Emory University), with a register that belongs to literary criticism, replete with the scholarly apparatus that signifies its institutional status (references, citations, bibliography, index, etc.), and accordingly disseminated (first published by a university press, allocated space in scholarly productions and categories of book shops and libraries, introduced in scholarly reviews and curricula, etc.). In the above quoted passages the self-evident institutional register and form of the book addresses itself naturally to its readership and spaces, and these are primarily academic institutional spaces – lecture halls, seminar rooms, classrooms. Now the academic book, and usually the kind of institutional spaces in question, may be targeted in various ways to particular readers but are generally intrinsically democratic spaces. The book may circulate in a manner that largely fulfils Felman's desire to 'speak *to* women', but it is always possible that others – any one – will find it somewhere, open it, and read it. Unless determined efforts are made to police the gates of classrooms, seminar rooms, etc. (which does happen occasionally), it is always possible that men will stray in and listen. At any rate, texts generally, just by appearing as such, are open to engagement without limitation. Felman's attempt to introduce silences and assume deafness from certain quarters in her performance (reading-writing) of this text inevitably runs counter to the democratic openness that is the nature of textuality, and that is inherent in its institutional presence.

Despite the contradictions and resistances raised by this mode of embodying an identity-based political position and aligning institutional practice with it, these are not unfamiliar strategies in the field of social constructionist identity politics. But is this – or for that matter Castle's book – social constructionist? Are they perhaps simply straightforwardly essentialist in tendency? The unarguable and undebatable and indeed exclusive tendency of the logic of embodiment in these passages, and the strategies through which they seek to realign the practice of institutional literary studies, leave their attitudes to other kinds of identity-based political positions unclear. Their status as social constructionist or essentialist is indeterminate. But these passages from Castle and Felman do demonstrate how particular identity-based political positions can be embodied and made consonant with institutional practice, and as such these are indicative of the kind of thing that is institutionally contained by social constructionist identity politics. It does not really matter whether Castle and Felman are being essentialist or social constructionist here; the point is that by embodying their positions and giving them an institutional turn these positions become amenable to incorporation within institutionalized social constructionist identity politics. It is that amenability that is worth noting; it is that amenability which allows social constructionist identity politics to extend its reach and spread the silences and presumed deafness in question.

I come soon to a couple of self-announcements which engage directly with social constructionist identity politics and the institutional practice of literary studies. But before that a final example of strategies for realigning embodied identity-based political positions with the institutional practice of literary studies. This time the example has to do with collective rather than individual embodiment, and this passage comes from a book published a few years later, in 1998.

Woods on the gay tradition

Gregory Woods's *A History of Gay Literature: The Male Tradition* (1998) presents an impressive and self-reflexive scholarly elaboration of its theme, not merely to take account of ostensibly gay literary production from a historical perspective, but also of the 'selection, production and evaluation'[24] that is implicit in the process of charting literary tradition. In introducing the study, and locating itself within its own remit, the following passage is given to describe a process of institutionalizing gay literary studies:

> Even given the effects of homophobia on the production, distribution and evaluation of texts, we are increasingly in charge of our own culture. We have our own requirements, and set our own standards thereby. This is why gay-edited anthologies and gay-authored critical works are the crux of the development of gay reading practices. Moreover, the specialist marketing of gay literature is greatly facilitated once specifically gay bookstores start opening in the major urban centres of the Western world [...]. As important as the text itself are the ways in which we come to hear of it, find a copy of it, read it, and keep it to ourselves or pass it on to others. Gay newspapers provide gay book reviews; many run their own mail-order book clubs. Gay literature emerges from a network of readers as from poets, playwrights and novelists themselves. The book you are reading continues this process.[25]

Woods goes on immediately to note the establishment of specialist publishing houses starting from the 1969 gay liberation movement onwards, and that 'gay literary studies began to flourish in the American academic world' and gay literary criticism 'set a high critical standard for gay academics in literary studies to follow'.[26]

It seems to me that the logic of embodying an identity-based political position works here as in Castle's and Felman's self-announcements, and as in those cases it is wedded to an institutional realignment of literary studies – but in a quite different manner. Where for Castle and Felman embodiment and institutional realignment is a process of creating a bind between the identity-defined authorial self and the identity-based theme of their texts, and the institutional alignment follows primarily in *enacting* this through the monograph itself and its transmissions, Woods assumes a collective identity-defined voice and *explicates* (rather than simply performs) the necessary institutional realignment. The collective identity-defined voice is still an embodied voice, as I explain below, but it loosens the claim of author-ity as the central locus; and correspondingly, the explication of an institutionally extended identity-based network puts institutional practice more into perspective and concretizes some of the complexity of institutionalization.

The manner in which the logic of embodiment operates in this passage is connected to the use of collective first-person pronouns. The insistent 'we'/'our' in that passage could be read in two ways depending on how the implied reader is constructed. On the one hand, if the implied reader can include himself (it is the male tradition in question here) in the collective pronouns then the passage is a statement of inclusive affirmation. This included reader is, however, presumptively understood to recognize the veracity of the claim here, to accept the 'our own culture' and 'our own requirements' and 'our own standards' that are mentioned there, to be participant in (already – this statement does not issue an invitation, it assumes that the invitation is already issued and to the right party) 'the ways in which we come to hear of it', etc. The affirmation of a collective achievement in this passage can only be accepted by the included reader, and conformed to. The retrospective syntax (appropriate to a history) does not leave space for an included reader to interrogate whether 'our own requirements' have already been met, 'our own standards' have already been acceptably set. The conformity and acceptance that is enjoined on the included reader gives this passage a celebratory air: the whole seems to issue from a collective voice that only incorporates gay readers within its already realized collective gay achievement. For the included reader the mode of reading this book as a whole itself – the strategies for filling in what Wolfgang Iser might have called the 'blanks' and 'gaps'[27]– are therefore already given. These strategies rest in accepting that this book itself 'continues the process' that is collectively assumed and largely achieved.

On the other hand, if the implied reader cannot include him or herself in those collective pronouns this passage comes as both a warning and an invitation. The assertion that 'our own culture', 'our own requirements', 'our own standards' are already in place and so clearly possessed by 'us' could be read as a warning not to bring 'your' (if not homophobic, at least not gay) culture and requirements and standards to bear on these matters. Nevertheless, the possessive pronoun does not exclude (not in the sense Felman's 'speaking *to* women' does, Woods is definitely 'speaking *for* the gay collective') but *addresses* those who are not gay without including them. That the implied reader could be gay or not-gay and generate different inflections to this passage is indicative of the openness of its (variegated) address. As such then, this passage, while warning those not-included readers not to go by their culture/requirements/standards, also invites them to recognize and respectfully accept the gay-possessed culture/requirements/standards that are discussed here, and that is exemplified by the appearance of this book itself. The not-gay implied reader is not quite rendered deaf, but is put in a position from which she or he can listen but not be heard. The gay-possessed autonomy of the network of gay literary circulation elaborated here can only be perceived but not responded to, and certainly not participated in, by a/the collective that is not-gay. This passage is an invitation to do just that to such an implied reader.

These, it seems to me reasonably clearly articulated, nuances of the above passage are akin to the kind of limitations on discussion and exchange that was associated with the logic of embodiment of identity-based political positions in Part I. In that respect it comes in the same category as the self-announcements by Castle and Felman discussed above. But by giving this self-announcement a collective rather than individual authorial weight, the institutional turn described in this passage takes a more explicit and differently nuanced character. Here the institutional turn is not simply performed in the academic form of the text, and nor registered in the transmissions of the text, but described as constituted within the collective voice. Since institutionalization, as understood here, rests primarily in the 'typification of habitualized action by actors', institutionalization here becomes coeval with the very presumption that allows a collective voice to be presented. Unsurprisingly, the quoted passage from Woods is essentially a description of gay-possessed and autonomously gay institutional processes for literary studies. It establishes a circulatory matrix for literary studies – incorporating production, selection, reading, evaluation, or extending across authoring, publishing, selling, reviewing, academically researching and teaching – which is *a priori* gay-possessed or autonomously gay. Every aspect of institutional practice that is conceivable for literary studies is incorporated into that description of a circulatory matrix. The realignment of literary studies with this collectively embodied identity-based position is effected through the registering, the description, of the gay-possessed, and autonomously gay circulatory matrix of gay literature/literary studies.

And yet, this clear apprehension of the institutional practice of literary studies cannot be entirely devoid of its broader open boundaries, its larger-than-specific identity-based embrace. Just as Woods implicitly addresses (without including) the not-gay implied reader through the collective pronoun, so the positing of a contained gay institutional literary studies gestures to the uncontained institutional reach of literary studies. In the circumscribed institutional space determined by the connections between 'gay literature', 'gay-edited anthologies and gay-authored critical works', 'gay reading practices', 'gay bookstores', 'gay newspapers', 'gay book reviews', 'gay academics', etc., that is described here, an awareness of larger institutional, and not gay-identified, notions of academic value and status intrude. Why, the gay and not-gay reader alike may wonder, is it important that 'gay bookstores start opening in the major urban centres of the Western world'? Or that specialist gay publishing houses started appearing in the USA or 'gay literary studies began to flourish in the American academic world'? Evidently, in these instances it is the institutional centrality of the geopolitical domains into which gay literature and literary studies find access that *confer* the latter suitable weight, are the markers of 'we' being 'in charge of our own culture'. Arguably, the association of geopolitical centrality in global institutional arrangements with the matter of 'being in charge', of possessing, is indicative of an attempt to associate status with corporate capitalist values which are not in themselves identity-based. When Woods lists early gay critical works that 'set a high standard for gay academics in literary studies to follow', by what measure were these of a *'high standard'*? If the gay literary circulatory matrix sets its 'own standards', then the measure of high quality would have no relative meaning; it seems appropriate to infer that Woods means that a high standard was set not in terms of being contained in the autonomy of gay circulation, but by wider standards of critical practice in academia. There is, it seems to me, a discernible tension between the autonomous institutionalization that the logic of collective embodiment enjoins and the open and democratic nature of reading-writing and academic institutionalization within which this identity-based realignment is effected.

Woods's book, that 'continues the process', comes after all with the weight that, and is squarely within the wide academic reach that, a reputable academic publisher such as Yale University Press – not particularly gay-identified – enables.

Feminist literary studies textbooks

To summarize: in this chapter so far I have exemplified the use of the logic of embodying identity-based political positions to realign (in a self-aware fashion) the institutional practice of literary studies by looking closely at certain self-announcements drawn from books by Castle, Felman, and Woods. In each of these, and inferably in all such instances, the exclusions and inclusions which are assumed in following the logic of embodiment have a resistant relationship to the field of institutional practice that is thereby realigned. The in-principle-open nature of that institutional field – the open access to discussion and debate in reading-writing, in research and teaching, in criticism and fora for critical exchange, in academic publishing and dissemination – is both where these identity-based political positions locate themselves and where the constraints they extend are inevitably held at arm's length, released to interrogation, inevitably work against the grain. In this instance 'against the grain' does not have the radical ring that its previous association with Theory might suggest; 'against the grain' is more in the nature of disguising dispersed essentialisms under the emancipative drive of social constructionist identity politics. I have observed that it is the sought after, enacted, presented, registered institutional realignment and amenability to institutional practice that leaves these embodiments of identity-based political positions at a cusp of indeterminacy – almost essentialist in tendency and yet not quite (otherwise how are they to be contained in this institutional space?). It is in embracing such identity-based political positions within the wider remit of institutional literary studies that the institutionalization of social constructionist identity politics, as understood in Part I, clarifies itself. To that end this chapter necessarily moves on to a couple of self-announcements that are both coherent with such embodied identity-based positions and encompass them within a larger frame. The most familiar and self-interrogative figure exemplifying this direction is undoubtedly Gayatri Chakravorty Spivak, and it is a few passages from an essay by her that I take up here.

Before that however it might be worth pausing on the tendency to disperse essentialisms through the logic of embodiment in institutional practice, and the tensions that arise from that. The explanations that attempt to gloss over such tensions are familiar to the cognoscenti. These incorporate the laboured debates that I have already mentioned about the status of male critics as feminists, and which often favour some notion of 'pragmatic essentialism' or 'strategic essentialism': i.e., an essentialist political gesture that is not what it purports to be and knows it, but is made nevertheless to shake up the prejudiced establishment. There are several levels of bad-faith (in the existentialist sense) self-evidently involved here. The political gesture that is not what it seems to be may be taken for exactly what it seems to be; or, at any rate, it is a con which defeats itself as soon as it articulates and explains itself. I have covered this in Part I and will not dwell on it again. Such glossing attempts are on more persuasive grounds where they remark a contextually and contingently defined arena where essentialist assumptions are so deeply and prejudicially grounded that no articulation is possible without acknowledging its presence. This occurs, for instance, when Walter Benn Michaels argued that 'The modern concept of culture is not [...] a critique of racism; it is a form of racism'[28] with reference to, and in some sense speaking from within, the 'logic of cultural pluralism' in the United States. Soundly rationalized as this is, it leaves the tension of identity-based political positions and institutional practice simmering with unresolved – and perhaps unresolvable – limitations. But it is not just in the conceptual edge of academic endeavour that these tensions are enunciated. From the later 1980s and through the 1990s these tensions were perhaps most cogently and unresolvably (at times with defiant irresolution) expressed in the self-announcements that appear in those most indicative of institutional transmissions: literary critical and theory textbooks. The consistency with which this occurred is worth registering here. It clarifies the contradictions within the process through which the institutionalization of the logic of embodiment of identity-based political position and thereby of social constructionist identity politics in literary studies took place.

This tension is consistently revealed, for instance, in textbooks of feminist literary criticism and theory; unsurprisingly, since feminist theory has obviously been one of the most dynamic and interrogative of identity-based conceptual fields over an extended period of time. The self-announcements, usually prefatory, of these textbooks are remarkable in their uneasy collision of institutional affiliations and identity-based location, in the irresolution (at times irritability) of their need to make perceivably essentialist tendencies accessible within institutional folds, in their defiantly weak gesture. Such a self-announcement is available in (invaluable textbook of the time) Toril Moi's preface to *Sexual/Textual Politics* (1985), in the agonized self-removals from the locations and subjects she addresses:

> Constructive criticism should, however, indicate the position from which it is speaking; simply to say that one is speaking as a feminist is not a sufficient response to that responsibility. Like many other feminist academics, I speak as a woman with only a tenuous foothold in a male-dominated profession. I also speak as a Norwegian teaching French literature in England, as a stranger both to France and to the English-speaking world, and thus as a woman writing in a foreign language about matters to which in many ways she remains marginal.[29]

This quixotic series of self-definitions are effectively, it seems to me, a series of withdrawals from self-definition. That Moi finds that her feminism (as a woman) and her institutional standing (as a female academic) do not cohere neatly is in keeping with the kind of tension in question. That she goes on to associate this position with the complexities of her national and ethno-linguistic dislocations seems to turn both into a complex of marginalities within which Moi simply withholds herself, where Moi's self-announcement paradoxically disengages her. This is a complicated if interesting manoeuvre, but it is in line with the kind of fissures in institutional self-locations that interest me here.

More straightforwardly, there is the indecision about institutional practice in the self-announcement at the conclusion of another feminist textbook – this from Mills, Pearce, Spaull, and Millard's *Feminist Readings/Feminists Reading* (1989):

> [While] we believe the desirable goal of feminist criticism to be a vigorous and complex gender analysis that is not reducible to the biological sex of the author, we are also aware that the utopian conditions for post-feminist scholarship are very far away. While we may welcome the fact that individual males are now eager to address issues of gender, or that occasional courses may choose to include such topics in their syllabuses, we hold that such activity can only be regarded as *supplementary* to the spaces won (at such great expense) to provide courses for, and about, women.[30]

The two contradictory avowals (what 'we believe' conceptually and what 'we hold' for teaching) are, it appears to me, exactly at the tenuously bridged fissure between the embodiment of a feminist identity-based political position and the institutional practice of the literary studies it seeks to realign. Where Moi removes the need for such contradictory avowals by strategies of self-withdrawal into a complex and distinctive marginality, the authors here choose the double-avowal in this institutional transmission (a sort of internalized schizophrenia in the academia where this textbook circulates). Mary Eagleton's edited reader *Feminist Literary Criticism* (1991) – not quite a textbook, but to similar purpose – comes with a similar introductory (and institutionally aware) sentiment:

> Just at the moment when women are discovering a sense of identity, history and credibility of their experience, gynesis tells them that it is illusory, and that their extensive work on the woman author, the female tradition, images of women is at best an interesting cul-de-sac. For the feminist at the chalk face of Women's Studies, those who are planning courses, and hoping for tenure, the distinction between the anti-feminist, who never thought feminism was academically respectable anyway, and the post-structuralists, who see the project as misconceived, may appear minimal.[31]

The issue causing unease here is different (not men as feminists but post-structuralist interrogation of certain feminist presumptions), but the point of unease is pretty much where the previous quotation's was. It lies again at the tensely joined crack between institutional prerogatives and conceptual prerogatives which is occupied by 'the feminist at the chalk face of Feminist Studies' – those who define the academic space by doing things within it. A similar, somewhat irate, self-announcement is available in the preface of Maggie Humm's 1995 textbook *Practising Feminist Criticism*. This was actually a follow up of an earlier textbook, *Feminist Criticism* (1986), in introducing which Humm had asserted that feminist literary critics should be 'women choosing to read women as women' and their work could 'well be the *only* literary criticism needed by women students'[32] [Humm's emphasis]. The confidently prescriptive tone of that had changed to a rather more careworn and defiant one by 1995:

> I make no apology for my women-centred perspective. It appears that feminist thinking has fractured into a poststructuralist rejection of the essentialism involved in such a perspective; attacks on the ethnocentrism implied by its exclusions; psychoanalytic attacks on a unified subjectivity; and anxieties about the heterosexism of a singular perspective. Yet a desire to focus on women's books is felt very

strongly, not least by students entering women's studies, and I share those feelings.[33]

Evidently, as Mary Eagleton had noted, Humm too finds that the unrestrained academic flows of debate and exchange and the institutional practice of feminist literary studies are not quite fitting. This too translates to fissures and bridges along the lines of embodied identity-based political positions in academia and the (in principle) openness of academic fora.

Other similar self-announcements can be adduced, but I think the point is sufficiently conveyed already. The awareness of institutionalization and institutional practice that is found in these marginal self-announcements derives from the nature of the books that they appear in the margins of. As textbooks, readers could expect from these both a report on the state of the established discipline and utility value in perpetuating institutional practices. Inevitably these marginal statements are self-announcements with regard to those expectations; they are statements of the authorial self as endowed with the authority to perform the expected textbook functions. They tell of authors as observers and participants of institutional practices and of feminist identity-based political positions; they are autoethnographic expressions – momentary and marginal ones, but notable nevertheless. And they reveal a constant preoccupation with a fissure that arises within their responsibilities and observations, with that tension between embodying an identity-based political position with institutional effect and yet within an institutional space and practice which is always open, or at any rate always open to challenges and even invasions. At its most simplistic, the consideration of institutional practice leads feminism consistently and simultaneously towards both an identity-based essentialist tendency and the denial of that essentialist tendency. These coexist and mutually define and mutually refine and repulse each other in institutional practice till essentialism is dispersed across the field in a series of contradictory and yet coexistent exclusions and inclusions, demands for authenticity and openness, respectful distance and invitations to understanding. That this occurs for other kinds of embodied identity-based political positions too as they negotiate institutionalization can be similarly demonstrated. Out of this dispersal appears the kind of social constructionist identity politics which is institutionalized in literary studies now, containing and embracing different identity-based political positions. Or, in Gayatri Spivak's terms, institutionalizing 'marginality'(one of those useful 'in-between terms' characteristic of social constructionist identity politics, see Chapter 4) in literary studies – which leads me to the next self-announcement.

Spivak on marginality and teaching

Since much of Spivak's writings are rich explorations of the complexities of assuming various identity-based political positions, in particular geopolitical and institutional contexts, a comprehensive discussion of this matter can easily become an extended preoccupation. In (almost inevitably) referring to Spivak here I delimit the scope of that discussion and render it coherent with the above by focusing on specific self-announcement-like passages, explicit about institutional factors, that convey her approach fairly veraciously. In this instance, the passages are taken from the essay 'Marginality in the Teaching Machine', which appears as the third chapter of her rather brilliantly titled book, *Outside in the Teaching Machine* – published, not irrelevantly for the present chapter, in 1993. Unlike other passages quoted above, the self-announcing passages in this instance are not taken from the margins of her book, from prefaces and introductions and conclusions, but are central to this essay and indeed to the book as a whole. This is only to be expected. As I said, for Spivak generally the matter of institutionally aware self-announcements and identifications is her theme, and in this book the title indicates that institutional practices are the issue, and locations 'in' but 'outside' the emphasis. Even the habitualized nature of the institutional space is conveyed by the conceit of the machine (for this essay and the book as a whole). For Spivak I do not need to look at the margins of her book; she puts the margins squarely in the centre of her work.

More specifically though, it *is* the margins of this essay that interest me: the manner in which Spivak introduces 'Marginality in the Teaching Machine'. It begins with a contention *about* how a politically effective ('radical') identity (in the first instance racial ones, such as 'Asian' or 'African', and gendered, 'she') and institutional standing ('academic') slide into and away from each other in the contexts she addresses ('British' and 'American' in the late 1980s):

> The radical academic, *when she is in the academy*, might reckon that names like 'Asian' or 'African' (or indeed 'American' or 'British') have histories that are not anchored in identities but rather secure them. We cannot exchange as 'truth', in the currency of the university, what might be immediate needs for identitarian collectivities. This seems particularly necessary in literary criticism today, with its vigorous

investments in cultural critique. If academic and 'revolutionary' practices do not bring each other to productive crisis, the power of the
script has clearly passed elsewhere. There can be no universalist
claims in the human sciences. This is most strikingly obvious in the
case of establishing 'marginality' as a subject-position in literary and
cultural critique.[34] [Spivak's emphasis]

Several relevant steps, from this study's point of view, are quickly taken
in the thickly connotative phrasing of this passage. The density of quotation marks here establishes the provisional nature of claims. This is
immediately supported by a universalist-sounding statement that there
can be 'no universal claims in the human sciences', thus capturing the
political drift of Theory's travels vis-à-vis the British/American new left
in the 1980s. The kind of racial and gender identities that are cited are
embraced into the dynamic of social constructionist identity politics, the
'immediate needs for identitarian collectives', the 'establishing of "marginality"'. A gesture is made towards the provisionality of such singular-
izing of identity-positions themselves by noting that histories are not
'anchored in' but rather 'secure' identities – or, as it soon becomes evident, 'establishes' them. And yet the universalist ring of the denial of
universal claims is simultaneously referred to the matter of 'establishing
"marginality" as a subject-position'; unless establishing marginality's
subject-position is not a universally provisional matter it cannot show
the irrelevance of universal claims. It is a familiar set of contradictions
and rapprochements that are presented here; in fact, precisely the con-
tractions and rapprochements that have been discussed at length in Part
I, and that *is* social constructionist identity politics. What is interesting
about this passage, however, is that this is performed deliberately with
regard to the institutional practice of 'literary and cultural critique', the
'currency of the university', 'the academy'. What is also interesting is
that in talking *about* this institutional space, and *about* the marginal
identity-based subject positions that can be assumed therein, it is somehow taken for granted that *marginality is necessarily radical* (with an
emancipative ring to 'radical'), and academics who assume – can
embody – such positions are probably being 'revolutionary' (with an
emancipative temper, albeit with quotation-mark-provisionality).

Though these steps are presented as *about* institutional self-
announcements, these immediately merge into – and gain weight from –
Spivak's performance of institutional self-announcements on her own
behalf. This again is familiar territory for her, oft found in her writings.
By way of examining the implications of identity-based claims in

particular contexts, Spivak moves after the above passage to a series of self-announcements in particular contexts, or, more precisely, she mesh-es a series of self-identifications and located anecdotes that amount to self-announcements. She reflects on speaking in a conference in London in 1988 'As a politically correct Asian [...], a well-placed Asian academic'; she notes that 'In the United States, where the speaker lives and teaches, her cultural identity is not 'Asian' [...]. In the United States, she is 'Indian''; she allows that insofar as cultural identity pre-supposes a language, 'I suppose I feel Bengali.'[35] This is where the advantages of the logic of embodiment are both reflected on and used. These self-announcements are made by Spivak precisely for the pur-pose of examining the implications of such self-announcements, i.e., ones that assume identity-based political positions within institutional practice. Because she addresses this as her theme, lays it open to rational scrutiny, assumes a critical stance towards such self-announcements, she does not simply offer a specific identity-based political position, she moves to a more encompassing view of the matter. She rises to an espousal of social constructionist identity politics, of the critical insti-tutional value of marginality rather than of a potentially essentialist particular identity-based political position. To this extent, Spivak *reflects on* self-announcements, with her own as exemplary. At the same time though, the fact that these reflections on identity-based self-announcements are also her own self-announcements brings an addi-tional weight to her voicing of these arguments. Spivak is reminding her audience/readers here that she *is* an 'Asian' in Britain, an 'Indian' in the USA, a 'Bengali' to herself, 'a well-placed academic', and she goes on later to speak 'as a teacher', 'as a feminist', as 'postcolonial', as a 'radical academic'. In the body of the paper, and indeed in much of Spivak's writing generally, this embodiment of what Spivak *is* as the locus of an authority for pronouncing on the matter of being those things (broadly, minority academic) remains a persistent *lietmotiv*, and actually is the operative presumption of her argument. Because she is identifiable in a particular racial and cultural fashion, as a feminist, as minority, as academic, what she says is the 'real' thing: she has embod-ied her argument, in the terms of this study, or makes her argument as if voiced by her self rather than her rational capacity. If she says that being 'marginal' in institutional academic literary studies in Britain and the United States is a promisingly and inherently 'radical' position, more than her reasoning the claim comes with the weight of who she *is*. Similarly if she is critical of or expresses misgivings about the commodifications and appropriations of 'marginality' in academia, in institutional practice, in particular geopolitical areas, that too matters because she is who she, so emphatically, *is*. She embodies her argument, much as Castle and Felman and Woods did above.

But Spivak's mode of embodiment is not with regard to a specific identity-based political position but to a range of such positions – or to such positions generally – in the embrace of social constructionist identity politics. It is this extended scope within which her self-announcements, embodiments, are performed that allows her a more critical perception of what she embodies. Or, put otherwise, it allows her a clear and explicit sense of the social constructedness of such identity-based political positions – ergo of identity politics, of the politics of marginality, generally. Her conviction in the radical potential in espousing a marginal position in the academy is also recognized as a construction, and comes with the anxiety that such constructions can be (as constructions are apt to be) remoulded/bought out/simply occupied by those who do not embody as marginal academics can, or do not embody with good faith, or do not embody at all and serve (let us call it) 'majoritarian' interests. So, after the self-announcements, and still with the weight of embodying her arguments, the introduction to this essay comes with a peculiarly-Spivakian turning-upon-itself, an illuminating holding of marginality at arm's length:

> If there is a buzzword in cultural critique now, it is 'marginality.' Every academic knows that one cannot do without labels. To this particular label, however, Foucault's caution must be applied and we must attend to its *Herkunft* or descent. When a cultural identity is thrust upon one because the center wants an identifiable margin, claims of marginality assure validation from the center. It should then be pointed out that what is being negotiated here is not even a 'race or a social type' [...] but an economic principle of identification through separation.[36]

This is a critical comment on the construction of marginality which only a social constructionist position can enable; and yet, at the same time, also this is a critical comment that underlines and emphasizes the logic of embodiment on which so much of Spivak's voice hinges. What matters, it seems to be suggested, is who is doing the constructing. If it is someone, it follows from this argument, *within* the margins then that is all right, if it is someone at the centre then it is time to worry. If one can embody one's marginality one should talk about marginality, if someone who cannot do so talks about marginality be suspicious.

Behind that inference lie all the exclusions and compromises which make the logic of embodiment a deeply questionable one (the substance of Part I). In these self-announcements Spivak effectively weds the logic of embodiment to social constructionist identity politics (rather than just an identity-based political position) *within* the institutional practice of literary studies and cultural critique. Her self-aware avowals are central to this study.

The implications of Spivak's arguments as laid out above are rather neatly summarized by Huggan in observations on another essay by her[37] (which may as well have served the purposes of the present chapter as the one I have chosen):

> With characteristic brio, Spivak sees marginality as an advantageous subject-position, to be manipulated for maximum leverage within the postcolonial academic field. At the same time, she is anxious that the uncritical endorsement of marginality might play into the hands of a 'neo-colonial educational system' wishing to assimilate it for its own interests. [...] It is not that Spivak rejects marginality *per se* but that she rejects it as exotic – as a vehicle for patronising views of minority representation and recruitment in the academy and, above all, as a legitimising category for palatable versions of cultural other-ness in society at large.[38]

This is a fine summary of the matter, but it is oriented towards Huggan's preoccupation with the 'postcolonial academic field', and the distinction between 'postcoloniality' and 'postcolonialism' that he offers and the critique of 'exotic' that follows from that. Though the 'postcolonial academic field' itself is one that seems to extend optimistically in (postcolonize?) all directions (or is it colonize?) – and serves, I observed in Chapter 4, as an 'expansive term' in concert with social constructionist identity politics – it is nevertheless a limited field. It comes with a set of limited associations in the institutional practice of literary studies, a particular history of research and curriculum-setting, a particular set of appointments and authorities, a circumscribed frame of references. Spivak's social constructionist espousal of marginality in literary studies is part of the *modus operandi* of the term 'postcolonial's' expansion – but it is more than that. Even if the particularity and limits of the association of 'postcolonial' in institutional practice is recognized and accepted, the institutional practice can be discerned as happening outside that remit. The logic of embodiment in Spivak's institutional valorization of marginality is, even with such recognition and acceptance, effective for the general field of literary studies. Put otherwise, what can be inferred from the above passages is something of moment in the institutional practice of literary studies generally, the entrenchment of social constructionist identity politics therein, irrespective of whether one understands or fails to understand or refuses to understand the fluid connotations of 'postcolonial academic field'.

Further, between what Huggan phrases as Spivak's acknowledging the advantage of marginality as a subject position and Spivak's anxiety about its assimilation in a neo-colonial educational system there is a link. The anxiety and the advantage are thrown up by the strategy that gives weight to both: the logic of embodiment with which the marginal subject position is assumed and enunciated. Without being able to embody marginality Spivak's advantage and anxiety can have little leverage. That seems to me a serious problem, because it curtails free flow of debate and exchange and spreads limitations thinly across the institutional practice of literary studies, it withdraws the rational potential of communication and the in- principle-openness of the academy. It is the link, that is, Spivak herself, embodied in her argument, which calls for critical attention, perhaps before the two-fold observation on marginality (radical advantage/centrist categorization) can be considered.

Gubar's millennial assessment of feminism

The incorporation of the logic of embodiment for specific identity-based political positions within the broader reach of social constructionist identity politics, exemplified in Spivak's self-announcements here, leads both to a resolution of some contradictions arising from the institutionalization of identity-based political positions and to a spreading of those contradictions. The remaining two passages which I pick up here enable an examination and present instances of this.

The first comes from Susan Gubar's survey and critical analysis of feminism in literary and cultural studies at the beginning of the new millennium, *Critical Condition: Feminism at the Turn of the Century* (2000). Gubar's is, it is well-known, a name that is firmly associated with second wave feminist literary criticism, particularly through the impact of *The Madwoman in the Attic: The Woman Writer and the Nineteenth Century Literary Imagination* (1979),[39] which she co-authored with Sandra Gilbert. For Gubar writing *Critical Condition* is, as she notes in the introduction, a reckoning with the field of feminist literary criticism in the intervening twenty years. The introduction makes it clear that this reckoning is essentially a matter of moving from the feminist identity-based political position that she had influentially located herself within towards a wider field of social-constructionist identity positions. Or, to be more precise, this movement is necessitated by the nature of institutional realignments that had occurred in the interim. In the late 1970s the institutionalization of feminist identity-based politics within literary studies was still a goal, whereas with the approach of the 21st century Gubar feels that it has been achieved to a degree (she regards it as an 'indisputable fact that the situation of women in higher education has completely changed for the better'[40]), and that the institutional turn of the time is to accede to a larger achievement – the institutionalization of different marginalities, or in our terms the institutionalization of social constructionist identity politics. She considers this matter from *within*, so to say, feminism:

> [...] what made [the title] *Critical Condition* seem honest was its equivocation, which captures my sense of being poised between causes for regret and for celebration: now institutionalized in a variety of humanities departments, feminist studies have multiplied into various forms of enquiry in which every category linked to gender so as to make our investigations more sophisticated has itself undergone critical redefinition. Just as proponents of identity politics enlarged the meaning of the term 'women' by combining such categories as race and sex with gender analysis, poststructuralist thinkers used gender analysis to display the instabilities of such categories as race and sex. In other words, the terms that happen to interest me in the first four chapters – race, sex, religion, caste – started out as fixed phrases vis-à-vis gender, but considerations of gender quickly complicated their meanings.[41]

On the one hand, we have here a change in tone from that of, for instance, the self-announcements in later 1980s and early 1990s textbooks of feminist criticism quoted above (Mary Eagleton, Maggie Humm, etc.). Whereas the latter expressed anxiety about infringements upon and challenges to embodied feminist identity-based politics that came with its attempt at realigning institutional practices, these infringements and challenges are actively and self-consciously embraced by Gubar here. There is an attempt to reposition feminist identity-based political positions as impinging upon and being impinged upon by other identity-based political positions; and it is recognized that this repositioning is inevitable given the disposition of institutional practice.

It is the case that feminism is 'now institutionalized in a variety of humanities departments', bringing the mutual perceptions, and effects, of other identity-based political positions with feminism to the fore. It is the survey of this institutional practice, the enterprise of *Critical Condition*, which inevitably brings race and sex into consideration alongside and interpenetratively with feminism. The institutionalization of social constructionist identity politics is both apprehended, and seen to exert critical pressure on feminism – on Gubar's own project. On the other hand, this also comes with the anxiety that arises from the retention of the logic of embodiment vis-à-vis specific identity-based political positions within the embrace of social constructionist identity politics. It is clear in the above quotation that Gubar feels equipped to deal with those other margins of sexuality and race and religion and caste only insofar as they do interpenetrate with feminism, insofar as the 'meaning of the term "woman"' is affected by and affects those. So she accedes to the greater reach of the now institutionalized social constructionist identity politics, but with the doubts and confidence that her critical self-identification as a woman – and therefore an embodied feminist – allows. This anxiety is, in fact, highlighted *by* questioning and even apparently abandoning the logic of embodiment soon after:

> From what sort of background, with what sort of investment, with whose imprimatur do I approach such subjects as African-American and lesbian modes of expression? Implicitly this collection asserts for the critic what many creative artists have always claimed, namely that interest and imagination provide sufficient license for intellectual scrutiny – besides doing the requisite homework, of course – investigations ought not to be and really cannot be policed. That you don't have to be black to write about blacks or a lesbian to write about lesbians follows logically from these two essays, which demonstrate exactly how unstable, how slippery those terms ('black' 'lesbian') are, especially as identity categories. Shaped by my commitment to making scholarship activist in the dismantling of racist and homophobic mindsets, my stake in writing about African-American and lesbian art also derives from a passionate belief that the pedagogic function of feminist studies depends on abrogating scholarly ghettoization and that its future vitality hinges on our ability to bring gender into play with different sorts of differences.[42]

Recognizing the slipperiness and unstable quality of identifications like 'black', 'lesbian', and by the same rationale 'woman', is, as I have noted earlier, implicit in social constructionist identity politics. In considering the debate between essentialism and social constructionism in identity politics in Chapter 3, I had also observed that the logical corollary of social constructionism should be the dissolving of the logic of embodiment – which however does not quite happen (the opposite happens) in the current institutionalization and pervasiveness of social constructionist identity politics. Instead, the fluidity of identifications results in a dispersal of embodiments *as* embodiments across the field, as a spreading of limitations and exclusions on debate and exchange being given institutional form. That is precisely the problem the present study is addressed to. Gubar here actually draws the implications of social constructionist identity politics to the logical conclusion that dissolves the necessity to embody identity-based positions: 'you don't have to be black to write about blacks or a lesbian to write about lesbians' in considering and advocating against prejudicial 'mindsets'. For Gubar, indeed, it is the realignment of the institutional space itself, the enterprise of making 'scholarship' itself 'activist', that suggests the dissolving of the logic of embodiment. And yet, even through that admission, paradoxically the weight of the logic of embodiment is given its due, and is tacitly endorsed *for institutional purposes*. I do not say that in a spirit of disbelieving what Gubar obviously says, taking, like Freud, her no as yes. I say this because, it seems to me, a tacit endorsement of the logic of embodiment is just as obviously written into that quotation as her scepticism about it.

Asking the question, 'From what sort of background, with what sort of investment, with whose imprimatur do I approach such subjects as African-American and lesbian modes of expression?,' is itself a gesture that acknowledges the pressure that the logic of embodiment exerts within the wide field of social constructionist identity politics. The recognition that the constructedness of social identities alleviates her anxiety about this pressure is, nevertheless, tempered by a vivid sense of the limited reach of her 'interest and imagination' and 'requisite homework'. It is suggested that there is some sort of (unjust? implausible?) 'policing' – a peculiarly indicative term – at work. More importantly, though Gubar cites her commitments to social constructionist identity politics in the widest sense as one of the movers of her questioning of the logic of embodiment, it is not the prime mover. A 'passionate belief' that the 'pedagogic function of feminist studies' has to be retained – in other words, that the institutional practice of feminist studies has to be maintained as such – makes this compromise (that is what it is) necessary. There appear, therefore, two contradictory strains of explanation for Gubar's attitude to the logic of embodiment: it is necessarily abandoned in institutional practice following her social constructionist commitments; it is abandoned as a compromise to maintain a place for feminist identity-based politics within institutional practice. The reasoning underlying the former strain (recognizing the instability and slipperiness of identity), is – here and as the introduction develops further – superseded by Gubar's 'passionate belief' in the latter frame (emotion and unquestioning conviction, in the nature of 'belief', attach to feminist pedagogy). The latter strain supersedes the former, does not need to be reasoned, because none can question her claim to expressing such a 'passionate belief'. She does not need to ask that question of herself insofar as she is a feminist; that, at any rate, the autobiographical tenor of the introduction clarifies, she does embody. None can ask this question of her insofar as feminism goes. In brief, what she cannot embody she has to reason about, what she can she does not. When she cannot embody she becomes social constructionist at the expense of the logic of embodiment; when she can embody her identity-based politics she does so with supersedent and overarching effect with regard to institutionalized social constructionism. The schism is held together in the performance of this carefully plotted academic discourse.

What is perhaps most interesting about Gubar's self-announcements quoted above is that their strategies, their bridging and holding asunder of contradictions, occur with regard to her apprehension of the institutional field. It is the institutionalization of social constructionist identity politics extending over the institutionalization of feminist identity-based political position which, in a way, forces her hand. It makes her recognize the logic of embodiment that operates across several marginalities within the social constructionist identity politics of academia; it makes her protest against it by extending her critical gaze beyond embodied claims; it makes her accede to it by asserting her embodied claims on behalf of feminist institutional practice – all at the same time. In effect, Gubar reintroduces the schism between institutional practice and the logic of embodiment noted for Felman, Castle, Woods, and those textbook writers above, *while compromising with the institutional orientation towards social constructionist identity politics*. The institutional disposition of literary studies towards social constructionist identity politics contains this contradiction without erasing it. The unease of this sort of institutional pressure becomes increasingly evident in the autobiographical reckonings that follow after that passage in the introduction to *Critical Condition*. Ultimately, a somewhat careworn complaint at the schizoid position she has been put in, strongly reminiscent of the self-announcements of Humm and Eagleton above, comes through:

> [...] looking back on my own intellectual trajectory, I realize how much I wanted to disentangle my critique of the field from a purely defensive posture. Yes, it was painful to be divided, but I did not then and do not now want my personal discomfort to be used to discount what I believed and still believe to be a just representation of a generalized chagrin among many other feminists about an unproductive divisiveness in feminist scholarship.[43]

Ultimately, Gubar says, there is a gap between what she critically avows and what she feels. It may not be manifest in her critical analysis in *Critical Condition*, she suggests, but she does speak as a feminist for (many other) feminists. The thing is that this schism is manifest in her critical analysis throughout the book as a well-dispersed and constantly retained schism. It becomes evident through close readings of other passages from this book as it does through the last-but-one quotation above.

Eversley on authenticity

The final self-announcement that I take up here appears in the concluding paragraph of the 'Postscript' of Shelly Eversley's *The 'Real' Negro: The Question of Authenticity in Twentieth-Century African American Literature* (2004). In this the self-announcement is positioned clearly in view of the social constructionist nature of race, in a sequence of analogues and equivalences with other identifications of minority positions. Moreover, it asserts that where art is made conditional to such identification (is given 'authenticity' as such), where the embodiment of art as so identified is *a priori*, the logic of embodiment involved negates the apprehension of art as art.

> The imposition of black authenticity repudiates the possibility of any art made by an African American. Art requires invention, artifice, something not natural, but something made from the imagination. In this way, racial authenticity is an invention masquerading as the natural, ontological 'truth' about people of colour. As 'truth,' anything read as 'authentic' becomes not art, but reality – a reality that makes the creativity of African Americans, women, homosexuals, Latinos, Chicanas, Asians, Indians, etc. not art or intellect, but reportage. It

becomes evidence of being, something unlearned and always there. Even as authenticity promises consciously and unconsciously a kind of cultural capital to black writers, it also imprisons them in a logic that positions a myth of racial being as their contribution in art. It is a prison, however comfortable and seemingly natural.[44]

There is an interesting double take involved in this statement. First, the constructedness of identity is given clarity by seeing an analogue in it with the constructedness ('invention, artifice') that is self-evidently art. Second, the attempt to make art conditional to (emanant from) identity is seen as a misrepresentation of identity – by assuming that identity is essential (a mode of 'being', 'something unlearned and always there') – and indeed a negation of art – by making the artistic product appear to be a product of reportage (a representation of 'reality'). It is at the surface of the constructedness of both art and identity that the politics of embodiment is played out here; the strategy of embodiment underlies the claim of authenticity, and the politics of that is neatly unpicked here as an invidious one.

So far so good; the question that remains, however, is whether the negation of art (say literature here) through the logic of embodiment, could be indicative of the invidiousness of institutional literary studies. What occurs, to pose the question otherwise, between the critical apprehension that recognizes the constructedness of art in the academy and the critical apprehension that realizes the constructedness of identity out there, in the real world, so to say? How does this critical voice pitch itself, in its distinctively institutional mode, between art and world? What sort of space is it that structures such a statement? It is at the critical juncture of such questions that a remarkably self-aware self-announcement is presented: one that tries to negotiate the authorial subject between social constructionism, institutional literary studies, and the world. This self-announcement reverts to a consideration of the hoped-for 'worldliness' of literary studies, a reference to the direction through which (as argued in the previous chapter) social constructionist identity politics has come to be institutionalized in literary studies. This self-announcement, with willing deference to the complexity and necessary open-endedness of its task, comes through anecdote – a narrative that is itself open to interpretive possibilities:

> The idea of this book happened in a barbershop in Baltimore. A week before the Million Man March was to take place in Washington, DC, this student needed a haircut. Uneasy in her barber's chair, she listened

to the men, all black, in the shop discussing their plans to make a political statement and take a day off work and march on Washington. They were celebrating their possibility, their chance to make a statement as a group. This student, a self-proclaimed feminist, was uncomfortable and her barber knew it. He asked her why, and in her best graduate student-speak, she described the ways in which the March seemed to imagine a neo-conservative vision of black patriarchy as the solution of collective empowerment. For a few seconds, the men in the shop stopped, seemed to listen, and then continued with their conversation. Her barber, a great intellectual, teacher, and entrepreneur, whispered in her ear: 'try again, college girl.' She tried again. In the legacy of Zora Neale Hurston, she offered a picture of her thoughts. She wanted to show them an image of what she understood was a collective sexism and homophobia that mirrored the logic of white supremacy. The men heard her, and upon her departure, one man said to her, 'you are still 100% black,' and her barber told her, 'your credit's still good here.' On her way to the library, this student felt simultaneously triumphant and sad: the men in the shop had read the education in her language as proof of her 'imitation whiteness,' and when they saw her ability to shape her academic self-consciousness, they accepted her as part of the group, as authentic, and they accepted her membership as credit. The economy of race in language had not been so clear to her. She had profited from its benefits, and when she arrived on campus (a racial and cultural distinction from the barbershop), she felt its disadvantages.[45]

There are several noteworthy features to this anecdotal narrative as a mode of self-announcement. *One*, the primary identification here of the authorial subject is as an institutionally located one, as a 'student'. She presents herself as such, self-consciously possessed of 'graduate student-speak', and is recognized as such through 'the education in her language'. *Two*, she is able to demonstrate her conformity to the social constructionist bent of identity politics (rather like Spivak) by embracing two possible marginal identifications: as black and as a woman and 'self-proclaimed feminist'. Irrespective of whether she deliberately embodies her arguments as such, her arguments in the barber's shop are so embodied by her being able to play off one against the other in the complicity of her presence and voice. She is received there as black, her membership in the black identity-based political alignment is questioned (and later allowed) because she is black, and she is able to convey her qualms (decentre that identity-based political position by the juxtaposition of another) because she is also a woman. By the same dint, however deliberately degendered and deracialized the appellation 'student' might appear, and however carefully distanced the student-author's self-presentation from a logic of embodiment might be, just by giving the above anecdote, by 'postscriptedly' self-announcing herself thus, she has implanted the possibility of her argument in the book being accorded an embodied weight. There is no point in asking whether the 'postscript' self-announcement is necessary for reading the preceding script, any more than wondering whether any of the quotations in this chapter were necessary. The point is that they are there, in their (usually) marginal locations – increasingly a habitualized practice in such institutionally valid expression. Eversley naturally knows this; it is there in her equation between the 'barber's shop' and the 'campus'. *Three*, the barber shop (as real world) and the campus (as institutional academic space) have a resistant relationship. They are concretized at different linguistic registers, for one thing: one in 'graduate student-speak', and the other in, for instance, symbolic populist gestures like the Million Man March and (the one the student-author is able to bridge) a language of pictures and images. But also, the resistant relationship is in the mutual constructions that exist between 'barber's shop' and 'campus'. Those in the barber's shop see the student-author as embodying her institutional presence and associate it with the false-consciousness of 'imitation whiteness'. They turn their black identity-based political position, with reductive effect, upon the institutional embodiment which they perceive. In a similar fashion, the student-author constructs the 'barber's shop' as real world by performing this narrative – this anecdote – in this 'postscript' context of her book. And just as she (with failure implicit) breaks through momentarily on the black identity-based political position in the 'barber's shop', so, by this performance, she is able to confirm (successfully) her allegiance to the social constructionism that coheres with the institutional weight of this book. *Four*, along with the resistant relationship between the 'barber's shop' and the 'campus' there is also a certain continuity between the two. Both spaces presume the efficacy of the logic of embodiment, whether in assuming a specific identity-based political position or in containing several of these within the embrace of social constructionist identity politics. The 'economy of race in language' which Eversley mentions deals with the same currency of authenticity, albeit in distinct and even resistant ways. The fact that the student-author is able to translate her 'graduate student-speak' effectively into the 'barber shop' language of picture and images on the basis of who she *is*/who she is perceived to *be* argues the coherence of the 'barber's shop' and the 'campus' in this matter. Identity-based political positions, the logic of embodiment, an embracing social constructionist identity politics do not present lines of separateness between the real world and institutionalized literary studies – the political pretensions and 'worldliness' of Theory would be defeated if it were. Misguidedly, though, it appears that the common ground lies along the schismatic logic of embodiment in the real world as in the academy. The reader senses, for a transient moment, in the narrating of the above anecdote the growing loneliness of the student-author who is aware of the power of constructions of authenticities and the efficacy of embodiment on both sides. The story of the 'barber's shop' is one of a compromise, one in which the logic of embodiment is deployed and received effectively after an initial failure. The entwined story of her institutional career is also one of such a failure turned to success by the logic of embodiment. What begins in the above quotation as recognition of her 'disadvantages' in the campus is turned to a resounding success, that is, the writing of this book (institutionally validated product, sound academic credit). The final lines of the book present the compromise with the logic of embodiment that operates in 'graduate student-speak' in the cause of social constructionist identity politics that is this (more than student-like in its achievement) book:

> She wanted to explore the 'universal particularities' that Alain Locke had named but she had not yet read. She pursued her voice, and in the beginning, like Maud Martha, she kept it to herself. When she sensed Hortense Spillers's declarative rereading of 'double consciousness,' that 'it was not enough to be seen, one was called upon to decide what it meant,' she began to write.[46]

I will not dwell on the references in that quotation – the connotations of these are best gauged by reading Eversley's book. The point to note is the manner in which the student-author takes possession of '*her* voice', from within 'herself', as the impetus for this book. At this last moment the logic of embodiment is invested in the book, in its institutional location, in particular identity-based political positions (predominantly black, also feminist), in its social constructionist identity politics. This taking possession of 'her voice' is implicitly that of an academic voice, tempered and moderated by a set of scholarly allusions. The scholarly allusions (from Alain Locke and Hortense Spillers), which are more than references in determining the modulation and setting the arena of this student-author's voice as literary critic, draw upon noted literary scholars and intellectuals: one embodying a black identity-based political position, the other complicating that by embodying both black and feminist identity-based political positions.

An attempt to summarize the arguments offered through close readings of the passages selected above would be a self-defeating one. It is the detailed process of the readings, the discernment of the nuances of their phrasing, the exemplifying (if occasionally opportunistic) selection of and juxtaposition of and generalized inferences from these passages which make the arguments of this chapter. These cannot, it seems to me, be stated briefly without doing them damage. What all the quoted passages share can, however, be noted again. These are all self-announcements, usually at the margins of academic tracts, which revolve identity-based political positions and/or social constructionist identity politics in the same breath as they reckon with the institutional practice of literary studies. These are all, put otherwise, 'autoethnographic expressions' which display the logic of embodiment in the matter of being identified/identifying themselves with political effect, and concurrently being academics practising literary studies. The concentrated bringing together of identity-based and institutional preoccupations that the passages, and many other such passages from other recent academic tracts, present is an indication of the prevailing entrenchment of social constructionist identity politics in literary studies.

8
Theory Textbooks and Canons

Definitions and distinctions

I began the previous chapter with a rather glib distinction between two kinds of text-based material that could be used to both demonstrate and clarify the institutionalization of social constructionist identity politics in literary studies. One of these is self-announcements in literary critical texts, which present self-aware reflections on institutional practice. These appear, I had suggested, in the register appropriate to peers in conversation (or masters talking among themselves). The previous chapter was devoted to looking closely at some such self-announcements. The other kind of relevant material is literary theory textbooks, I had maintained, which are:

> couched in a register appropriate to exchanges between master and novice, where the master's voice represents the discipline itself for the novice, becomes the discipline's self. Such [texts] have, for this study, the great advantage of making explicit the shared disciplinary knowledge that is so obvious that it is seldom expressed among peers. Such statements have the added advantage of being designed to consolidate the institutional character of the discipline, to be pitched for institutional transmission.

This self-quotation has a purpose other than that of a reminder: to draw attention to the glibness of it, and complicate or refine matters before giving such texts necessary attention in this chapter. There are some grey areas in that assertion. It is unclear whether this statement, for instance, should be regarded as relevant to all textbooks irrespective of discipline and context, or whether this is a generalization about literary theory textbooks in particular. It is well worth asking whether textbooks should be presumed to 'make explicit the shared disciplinary knowledge that is obvious' or whether it is possible that textbooks in fact often *constitute* shared disciplinary knowledge or even *contribute* a kind of knowledge that is not conveyed/subscribed to in other kinds of disciplinary texts. Perhaps textbooks should not be thought of as consolidating the institutional character of the discipline, but as being central to the institutionalized practice of disciplines. These and such questions need some consideration before I proceed with the task of this chapter, i.e., examining particular theory textbooks with the institutionalization of social constructionist identity politics in literary studies in mind. This much follows from Chapter 6: literary theory textbooks provide the particular area of literary studies textbooks where the entrenchment of identity politics is most likely to be clearly discernible.

Any attempt to generalize about textbooks, across disciplines and contexts, is usually an indeterminate exercise: as Issitt puts it, 'In pursuit of a textbook definition of textbooks, [...] the questions and complexities are legion and the solutions decidedly unsatisfactory'.[1] Issitt's useful essay, 'Reflections on the Study of Textbooks' (2004), presents both a somewhat strenuous defence of the study of textbooks, a theme that is often regarded with condescension by researchers, and a survey of textbook history, i.e., the history *of* textbooks and not history textbooks. With regard to its former objective Issitt notes that textbooks are often presumed to have a clear definition but on closer inspection fail to present obvious definitional features of general application. This does not, naturally, deter Issitt from attempting some definitional observations for the 'fuzzy category' of textbooks in general:

> It is precisely because they slip over and escape standard disciplinary, genre and analytic categories that they are so rich. In their creation they take their impulses from a mix of sources including configuration of dominant ideas and social values, the commercial impulses of the publishing industry, particular academic disciplines and conventions of authorship, and from progressive technologies of media production. Once created, they assume a position within a spectrum of genres and they achieve a temporary status as a legitimate form of knowledge by virtue of a synthesis of these factors. The definitional issues are acute and revealing because textbooks themselves lay a definitional claim to the knowledge they contain – they claim that 'this is certain knowledge and this is the knowledge you need'. Embedded in textbooks therefore is a foundational epistemological

assumption – that they have a status, a bona fide status with a potential for universal application.[2]

This is backed up by some further observations later in the essay: 'In general, the particular voice of the textbook author is subsumed within a monotone of expository clarity';[3] 'Textbooks as a teaching vehicle are legitimized in the business of education by the assumption of political neutrality';[4] and yet textbooks are *used* 'where the agencies of teacher and learner act',[5] which is seldom politically neutral. What strikes me about these rather agonized definitional observations is that something 'slips over and escapes' these while being effectively conveyed by these. The urge to define may be thwarted if it is confined to 'standard disciplinary, genre and analytic categories', or if it is restrained by simply *looking at* textbooks, but gradually gains in clarity if attention is directed to how they are *framed*. Textbooks are brought into general definition to some extent not simply in terms of what they contain, but in terms of what are expected of them, what purposes they serve, what sort of ends-orientation they have – how they are framed in the processes of production, transmission, and reception. And they are, following Issett, always pre-framed. He marks the pre-framings out: social values, commercial impulses, disciplinary norms, pedagogic purposes, etc., converge, according to Issitt, on a purposive assumption that always precedes and frames the actual reading of textbooks: 'this is certain knowledge and this is the knowledge you need'. This assumption stands at the heart of Issitt's definition, fuzzy as that is, and expands into the further clarifications. But that core itself – and this is what slips through and is yet clear enough in the above quotations – has a framed quality. The certainty and usefulness of the textbook discourse, extended through 'expository clarity' and apparent 'political neutrality', is a matter of status, 'bona fide status', repeatedly of 'legitimacy', of immediate 'use' (not opaquely drawing critical attention to itself, but transparently channelling legitimate knowledge). And what – to pose the obvious rhetorical question – is thus legitimized or given status? It is not knowledge in itself; every kind of knowledge has its own modes of self-legitimation, through authority or reason. It seems reasonable to say that Issitt is here tacitly pointing towards the *institutional character* of knowledge production and consumption: textbooks, he does not quite say explicitly but conveys nevertheless, are at the cusp of the institutional practice of knowledge production and consumption, incorporating a complex network of institutional agencies and prerogatives. Textbooks in general dispose knowledge for 'a reciprocal typification of habitualized actions by types of actors' across a range of institutional spaces (publishing houses, universities, education ministries, and so on).

Perhaps that is a reductive reading of Issitt, but it draws attention to at least an emphasis in what he says, and both clarifies the general aspect of what I meant in that self-quotation and explains my recourse to literary theory textbooks here. That literary studies, and particularly literary theory, textbooks have a distinctive character as textbooks, i.e., distinct from/within textbooks in general, is occasionally remarked. In literary studies usually three major forms of textbooks are recognized: the anthology (a selection of texts), the introductory literary history (usually a chronological introduction to national or 'world' literature, or literature in terms of genre, period, theme, approach, or some combination thereof), and the simplified and explanative narrative (covering all those terms I mentioned for introductory literary history, and often incorporating literary history, but more centred on conceptual explanation than chronological/contextual placement). However, it is not so much the formal construction that guides observations of the distinctiveness of literary studies, and particularly literary theory, textbooks as their disciplinary peculiarities – though these observations often appear with regard to one or the other of these forms. In a sceptical paper on literary theory guidebooks, 'Having Your Assumptions Questioned' (1993), Parrinder drew attention to the distinctiveness of their ideological assertiveness and self-contradictions (of which more later) as compared to ostensibly ideologically neutral and coherently paradigm-centred scientific textbooks described in Thomas Kuhn's *The Structure of Scientific Revolutions* (1962/1970).[6] Parrinder's comments on this express unease with the direction of literary theory textbooks in contrast to the scientific, but in the same breath acknowledge the distinction between sciences and humanities for grasping the distinctiveness of those literary theory textbooks: 'Writing about the natural sciences rather than the humanities, Kuhn evidently fails to conceive of textbooks which openly present their discipline as one riven by conflicts, and which themselves seem designed to function as weapons in the "theory wars"'.[7] The context in which this was written in the early 1990s, when the worldly desires of Theory were being challenged and asserted most vehemently (see Chapter 6), explains the tone of this essay for the moment – I return to some of Parrinder's arguments shortly. More to the point here, marking the distinctiveness of literary studies, especially theory, textbooks against scientific textbooks (with reference to Kuhn) is a recurring theme in the field. An extended treatment of the matter appears in David Downing's consideration of literary theory anthologies, 'The "Mop-up"

Work of Theory Anthologies' (2000). Arguing, not unlike Parrinder but with rather more conviction in Theory, that literary theory anthologies have served to tame or play down the subversive and radical potential of Theory he finds that this misdirection has been inspired by misreadings of Kuhn and misapplication of his natural science-based model. Kuhn is, he observes, often read as a theorist of the history of science who challenges a-historical and decontextualized notions of science and therefore serves as a model for the humanities. However, Kuhn was at bottom conservative in his adherence to the idea of a normalizing paradigm, in a way that simply does not hold in the humanities ... in literary studies ... especially for literary theory.

> According to Kuhn, textbooks in the sciences represent 'normal practice': they 'mop up' the predictable results of paradigmatic problem solving once a new paradigm has been established and exemplified. Theory anthologists no doubt experience some of this satisfaction. Their 'mop up' work consists of selecting representative essays that have been written by a wide range of writers in different social, historical, and intellectual contexts, for different audiences, and for different purposes, and somehow re-present them as exemplary models of relatively stable schools and methods.[8]

The splitting in 're-present' indicates doubt, and comes with a touch of 'misrepresenting', and has the effect of 'disciplining theory' (as the title puts it). But that aside, it also marks the distinctiveness of the literary studies – literary theory – textbooks against science textbooks, or rather (following a well-known disciplinary tradition) marks the undesirability of transporting Kuhnian perceptions of textbooks from their place in natural sciences to literary studies. Marking the distinctiveness of the literary studies, literary theory, textbook against (Kuhnian) formulations for the scientific textbook falls in, as I have parenthetically observed, with the traditional disciplinary pressure and resistance that literary studies acknowledges within itself in relation to science. This tradition is traced illuminatingly in Stein Haugom Olsen's 'Progress in Literary Studies' (2005),[9] which charts the self-questionings and modifications which the discipline has gone through by both matching itself to and distinguishing itself from the standard-setting models of knowledge derived from the natural sciences since the 19th century. Relevantly for this chapter, Olsen traces this with reference to well-known English Literature histories – often introductory literary histories which have been or are used as textbooks.

But there is, so to say, a third degree of distinctiveness to be discerned, and one that takes me squarely to the subject of this chapter: the distinctiveness of literary theory textbooks within/from literary studies textbooks in general.

This level is largely written into the trepidation expressed by Parrinder and Downing in the above quotations. The space of literary theory is, as previous chapters have maintained, both a relatively recent one and a peculiarly self-aware one within the institutional area of literary studies. The against-New Criticism turn of literary theory in the 1960s and 1970s, the two-fold construction of Theory in the late 1970s/early 1980s, the travel of Theory towards 'against Theory' (the so-called 'Theory wars') and 'after Theory' in the course of the 1980s and 1990s, are all marked by self-reflection about the institutional transmission, institutional implications, institutional programme, institutional space of literary theory vis-à-vis literary studies. It is, even in its gradual expansion and consolidation, a continually contested and interrogated area. Poised as they are in the cusp of institution-ness, held at the juncture of articulating the discipline and concretizing disciplinary practice, literary theory textbooks have been and continue to be crucially under the gaze of Theory itself, *within* literary theory as well as *addressing* literary theory. Literary theory textbooks have therefore been subject to the attention of literary theory, and have been a space for ideological advocacies in tune with the travels of Theory. But that has also gone against the grain of their textbook character. This proneness to explicit ideological advocacy and worldly commitments are contrary, for instance, to the features that Issitt above identifies as belonging to textbooks in general. Or, to flip that observation around, when a general textbook-like character has been adhered to in literary theory textbooks they have opened themselves to the charge of betraying literary theory itself. This almost inevitable fissure in literary theory textbooks is precisely the brunt of both Parrinder's and Downing's critique, though they stand on opposed ends in the 'Theory wars'. For Downing a 'taming of theory' takes place in literary theory anthologies which goes against the worldly bent of Theory. For Parrinder the questioning of assumptions championed in literary theory textbooks apply to them too, and usually to their own detriment. They question literary canonicity, for instance, while erecting canons of Theory along like lines. They assert the indeterminacy and multiple possibilities of literary texts, for another instance, in a distinctly determinate manner and monological tone. Parrinder (unlike Downing) makes his discernment of the fissure in literary theory textbooks the occasion for extending his scepticism about the entire post-1970s enterprise and institutional extension of literary theory itself. The

contradictions of textbooks lies at the heart of his 'against Theory' position: his title essay in *The Failure of Theory* (1987) was exemplified by two
case studies,[10] both of popular literary theory textbooks with confidently stated ideological positions (Catherine Belsey's *Critical Practice*, 1980,
and Terry Eagleton's *The Function of Criticism*, 1984); the essay 'Having
Your Assumptions Questioned' (1993), which I have quoted above,
self-evidently extended to other textbooks in a similar spirit. Downings's
is more a performance of literary theorizing at the expense of literary theory anthologies. Both demonstrate effectively the point relevant here:
that *the fissure in question is itself a distinctive feature of literary theory textbooks, and marks it out from/within literary studies textbooks.*

   Thus literary theory textbooks construct the institutional field of literary theory (just as de Man and Said constructed Theory) and yet do so
at odds with the practice that literary theory struggles for and espouses.
These textbooks are therefore sites on which Theory institutionalizes
itself and with regard to which Theory expresses its frequently anti-
institutional worldly desires. This is expressed in specific ways when
literary theory textbooks come within the gaze of literary theory itself –
specific ways which critically put into relief distinctive, even institutionally standardized, characteristics of literary theory textbooks. In a
discussion between Gerald Graff and Jeffrey R. Di Leo (2000) on the
effect of literary theory anthologies in teaching literary studies, Di Leo
homes in neatly on one of these ways:

> [...] what I call the 'cookie cutter approach' to theory [...] works some-
> thing like this: apply literary theory 'A' to literary text 'B'. Result: a valid
> interpretation of literary text 'B' (and a successful use of literary theory
> 'A'). On this strategy, students think that criticism and theory are some
> kind of game wherein points are scored for the production of valid
> interpretations. Textbooks like many of the volumes in the Bedford
> series in Case Studies in Contemporary Criticism that have primary
> texts along with selections like 'What is Deconstruction?' and 'What is
> Feminism?' promote this type of trivial use of theory, albeit I think
> unwittingly.[11]

Graff agrees with this observation in his response, and then goes off at
a tangent by taking this as proof of a continuing penchant for New
Critical close reading. That Di Leo's thoughts about the 'cookie cutter
approach' as a characteristic of many literary theory textbooks do not
necessarily mean that he and Graff can find an alternative model for
literary theory textbooks – they can enunciate what they want, but not

what that would concretely contain – also becomes clear as the exchange progresses. In fact the 'cookie cutter approach' of literary theory textbooks is arguably a distinctive and characterizing feature of almost all such textbooks now, the form of the institutional space of literary theory. The thrust of Di Leo and Graff's doubts about this approach is best conveyed by recalling Jonathan Culler on the prospects of literary theory a couple of decades earlier, in *The Pursuit of Signs* (1981), when Theory's institutional programme was still under formation and open to debate:

> Perhaps the favourite way of relating literary theory to the discipline is to offer some kind of seminar on 'methods' of literary criticism, in which beginning graduate students read a certain amount of theory. I do not want to suggest that such courses may not be extremely valuable to those who take them, and no doubt in departments where they provide the only context for literary theory they are invaluable. But I do think that courses in which students read theorists as a series of 'approaches' to literary works are predicated on two interconnected but fallacious assumptions: that the function of literary theory is to make possible better interpretations of literary works; and that one cannot become a skilled interpreter without being exposed to the principal writings of literary theory.[12]

The 'cookie cutter approach' in literary theory textbooks actually developed gradually, and in that development can be traced the patterns of institutionalization of literary theory in literary studies. And this development is, as will become evident below, of particular interest to this study, for tracing the institutional entrenchment of social constructionist identity politics in literary studies.

The institutional function of literary theory textbooks

The development of the 'cookie cutter approach' can be traced fairly clearly in narrative literary theory textbooks which trace the travels of Theory since the 1970s. The earlier instances of these, such as Catherine Belsey's *Critical Practice* (1980) and Terry Eagleton's *Literary Theory: An Introduction* (1983), were more or less linear narratives which summarized and synthesized a range of approaches. I do not simply mean that they presented different 'schools' of literary theory in a chronologically linear fashion (that occurred insofar as possible), but that they developed a continuous linearly progressive argument in their books, in the course of which a number of theoretical approaches were discussed. Catherine Belsey clarified as an overarching theme in her book the recent emergence of a 'new critical practice',[13] deriving from scepticism about New Critical and formalist approaches, and drawing upon the ambiguities of language and the drives of ideology. Terry Eagleton delineated different approaches of literary theory as conditional to their historical and political contexts, and framed these within an overarching argument: 'I have tried to popularize, rather than vulgarize, the subject. Since there is in my opinion no "neutral", value-free way of presenting it, I have argued throughout a particular *case*, which I hope adds to the book's interest'.[14] The case made had to do with an understanding of what literary value and institutional literary history (the two opening chapters) consist in and what sort of political agendas for literary theory can be inferred from this survey (the concluding chapter).[15] For both Belsey and Eagleton each theoretical approach was exemplified by providing summaries of key theoretical texts, and sometimes textual corpuses of theorists, and their implications for literary interpretation was clarified by citing specific literary works. But these summaries and applications were conditional, indeed ancillary, to the overarching design of the book: broadly, the advocacy of literary theory as a coherent enterprise, following a direction (the connecting argument of their narratives), which conveyed a sense of literary theory's ongoing travel, and some underlying interest in the rejuvenated prospects for institutional literary studies. Necessarily, such an arrangement of the narrative meant that the different approaches were constantly understood with regard to each other, as deriving from and questioning and needing to be weighed in terms of each other: literary theory was presented as a dynamic and fluid space, with a direction, where the convenience of identifying approaches was only for the larger endeavour of seeing how they intermeshed and resolved each other.

From about the mid-1980s and into the 1990s, in narrative critical theory textbooks which appeared in quick succession – indicative of the need to address rapid institutional acceptance of Theory – the 'cookie cutter approach' became the structuring device. Raman Selden's *A Reader's Guide to Contemporary Literary Theory* (1985) exemplifies this direction in narrative literary theory textbooks. It presented a sequence of schools or categories of literary theoretical approaches which seem to be more or less discrete conceptual wholes, accessible with reference to select representative texts and writers of each persuasion. Selden did – and others who follow his structure do – mark out the overlaps and cross-allusions that operate across all the categories, the field at large; but the disposition of literary theory into a sequence of conceptual wholes and *without* an overarching argument presented the field as a divided house, with every room containing its own realized and potential extensions. Russian Formalism, Marxist theories, Structuralist theories, Post-structuralist theories, Reader-oriented theories, Feminist criticism occupied here their own chapters and reading lists, and shouldered each other with grudging acknowledgements of their debates and differences and mutually regarding progressions. The introduction offered an argument for taking literary theory seriously within the practice of literary studies, as opposed to not taking it seriously or disregarding it, and let the matter rest there. Little effort was made to discern a direction – conceptually or institutionally – for literary theory, or for the progressive interactions, overlaps, and resolutions between the various approaches. Placing the different approaches of literary theory within the pragmatics of reading literature and pursuing literary studies amounted, for Selden, to understanding that:

> One can think of the various literary theories as raising different questions about literature. Theories may ask questions from the point of view of the writer, of the work, of the reader, or of what we usually call 'reality'. [...] At their best none of the approaches totally ignores the other dimensions of literary communication.[16]

The dynamic of the field of literary theory was reduced to the discreteness of separate approaches, only grudgingly aware of each other, with their largely separate emphases.

With the dilution of the argument that placed different approaches vis-à-vis and interactively with each other, and with the emphasis on different approaches as more or less conceptually discrete, the legitimizing impulse behind literary theory textbooks changed – naturally reflecting changing demands in institutional practice. If Belsey's and Eagleton's textbooks were meant as interventions within the travels of Theory – constructing and discerning a teleology in literary theory while advocating for a more considered place for literary theory in the curriculum – Selden's kind of move marked a desire to cater to an established institutional practice of literary studies. It reached out more clearly towards Issit's sense of what a textbook in general should be: consolidating institutional practice, maintaining social values, and appearing to be politically neutral.

But that move also opened up a need: if literary theory is to be, even tendentiously, for institutional consumption then its institutional *raison d'être* needs to be given and immediately apparent. This need is not answerable within the debate about Theory, the ongoing argument that challenges institutional assumptions, that *is* the travel of Theory; the need could be answered only if Theory could be perceived as a *contribution* to the existing institutional practice of literary studies. Selden's guide did the 'cookie cutting' of specific theoretical texts and theorists; thereafter the undertaking was to make literary theory, in the happily disposed and discrete categories, applicable to the fundamental function of literary studies – reading literary texts. As observed above, it was this compromise with the pre-existing habits of institutional literary studies that worried Graff and Di Leo in their exchange, and troubled Downing in his observations about literary theory anthologies 'taming' Theory. But the application of different approaches of literary theory to specific literary texts, so that Theory is legitimized by fitting the institutional ends of literary studies, was an organizing principle of most 1990s narrative literary theory textbooks. Subsequent editions of Selden's guide upped the emphasis on such application to literary texts. The natural outcome of this tacit programme for legitimizing literary theory for institutional purposes was to harden the discreteness of each conceptual approach ('school') as separately valid for reading literary texts. The idea seemed to be that if each could be shown to be useful for reading literary texts, then each would justify the attention sought for it, and therefore the space of literary theory as a whole would be justified. By a fallacious leap, this led to the *reductio ad absurdum* that the maximum validity of each approach could be demonstrated if each could be shown as producing valid interpretations for *one* literary text (or, at least, a small number of works of fiction or poetry). Thus Steven Lynn's *Texts and Contexts: Writing About Literature with Critical Theory* (1994) started off, in the first chapter, by demonstrating how each of the theories he was going to expand on thereafter could be applied to one text, Brendan Gill's *Here at the New Yorker*.[17] Lynn's view, in taking this approach, was that: 'Critical theories are like the different travel agencies through which the various tour guides generally work.'[18] With the demands of given institutional practice vividly in mind, Michael Ryan's *Literary Theory: A Practical Introduction* (1999) was the first to announce its organizing principle as precisely that of the presumption stated above:

> I felt that students would be aided by seeing theory at work in the practical reading of texts. And I felt the important differences between theories – the way each illuminated a different aspect of a work of literature – would be clearer if they were comparatively

applied to the same literary work. But it turned out to be difficult to find readings of varying critical perspectives of the same work. Each school seemed to favor certain kinds of texts, with, for example, the deconstructionists favoring symbolic poetry and the Marxists realist novels. I decided at that point – around the mid-1980s – to write my own readings of the same text, each of which would assume a different critical stance or theoretical perspective.[19]

This mid-1980s decision had several noteworthy assumptions: that each approach is equally useful for reading the same text; that each approach is therefore a separate conceptual construction, separate from other approaches, which emphasizes different aspects of the same text; that each approach exists in a kind of ahistorical literary continuum which makes each extendable to any text (it does not matter that each seems to favour certain texts and not others); that each approach has a separate validity which is comparable to the kinds of validity that other approaches present, each parallel to the others; that the only reason these approaches should be engaged with in literary studies is to facilitate the reading and interpretation of texts. That seems to cover the questionable assumptions of the 'cookie cutter approach' to literary theory pretty comprehensively.

An additional twist in the development of the 'cookie cutter approach' in literary theory textbooks involves ridding the dynamism and differences *within* each approach when taken as separate and parallel conceptual spaces. This evolved gradually through most of the above-mentioned (and other such) textbooks, Selden onwards. The idea here is that each approach can be reduced to a set of summary and characteristic practices, cutting across their differentiated expressions in specific theoretical texts. The possibility of generalizing an approach or school thus facilitates both its functional status with regard to the primary matter of reading literary texts, and hardens to the point of passivity its discreteness. A ruthless application of this is found in Peter Barry's *Beginning Theory: An Introduction to Literary and Cultural Theory* (1995)[20] – a book that in general manages to reduce the alive mass, that is, literary theory into a collection of well-ordered dead bodies. Perhaps most effective to that end are the sections found in this, subtitled 'Some recurring ideas in critical theory', 'What structuralist critics do', 'What post-structuralist critics do', 'What Marxist critics do', etc.

With these preliminary observations on the place of literary theory textbooks in the institutional practice of literary studies, I can proceed to the main point of this chapter: tracing the institutionalization of social constructionist identity politics in literary studies through the medium of literary theory textbooks.

Subsequent editions of literary theory textbooks

In view of the complexity and variety of literary theory textbooks, the frame of reference in this section should be carefully circumscribed. The kind of literary theory textbooks that I refer to here are explanative and simplified narratives, not anthologies or general literary histories. This means that, unlike anthologies, these are presented in a mono-vocal manner, as issuing in a self-consciously regulated voice throughout serving the coherent purpose of constituting a textbook. The institutional self-location and design of this voice, inevitably assumed in any textbook, is maintained consistently, i.e., with fixed presumptions. In most instances (barring moments in Belsey and Eagleton) these are voices that personify the discipline for the student, come with the address of initiate to novice, and often affect ideological and critical neutrality. Further, the textbooks I pick up here are specifically those that have gone into several editions (more than one) in the course of the 1980s and 1990s. This offers the possibility of tracing the manner in which developments in the field of literary theory were registered over this period from more or less coherent perspectives. It may be assumed that if similar developments were registered in more than one such textbook as it went through several editions then that sort of development could be regarded as becoming institutionally legitimized. Some of the textbooks I have touched upon already in noting the evolution of the 'cookie cutter approach' figure prominently here.

Let me begin with Belsey's and Eagleton's textbooks again. Interestingly, though the usefulness of these as textbooks was recognized as soon as they appeared, and though they have remained consistently popular since they appeared, these have been republished in the least number of new editions – one of each. They have been reprinted as first published with a frequency that marks their popularity. But Belsey's *Critical Practice*, originally published in 1980, was only republished in a revised and updated new second edition in 2002; and Eagleton's *Literary Theory*, first published in 1983, appeared in a similar new edition only in 1996. Perhaps this was because of their distinctiveness as textbooks, or their departures from the mould of textbooks in general: both were more programmatic, more devoted to setting out the agenda of a 'new critical practice' or to arguing 'a case', than expected of textbooks. It may be surmised that these therefore offered contradictory possibilities for the pedagogic practices to which they were available. On the one hand, a 'cookie cutter approach' could be imposed on them: students and teachers could use them selectively, singling out summative and explanative passages on 'different theories' as required, as a reference book or a sort of transparent window to all those theories shouldering each other out there. On the other hand, as whole texts they could opaquely draw attention to their own specific and consistently maintained arguments, and overtly conduct their own ideological advocacies as interventions within the travel of Theory. As such they did not conform to the 'cookie cutter approach' as textbooks; they become texts that could (and did) figure as exemplars of one or the other such theories as are comprehended in a 'cookie cutter approach'. The two-fold value of these books for pedagogic practice probably meant that their integrity as texts was treated with greater caution than textbooks generally receive. It is not uninteresting that when they were republished in new editions, they both came with marginal comments reiterating defiantly their original arguments. Belsey thus reiterated in the 'Preface' to the second edition of *Critical Practice* the objective of the first edition: that she was concerned not with the politics of reading but with 'the reading process itself'.[21] Eagleton's 'Afterword' in the second edition of *Literary Theory* presented not so much an updating as a critical dismissal of some of the literary theory 'schools' that had appeared in intervening years.[22]

Of particular interest here, and still on a speculative note, are the pressures under which second editions of these well-known textbooks were published, after protracted periods of continuous availability and familiarity in their first editions. There was no particular need for these to be revised to extend their reach in the market. If that was the intention, these second editions must have been commissioned with some expectation that they would be revised and updated as other, by now familiar and much revised and republished, literary theory textbooks with 'cookie cutter approaches' had been in the interim. If such an expectation was there among the publishers, it would probably have derived from their misreading or partial understanding of Belsey's and Eagleton's books. In both cases, the second editions were characterized by the authors' refusal to make significant revisions, and by their recognition of the expectations of revising and updating and explicitly uncompromising response to that. Both made only cursory revisions (the occasional phrase, a bit of reorganization), and more importantly where they actually put in new text it was mainly to address those expectations sceptically (if not with downright disgruntlement).

Since these second editions appeared after considerable gaps of time (22 years for Belsey, 13 years for Eagleton) both the cursory revisions and the additions provided scope for the authors to take stock of developments in the field in the interim and do that *within* the consistently and explicitly developed programmatic arguments in their first editions. Belsey and Eagleton approached this task without compromising with expectations in a 'cookie cutter approach' mould. As it turned out, these responses were primarily recognitions of and sceptical critiques of the place social constructionist identity politics had recently acquired in literary theory and literary studies generally. That maintaining their original programmatic positions, and not subscribing (compromising with) a 'cookie cutter approach', also means taking account of the place of social constructionist identity politics in literary studies suggests a link between the two. A closer look at what precisely Belsey and Eagleton did with their second editions in relation to the first may clarify that link, and bring us to the main point of this chapter.

Belsey's 'Preface' to the second edition of *Critical Practice* brought together succinctly both her view of interim developments in literary theory and her response to any anticipated 'cookie cutter approach':

One of the changes since I wrote the book has been an expansion of critical positions: feminism was well-established at that time, but not queer studies or postcolonialism. As far as I am concerned, the new developments are extremely welcome: the more radical readings there are, the better. But committed as I am to the success of queer and postcolonial politics, I have not isolated them in the second edition as distinct practices, any more than I isolated feminism in the first, though it was repeatedly present in the examples I gave. With the best of intentions, the understanding of critical theory as a succession of 'isms', the text now read from one political position, now from another, has done, in my view, more harm than good, giving the impression that reading is a matter of personal values.[23]

The main inference that could be made from this is that Belsey seems to divide critical theory into two provinces. The first was the substance of her first edition, and comprehends the formal and normative assumptions that have guided literary production and reception until and including the New Critics, the reading process itself, the nature of literary texts in general, slippages/ambivalences in language, and implicit ideological nuances. It is within this province that she had elaborated the 'new critical practice' in the first edition – and it seems understood here that few developments in *this* province had occurred in the interim to the second edition. The validity of her argument in the first edition within this province, therefore, stands largely unchanged. The second province has to do with political interventions of a particular sort, associated for Belsey with feminism, queer theory, and postcolonialism. It is mainly in this province that developments have taken place in the interim, primarily in a proliferation of political positions. To explain her reluctance to take these into account in the second editions, Belsey here effectively offers three interlinked arguments. (a) These are all in the province of identity politics, and while they multiply possibilities for radical reading, they do not add much to the general practice of radical reading that was outlined in the first edition. The proliferation of radical readings is a kind of confirmation of the argument of the first edition, not alternative to it or a development upon it. (b) Belsey seems to apprehend the social constructionist nature of identity politics as a holding apart of different specific identity-based political positions while bringing them together through analogues and equivalences. Her sympathy for social constructionist identity politics is emphasized here, and she suggests that in any case this sympathy was evident in the first edition too – implicitly expressed with regard to her feminist commitments. At the same time she is clearly sceptical of the divisive yet encompassing direction of an expanded social constructionist identity politics in literary studies. This lends itself to a 'cookie cutter approach' which undermines the integrity of the text, the general reach of her argument, which she regards as doing 'more harm than good'. In effect, she here notes a structural sympathy between the 'cookie cutter approach' and the divisive yet encompassing disposition of social constructionist identity politics which is germane to this chapter. (c) Belsey's explanation of her reservations about the proliferations of identity politics in literary studies (and therefore of the possible 'cookie cutter approach' that goes with it in literary theory textbooks) has particularly to do with 'the impression that reading is to do with personal values'. In objecting to the intervention of personal values, of a politics of individual constructions and identity-based position-taking, it seems to me that Belsey is objecting to what I have called the 'logic of embodiment' in this study.

However, while rejecting the extension of her textbook in line with the expected 'cookie cutter approach', Belsey did express her commitment to social constructionist identity politics. Though she did not adduce separate sections on interim proliferation of identity-based political positions in literary theory, she did occasionally attempt to rephrase passages in the second edition to register those developments. The rephrasing was meant to give an implicit thumbs-up to these developments, just as feminism was given salutary but implicit notice in the first edition. These rephrasings were revealing in this context, and worth noting. Compare, for instance the following passages: the first is from the 1980 edition, the second from the 2002 edition. Both follow reflections on the difficulties of finding singular and coherent subject-positions for women.

> Women are not an isolated case. The class structure also produces contradictory subject-positions which precipitate changes in social relations not only between whole classes but between concrete individuals within those classes. Even at a conscious level, although this fact may itself be unconscious, the individual subject is not a unity, and in this lies the possibility of deliberate change.
>
> [1980 edition][24]

> Women are not an isolated case. The survival of racism in a multi-cultural society also produces contradictory subject-positions, which precipitate changes in social relations not only between whole ethnic and cultural groups, but between concrete individuals within those groups. Even at a conscious level, although this fact may itself be unconscious, the individual subject is not a unity, and in this lies the possibility of deliberate change.
>
> [2002 edition][25]

The simple replacement of 'class structure' by 'racism in a multicultural society', and of 'classes' by 'ethnic and cultural groups', tells a somewhat different story from the prefatory pronouncements. Though Belsey did not extend her second edition textbook 'cookie cutter'-style because of her focus on the 'reading process itself' (what I called the first province above), *insofar* as she did gesture towards social constructionist identity politics (what I called the second province) it was with an implicit 'cookie cutter'-ness about it. Women, classes, ethnic and cultural groups exist for Belsey apparently as so may separate and switchable coins of roughly the same value, in which comparable subject-positions provide a thread of equivalences. The kind of uncritical holding asunder of separate identity-based political positions while embracing them all under social constructionist identity politics that was delineated in Part I, is tacitly performed by Belsey in this switching of terms. It does not seem to matter that the articulation of subjectivity, and the ambivalences therein, are quite different for 'ethnic and cultural groups' and socio-economic 'classes'; these are all thrust and rolled together as if it is all just a matter of differently embodied identities taking different subject positions. Implicitly, Belsey's approach to the second province is very like, for instance, Mouffe's radical democratic pronouncements. Further, Belsey's switching of words in their chronologically separate contexts suggests that understanding this matter of subjective position-taking is simply a matter of assuming the appropriate contextually-fashionable register: it used to be 'class', now it is 'race'/'ethnic and cultural groups', and 'women' are the constant. For Belsey, the matter of updating her textbook with its coherent and programmatic argument was, in short, to rephrase that argument in the currently fashionable terms, and that meant subscribing to the terms of social constructionist identity politics in a new left way rather than class analysis in an old left way.

Eagleton's approach to this matter was, as one might expect, different. Where there were opportunities for such rephrasing or switching to a currently fashionable register in the first edition of *Literary Theory*, he chose to leave it untouched in the second. The following passage at the end of the chapter on post-structuralism may have invited such switching of terms:

> With post-structuralism, we have brought the story of modern literary theory up to the present time. Within post-structuralism as a 'whole', real conflicts and differences exist whose future history cannot be predicted. There are forms of post-structuralism which represent a hedonistic withdrawal from history, a cult of ambiguity and irresponsible anarchism; there are other forms, as with the formidably rich researches of the French historian Michel Foucault, which while not without their severe problems point in a more positive direction. There are forms of 'radical' feminism which emphasize plurality, difference and sexual separatism; there are also forms of socialist feminism which, while refusing to view the women's struggle as a mere element or sub-sector of a movement which might then dominate and engulf it, hold that the liberation of other oppressed groups and classes in society is not only a moral and political imperative in itself, but a necessary (though by no means sufficient) condition for the emancipation of women.[26]

By 1996, one might have thought, the 'present time' of modern literary theory would need to be presented anew, and there was ample scope here for mentioning those other specific identity-based political positions under the embrace of social constructionist identity politics. But a little consideration shows that Eagleton could not do this: neither in 1980 and nor in 1996 did he regard specific identity-based political positions as switchable, and he consistently has little sympathy with the logic of embodiment in identity politics (which Belsey's notion of subjectivity allows space for). Eagleton's understanding of feminism, in its various forms, is not simply as an identity-based political position (it can be that, and he identifies that with 'radical' feminism) but also an extensive conceptual field in a socialist direction. The socialist extension is, for Eagleton, obviously so much more preferable to embodied identity-based political positions ('plurality, difference, and sexual separatism') – the normatively positive aspects of post-structuralism so much better than the normatively negative aspects – that the introduction of a currently fashionable new left social constructionist terminology is out of question. Eagleton's argument simply had a more pronounced socialist thrust to it to compromise even to the extent that Belsey did in her rephrasings in tune with identity politics.

Eagleton's comments on writing the second edition, when it comes in an 'Afterword' (as opposed to the prefatory remarks of Belsey), present both a structural similarity in approach to Belsey's and also sharp differences from Belsey's. This is more or less a tirade against developments in literary theory along the lines of identity politics, a more extended version of which appeared almost simultaneously in his *The Illusions of Postmodernism* (1996)[27] and then again a few years later in his *After Theory* (2003). Since I have summarized the arguments from *After Theory* in Chapter 6, and these are substantially the same as those in the 'Afterword' of the second edition, I will not go into this again. Worth noting briefly is his own placement of the writing of *Literary Theory* in the first edition (in 1982) as 'at the watershed of two very different decades'[28] – thus placing the first edition at the critical moment when Theory was constructed (a process in which *Literary Theory* undoubtedly had a role to play). A sweeping statement of the chronological phases of literary theory's travels in the 'Afterword' both remarks the rise of the logic of embodiment in 1990s social constructionist identity politics within literary studies, and places that as a loss of political direction rather than a valid political direction itself: 'Theory had shifted overnight from Lenin to Lacan, from Benveniste to the body; and if this was a salutary extension of politics into areas it had previously failed to reach, it was also, in part, the result of a deadlock in other kinds of political struggle'.[29] In postcolonialism and cultural studies he sees here the capture of a debilitating relativism, against which he defends the now embattled notion of 'universal values'. What comes through is a structural similarity to

Belsey's prefatory comments in the second edition of *Critical Practice* which enables him to refuse a 'cookie cutter approach'. Where Belsey championed the generality of the 'reading process itself' as a separate province from that of identity politics-inspired proliferations of 'radical readings', Eagleton sees the attempt to come to grips with universals in literary theory as a separate province from that of postmodernist post-colonialist multiculturalist identity politics. In this there are structural similarities. But where for Belsey the two provinces of Theory are simply separate, so that she can focus on one and sympathize with the other in implicit ways, for Eagleton they simply are diametrically opposed, so that in espousing one he inevitably has to oppose the other. Much of Eagleton's 'Afterword' in the second edition, and indeed *The Illusions of Postmodernism* can be read as a critique of Belsey's *Critical Practice*. At stake in both was an apprehension of the development of literary theory in keeping with social constructionist identity politics, institutionalizing identity politics in literary studies, and the pressures that this apprehension exerts on their textbooks. And for both this means rejecting any 'cookie cutter approach' style rewriting of their textbooks.

Meanwhile, however, numerous literary theory textbooks which had done exactly the kinds of things that Eagleton and Belsey refused to do in their second editions were becoming available. These both noted in an ongoing fashion the various proliferations in literary theory and did so naturally with a 'cookie cutter approach'. Since these were devoted not to elaborating a specific argument or a case (as in Eagleton's and Belsey's textbooks) but to noting developments in literary theory and summarizing arguments in an apparently ideologically neutral and even-handed fashion (often while denying that such a position is possible), these had relatively short shelf lives in individual editions and were rewritten and updated at regular intervals. The advantage of the 'cookie cutter approach', and the identity politics-based literary theory it has to thereby account, is that there is no need to revisit or revise arguments, there is little call for extensive repositioning and validating – new editions are mainly matters of *adding* sections and chapters (and occasionally but rarely removing) as new theories become institutionally accredited and enter research citations and teaching syllabi. The institutionalization of identity politics in literary studies, in concert with the 'cookie cutter approach', is therefore easily traced in subsequent editions of such literary theory textbooks.

A familiar example of this is, as already noted above, Raman Selden's *A Reader's Guide to Contemporary Literary Theory* (first edition in 1985). This has since been issued in three revised new editions: the second in 1989;

the third after Selden's demise was published in 1993 and updated and revised by Peter Widdowson, who appeared as co-author; and a further updated and revised edition was published in 1997, with Peter Brooker joining as third co-author. A reader was also put together by Selden to go with the second edition, *Practising Theory and Reading Literature: An Introduction* (1989),[30] which focused on readings of specific literary texts by specific critics by way of illustrating particular theoretical approaches. This was replaced with a new reader, entitled *A Practical Reader in Contemporary Literary Theory* (1996),[31] to go with the fourth edition. I will, however, not take up the latter, and confine myself to the general narrative of literary theory in subsequent editions of *A Reader's Guide*.

In the first edition (1985) Selden had confined himself to the following: Russian formalism, Marxist theory, structuralist theory, post-structuralist theory, reader-oriented theory, and feminist criticism. In coverage of approaches (without an overarching case being presented) this had some resemblance to Belsey's and Eagleton's textbooks. The idea seemed to be to emphasize those theoretical approaches where the writing and reading of literature are taken as general activities, with little attention to identity-based politics that may impinge upon this. Even the political possibilities that emanate from postmodernist or post-structuralist understandings of ideology, into which specific identity-based political positions and social constructionist identity politics were already being inserted, were little noted. The obvious departure here was the chapter on feminism. This is where the otherwise apparently detached narrative voice lapsed into its most ideologically demonstrative, or ideologically manifest, expressions. That feminism was included in this frame, it becomes evident, was more to serve a liberal political conscience (the textbook narrator's even-handedness) than as a distinctive approach which can shoulder the others in reach and scope – and it appeared as a concession from a presumptively male voice: 'It has proved difficult for feminists to develop theories without resort to male theorists. [...] Whatever the difficulties, women have the right to assert their own values, to explore their own conscious-ness, and to develop new forms of expression corresponding to their val-ues and consciousness'.[32] This assumes that: (a) feminists seek to elaborate a theory that is of interest to women alone, and is therefore of limited application (unlike the others); (b) that the use of male theorists somehow undermines the feminist enterprise (there is an essentialist streak in this); and (c) that feminists have a *right* to attempt this (the liberal concession is offered by the author on behalf of *his* readers). The introduction of the rights discourse to accommodate feminism is the most explicit ideological avowal on the part of the author that is available here. Identity-based political positions entered very uneasily into Selden's textbook sweep on literary theory (far more so than in Belsey's and Eagleton's textbooks), and probably reflected fairly accurately dominant institutional attitudes in literary studies at the time. On Selden's take on feminism in the first edition I have more to say soon.

In the 1989 second edition of *A Reader's Guide*[33] the chapter on feminism was left untouched, but importantly new sections appeared on postmodernism in relation to post-structuralism, on discourse, and on New Historicism. The summaries and references presented in these effectively presented precisely those ideological nuances of theoretical developments which would allow specific identity-based political positions under the umbrella of social constructionist identity politics to take hold within literary studies. There is little indication that Selden appreciated the extent of this, though the phenomenon was already well established and underway. However, the kind of in-between and encompassing and metatheoretical rhetorical structures that these theories provided – amenable, as I have observed in Chapter 4, to the institutional insertion of social constructionist identity politics – was remarked clearly enough, and again probably reflected the institutional disposition of literary studies vis-à-vis Theory appropriately.

The 1993 edition,[34] under the revision of now co-author Peter Widdowson, marked a significant break in both tone and direction of 'cookie cutter approach' expansion for this textbook. This date accords well with the travels of Theory towards the institutionalization of social constructionist identity politics in literary studies observed in previous chapters. This followed the now widely accepted version of the critical assumptions against which contemporary Anglo-American literary theory apparently delineated itself, and placed an introductory chapter on 'New Criticism, Moral Formalism and F.R. Leavis'. A section on postcolonial theory was appended to the chapter on postmodernism: 'From a postcolonial perspective, Western values and traditions of thought and literature, including versions of postmodernism, are guilty of a repressive ethnocentrism'.[35] The chapter on feminism was expanded to include a more substantial section on 'Black, Women-of-Colour, and Lesbian Literary Theories'. As significantly, the tone of the writing insofar as it touches upon identity politics was altered, mainly with the effect of downplaying the air of liberal patronage. This is apparent, for instance, when the following passages are compared from the chapter on feminism in the 1985 and the 1993 editions:

> In Aeschylus's trilogy, *The Oresteia*, victory is granted by Athena to the male argument, put by Apollo, that the mother is no parent to

her child. The victory of the male principle of intellect brings to an end the reign of the sensual female Furies and asserts patriarchy over matriarchy. Feminist criticism sometimes summons up the anger of the Furies in order to disturb the complacent certainties of patriarchal culture and create a less oppressive climate for women writers and readers. Sometimes feminist critics have employed wit to 'deconstruct' male dominated ways of seeing.

[Selden, 1985 edition][36]

In Aeschylus's trilogy, *The Oresteia*, victory is granted by Athena to the male argument, put by Apollo, that the mother is no parent to her child. The victory of the male principle of intellect brings to an end the reign of the sensual female Furies and asserts patriarchy over matriarchy. Throughout its long history, feminism (for while the *word* may only have come into English usage in the 1890s, women's conscious struggle to resist patriarchy goes much further back) has sought to disturb the complacent certainties of such a patriarchal culture, to assert belief in sexual equality, and to eradicate sexist domination in transforming society.

[Selden and Widdowson, 1993 edition][37]

The first passage suggests that Selden more or less went along with the male principle of intellect and female principle of sensuality divide, like the Greek Gods or Aeschylus. He saw feminist critics as Furies, or at best as employing 'wit' (distinct from rational argument). Selden also regarded (as I have noted before) feminist criticism as something that is confined to 'women writers and readers', and as a strand of literary theory that is happening in the present. Widdowson's amended passage sticks with the mythic allusion but to draw quite different links with feminist criticism. It serves to remind of the historic extent of feminist resistance to patriarchy. More importantly, it does not confine the implications of feminist theory to women alone: 'sexual equality' is obviously something that affects both sides of the equation, and the end-result is seen as a transformation of society itself. The political impact of specific identity-based political positions (especially as intellectually rigorous and searching an area as feminist theory) could not be taken lightly any more and their institutional transmissions had naturally become more positively phrased in textbooks. In general social constructionist identity politics was already recognized as central to literary studies. The trend was confirmed in the fourth edition that appeared in 1997.[38] There were further additions in the 'cookie cutter approach' mould, mostly in the direction of embracing more specific identity-based political positions under the increasingly social constructionist frame of contemporary literary theory, and thereby recognizing their, or according them, institutional status as is appropriate in a textbook. The chapter on postcolonial criticism became separate from the chapter on postmodernism, and had a substantial section of race and ethnicity. The chapter on postmodernism acquired a section on postmodern feminisms. Also to be found now was a new final chapter, 'Gay, Lesbian and Queer Theories'. If the literary theory textbook in Selden's hands in 1985 revealed a tacitly patriarchal and explicitly liberal grounding, by 1995 it had been transformed by Widdowson and Brooker to contain social constructionist identity politics, presenting elaborations of a range of specific identity-based political positions, and with a distinct new left inclination.

Such a tracing of the patterns of institutionalization of social constructionist identity politics through subsequent editions of 'cookie cutter'-style literary theory narrative textbooks can be conducted for other examples, and can be extended to literary theory anthologies. In doing this, certain differences would undoubtedly be thrown up: different textbook authors hold and sometimes reveal different ideological proclivities, some register developments sooner or later than others, the selection of approaches that deserve emphasis differ, and so on. But the direction is similar. To give this extensive demonstration would be an unnecessarily protracted and tedious affair. Nevertheless, it is worth considering, more sketchily, another instance to press the point home.

Steven Lynn's *Texts and Contexts: Writing about Literature with Critical Theory* is another instance of a literary theory textbook which has been republished in revised editions at regular intervals: the first edition appeared in 1994, a second in 1998, and a third in 2001. The 'cookie cutter approach' of this was clearly embraced and acknowledged by the author in the first chapter of the first edition: 'In an ideal world, an introduction to writing about literature would include every identifiable approach. The goal of this introduction is necessarily more limited: using a sampling of the most visible approaches, it aims to show how theory shapes practice – how assumptions stimulate and guide the process of developing critical essays.'[39] The ideal of total inclusiveness naturally works against any ambition to present a programme or case. The mode of selection – 'the most visible approaches' – registers the textbook ambition to reflect the most obviously institutionally sanctioned approaches to serve a clearly institutional function, 'developing critical essays'. Starting in 1994, the first edition of this finds itself at the institutional position where Selden and Widdowson's *A Reader's Guide* found itself in its third edition (1993). There was a strong sense of a normal literary theory sequence of general import (covered by chapters on New Criticism, reader-response, deconstructive, biographical and historical and New Historicist criticism, and psychological criticism), but there was also sufficient grasp of the increasing institutional weight of identity-based theories (particularly in the chapter on feminist criticism, which included a section on lesbian and gay theories, and in a section in Chapter 1 on other theories, which apologizes for not covering African American, religious, ethical, and Marxist approaches). Like Selden and Widdowson in 1993 he was inclined to see feminist literary theory – still the primary locus of identity-based political theorizing – as not a matter for women alone, albeit cautiously:

> At the risk of irritating or even outraging some of my readers, I think [...] that *anyone* can do feminist criticism – and do it honestly. One of the wonderful things about words is that we can use them to try out ideas, to speculate, to put on roles and explore. We construct arguments and conduct analyses not only to persuade others but also to investigate things about ourselves – if we have an open, critical mind, that is.[40]

The 1998 second edition of *Texts and Contexts* appeared again shortly after Selden and Widdowson's 1997 fourth edition of *A Reader's Guide*, and like the latter came with a stronger sense of the political agency of identity-based political positions. Though not quite expanding along 'cookie cutter' lines as Selden and Widdowson's fourth edition did, Lynn acknowledges this by reworking the chapter on feminist criticism to place it within a context of 'politically self-conscious reading' and while revolving the problem of identity.[41] The bringing together of specific identity-based political positions under a rubric of social constructionist identity politics is reasonably explicit here. The 2001 third edition of *Texts and Contexts* confirms this direction by doing further 'cookie cutter approach' expanding, and now gives extended treatment to African American criticism, postcolonial theory, multiculturalism, ecocriticism, queer theory, and addresses cultural studies. The remarks on multiculturalism, most obviously in the province of identity politics as understood here, are of particular interest:

> [Multiculturalism] seeks to appreciate, understand and respect the uniquely different viewpoints of different cultures – even if we disagree. Some practices and beliefs, however, seem so obviously unethical and erroneous that a simple multicultural celebration of

difference becomes problematic. At the least, a multicultural stance invites us to attempt to understand the subjectivity of our own culture as we look on other cultures.[42]

The trace of literary theory's institutional 'cookie cutter approach' travel in textbooks from predominantly general/universal concerns to increasingly registering specific identity-based political concerns to living with social constructionist identity politics as the primary growth area is pretty clearly in evidence in these rewritings.

It is not just the shifting emphases of the content of particular editions that is indicative here, but also the negotiations that Lynn engages in for the critical 'self' in the above-quoted passages (that is why I particularly quoted them). In 1994 the 'self' that could extend to feminist criticism honestly and irrespective of gender was a universal 'self' – one with an 'open, critical mind', the great 'we'. It is a 'self'-conception that still derives from a liberal tradition and comes with the complicated baggage of that tradition, but at any rate it is free of the patriarchal condescension of Selden's 1985 voice. In 1997 this 'self' has a particular sort of inflection: it is also *politically* invested and that has something to do with identity. By 2001 the 'self' is not so much in a position to extend where it does not seem to be but to focus critically on where it ostensibly is, to 'understand the subjectivity of our own culture'. It is not so much that the critical liberal 'self' of 1994 was necessarily above dishonesty, but that its possible engagement with debate and exchange has become curtailed by becoming absorbed or integrated into social constructionist identity politics. In these shifts the precise nature of the limitations imposed on open debate and exchange through the logic of embodiment in social constructionist identity politics is exemplified; that these shifts are textbook shifts registers their institutional character.

Before leaving the arena of narrative theory textbooks in multiple editions, there is a final point that is of interest here. I have noted above a particular sympathy between the 'cookie cutter approach' of textbooks (which are periodically revised, expanded, and republished) and the institutionalization of social constructionist identity politics. Those, like Belsey and Eagleton, who espoused a programme or case in their textbooks and resisted the 'cookie cutter approach' also seemed reluctant to recognize the expansion of literary theory along the lines of identity politics. Those who simply let different theories shoulder each other as of equal utility and in a spirit of registering the institutional moment for institutional pedagogic practice – i.e., follow the 'cookie cutter approach' – felt called upon to expand along the lines of accommodating different identity-based political positions within social constructionist identity politics. To some extent this sympathy derives, I feel, through the internal rationales of identity politics' embrace and 'cookie cutter approaches'. They both depend on a rationale of non-comparison or of inattention to relative evaluations or, simply, of holding-bits-apart. Identity politics hold different identity-based political positions apart while extending an umbrella over all of them as implicitly equivalent or analogous; 'cookie cutter approach' textbooks hold different theoretical approaches apart and extend an umbrella of institutional literary studies over them as if they are all equivalent or analogous. They just come together well. But there is another twist to this sympathy. Not all the approaches covered in literary theory textbooks of this sort are in line with identity politics. Criticism aligned to identity-based political positions (brought together as identity politics) and criticism concerned with general/universal literary concerns shoulder each other as if they are similar, and have equivalent utility, and are analogous in their institutional applications. There is a lack of discrimination here which, quite possibly, rubs off on identity politics in literary studies to its advantage. They all seem to feed into each other to produce a coherent field of literary theory where identity politics gains increasing legitimacy through monopolistic growth. For institutional purposes the contested nature of literary theory is quelled to give that monopolistic tendency sway.

Literary canons and anthologies

Taking a related but somewhat different direction, and still germane to the theme of this chapter, the institutional mediations of textbooks are usually grounded on institutional practices which centre on literary canons. Literary theory textbooks impinge upon the latter in two ways: they seem to construct a literary theory canon, especially as the 'cookie cutter approach' comes together; and they present interrogations of literary canons and pedagogic practice (particularly the constitution of curricula). Literary theory textbooks seem to, in a number of ways, shadow that important aspect of institutional practice in literary studies: the formation of canons and curricula. Unsurprisingly, just as social constructionist identity politics is traceable in the institutional negotiations of literary theory textbooks it is also available in related debates about canons and curricula.

The steps of this argument from narrative theory textbooks to canon debates are well-traversed ones. Parrinder's essay, 'Having Your

Assumptions Questioned' (1993), which I have referred to already, observed that: 'Many of the theory guides [...] denigrate the notion of a literary canon – the canon is frequently portrayed as a merely ideological construction – and this should lead us in turn to question the canon of theory'.[43] Theory textbooks appear to stand at the cusp of an institutional development – or inculcation of worldly desires – which gives shape to a Theory canon for pedagogic transmission while interrogating another canon (variously thought of as a received Western canon, Anglo-American literary canon, canon of European literature, canon of national literatures, etc.), the institutional weight of which is already established in a range of curricula – with their textbooks. Indeed, debates about the threat to these canonical formations, a perceived 'crisis' in the study of literature (particularly in American and British universities), was often regarded as the result of the onslaught of Theory in the academy. The 'canon wars', as they were popularly known throughout the late 1980s and 1990s, was construed within the path from the construction of Theory to the worldly travels of Theory to the formulations of 'against Theory'/'after Theory'. Narrative literary theory textbooks charted their institutional prerogatives in this path, and these institutional prerogatives were at each point seen as needling the institutional force of established canonical formations. The opening up of canonical formations to interrogation, the impassioned 'canon wars', in turn impinged upon the production and reception of literary studies (not theory) textbooks in two ways: (a) attempts were made to reconceive and realize a more inclusive, multicultural, mainstream canon (Western, Anglo-American, etc.) in curricula and supporting textbooks; and (b) proliferations of canons (a production of alternative or neglected canons), at odds with and filling the lacunae of established canons, were evidenced in curricula and supporting textbooks. The passage of narrative literary theory textbooks that is briefly delineated above, and the passage of curricular changes and new textbooks in literary studies of the 1990s, evidently moved together – not in terms of causal symmetries, but importantly by the unifying patterns thrown out through the entrenchment of identity politics.

In pulling this discussion of textbooks in the direction of the 1990s 'canon wars' the relationship between literary studies textbooks (which include Theory textbooks) and canons obviously needs clarification. From the beginning, both sides of the canon debates were strongly invested in pedagogic concern: both in defending the legitimacy of the Western or Anglo-American canon from the relativism of or the multicultural push of Theory (such as William Bennett, Harold Bloom[44]), and in calling for its reconsideration and opening up (e.g., Paul Lauter, John Guillory, and Gregory S. Jay[45]). To a great extent the connecting line between canon and curriculum in these rested in a notion of 'content', generally exemplified in the reading list (syllabus, curriculum) and often concretized in particular kinds of literary textbook, the anthology and general literary history. On the anthology and general literary history as sites for debate I have more to say soon. The focus on 'content' often revolved on a more or less simplistic notion of the canon as constituted by the texts it contains in reading lists. Such approaches were broadly inspired by Arnold's 'touchstones' or Leavis's 'great tradition',[46] but departed from them in increasingly sophisticated accounts of how or why canonical texts surface as such. At any rate, for Bloom, for instance, maintaining attention to the texts of the Western canon as a personal aesthetic frame ('the aesthetic is, in my view, an individual rather than a societal concern'[47]) was a matter of accepting an accrual of texts in a conservatively given reading list; whereas for Lauter, for instance, trying to bring a 'meaningful recognition of the character and importance of [America's] diversity'[48] was a matter of noting exclusions and ensuring inclusions in the mainstream Anglo-American canon, or questioning existing reading lists and introducing new and inclusive ones. More complex articulations of the relationship of canons to reading lists (in curricula or in syllabi) actually question the assumption that canonicity is *contained* in reading lists at all – it is averred that there is, at best, a transient and contingent relationship. Guillory's notion (1993) of the canon as something that materializes through the circulation of cultural capital presents this view most lucidly:

> The form of the canon belongs to the process of the reproduction of social relations, but it does not enter the process immediately. The canon does not accrete over time like a pyramid built by invisible hands, nor does it act directly and irresistibly on social relations, like a chemical reagent; in its concrete form as a syllabus or curriculum, the canon is a discursive instrument of 'transmission' situated historically within a specific institution of reproduction: the school.[49]

And a bit later:

> Canons of texts belong to the *durée* of the school as both an objectification of 'tradition' and as a list of texts (syllabus, curriculum) continuously changing in response to the fictional relations between individuals and social reproduction.[50]

This understanding of the canon in relation to the reading list inserts the political into the debate not merely as a matter of inclusion/exclusion in terms of social or aesthetic conscience, but as contingent upon the continuum of social transmissions and reproductions *within* which canons and reading lists are mutually constituted. With this in view, Guillory was inclined to be critical of both sides of the canon debate as resulting from a misdirected liberal tendency: both derived, he felt, from some notion of social conscience expressed as inclusion/exclusion in reading lists. For Guillory this necessitated the insertion of the radical political desire of Theory in canonical debates. Also in a sceptical vein as far as a simplistic equation of content (curriculum, syllabi) and canon go, and also feeling that a misdirected liberalism has characterized both defenders and 'openers' of the Western canon, Kolbas in 2001 presented a 'sociological and historical understanding of the canon that is confined neither to schools and universities nor to social representation but that stresses the material reproduction of culture in the process of canon formation'.[51] A wider emphasis on material reproduction (wider than Guillory's focus on schools and reading lists), and a sociology of the aesthetic (which Guillory had rather neglected), in canon formation led Kolbas to a conservative position in the canon debate (unlike Guillory).

Despite these shifts in conceiving the relationship between canons and reading lists (curricula, syllabi), in terms of *institutional practice* the content of reading lists in the classroom has been the focal point of the canon debates. Moreover, as textbook concretizations of reading lists in the classroom – concretizations of specifically that institutional nexus – anthologies and general literary histories have in particular been key sites of the canon debates. And, significantly for this study, debates on this site are characterized by a constant reckoning with the gradual entrenchment of identity-based political positions under the umbrella of social constructionist identity politics. This is traceable in much the same way as in self-announcements or narrative literary theory textbooks. This trace can be traversed expeditiously here without repeating the patterns I have described already.

The sheer number of anthologies devoted to specific identity-based political positions that appeared within the concentrated period of the 1990s seems to me indicative of the growing institutional disposition of literary studies: the publishing industry and the academic curriculum had gone into an overdrive of holding these apart and yet together in the structure of identity politics. That the 1990s is where this institutional disposition is symptomatized in this fashion is consistent with developments noted in previous chapters. The 1990s is also where the canon debates, briefly mentioned above, come to a head – the anthology and the debate were inextricably connected. A cursory list of major, perceivably canon-setting, anthological productions directed to the Anglophone market (particularly American and British) in the decade speaks for itself. The 1980s had seen the appearance of some major anthologies of women's literature: markedly *The Norton Anthology of Literature by Women* (1989), *Longman Anthology of World Literature by Women* (1985), and Spender and Todd's *Anthology of British Women Writers* (1989).[52] The 1990s saw a marked expansion in this direction. The turn of the decade saw the appearance of another canon-setting reference book, *The Feminist Companion to Literature in English* (1990), and by the end of the decade there were the second and revised edition of *The Norton Anthology of Literature by Women* (1996) (with subtitle changed significantly from *The Tradition in English* to *The Traditions in English*), *The Prentice Hall Anthology of Women's Literature* (1999), and *The Longman Anthology of Women's Literature* (2001).[53] A smattering of largely genre or period specific anthologies of gay and lesbian literature, gave way to more comprehensive anthological productions: Mordden's *Waves* (1994), Federman's *Chloe plus Olivia* (1994), Beemyn and Eliason's *Queer Studies* (1996), *The Columbia Anthology of Gay Literature* (1998), and Drake's *The Gay Canon* (1998).[54] Woods's *A History of Gay Literature* also appeared in 1998.[55] A strong anthological tradition of black or African American literature[56] was significantly updated in this decade with the appearance of *The Norton Anthology of African-American Literature* (1996), Young's *African American Literature* (1996), Hill et al.'s *Call and Response* (1998), and Powell's *Step into a World* (2000).[57] Cutting across the lines of race, gender, sexuality, primarily in the United States, appeared a number of equally ambitious canon-setting enterprises: at the intersection of black women – Busby's *Daughters of Africa* (1992), *The Prentice Hall Anthology of African American Women's Literature* (2005);[58] at the intersection of race, gender, and sexuality – Beam's *In the Life* (1986), Mckinley's *Afrekete* (1995), and Carbado et al.'s *Black Like Us* (2002).[59] Other ethnic minorities got their anthological dues: Heyek's *Barrios and Borderlands* (1994), del Rio's *The Prentice Hall Anthology of Latino Literature* (2001), Wong's *Asian American Literature* (1996), and Lim's *Asian-American Literature* (1999).[60] The identity politics of wider Anglophone literary production for textbook consumption in the West was captured in books like *The Arnold Anthology of Postcolonial Literatures in English* (1996) and Ross's *Colonial and Postcolonial Fiction in English* (1999).[61] If the naming of such 1990s identity-based anthological publications extends to those with further regional, chronological, and generic delimitations we will have a bibliography of very substantial proportions.

While this extraordinary and concentrated proliferation of canon-forming, curriculum-determining anthological production along identity-based lines was underway through the 1990s, the conventional canons of English and American Literature were also being expanded, to a significant degree by accommodating inclusions that resulted from identity politics. This is easily traced in the most influential and well-resourced strand of such production: in subsequent editions of *The Norton Anthology of American Literature* from its second edition in 1986, through its third in 1989, fourth in 1994, fifth in 1998, and (substantially expanded) sixth in 2003;[62] as well as in subsequent editions of *The Norton Anthology of English Literature* from its fifth edition in 1986 through its sixth in 1993 and seventh in 2000.[63] On a broader scale, such a desire for inclusiveness impinged also upon perceptions of the most inclusive of literary horizons, that of 'world literature'. The decade also saw a new edition of *The Norton Anthology of World Masterpieces*, which was followed soon after by *The Longman Anthology of World Literature* and *The Bedford Anthology of World Literature*.[64]

While these anthologies, produced as they were within a concentrated period, registered patterns of curricula and syllabi development in this period, they also dovetailed into simultaneously conducted canon debates. For institutional purposes such anthologies concretized canon formations, and also served as sites for debating the canon. The consideration of canon debates and anthological productions together paves the way for an insight into the most structured level of institutional interpersonal relations in literary studies ... in academia: the classroom. The targeting of these anthologies towards the classroom was perfectly clear. Many of the anthologies, for instance, came with companion guides for teachers: the Norton anthologies for American Literature, English Literature, and Literature by Women came with such guides, as did the later Longman Anthology of World Literature.[65] That these 1990s anthologies were powerfully invested in identity politics was constantly suspected in reviews, especially in general statements about anthologies. Thus, in a review Ilan Stevens observed in 2000 that:

> Anthologies are merchandise, and the politics behind many of them are clear. Eclipsed portions of the population (women, members of

minority groups, denizens of Third World nations, etc.) are far better represented in the anthology section than in the section on general fiction. Short selections about do it.[66]

Similar observations are found in reviews about a range of 1990s anthologies by Margorie Perloff.[67] Such anthologies were also the site of much theorizing and criticism which were almost invariably cognizant of the expectations of identity politics and the role thereof in pedagogy. Notably, for instance, special scholarly journal issues or sections of issues were devoted to analysing such canon-setting productions and their impact: e.g., a special issue of the journal *Symploke* 2000 was devoted to questioning the recent edition of *The Norton Anthology of World Masterpieces*, and another issue of the journal in 2003 carried a forum discussion on *The Norton Anthology of Theory and Criticism*.[68] An extended paper by Waïl S. Hassan in 2000 reviewing the 1997/1999 appearance of *The Norton Anthology of World Literature* demonstrated how 'a brief history of the anthology's eight editions [...] show how its Eurocentric definition of "world literature" itself has come to embody some of the most problematic aspects of multiculturalism'.[69] What all that gestures towards is how closely invested identity politics had become by this time – through the canon debates, through the anthologies (and their implicit curricula/ syllabi) – in structuring that interpersonal institutional space of the classroom.

This was inevitable given that the canon debates were in the late 1980s and through the 1990s conducted with careful attention to the composition and disposition of the classroom. Modes of self-awareness and identification were brought into the classroom through the canon debates, supported by such productions as of identity-based curriculum-setting anthologies, into the very heart of academically structured interpersonal relations and face-to-face interactions, into the transience of unrecorded exchange and communication. Textualized hints of resulting changes in the classroom are available occasionally in the stated intentions of teachers with investments in identity politics. Going back to the essay by Spivak that I discussed in the previous chapter, we find a clear statement of such intention:

> [...] the long-haul emancipatory social intervention is not primarily a question of redressing victimage by the assertion of (class or gender or ethnocultural) identity. It is a question of developing a vigilance for systematic appropriations of the unacknowledged social

production of a *differential* that is one basis of exchange into the network of the cultural politics of class- or gender-identification.

In the field of ethnocultural politics, the postcolonial teacher can help to develop this vigilance rather than continue pathetically to dramatize victimage or assert a spiritual identity.[70]

The postcolonial teacher's role, in other words, is to be *identified* within the classroom along social constructionist lines so as to engender an awareness of identity which is both emancipative and unappropriable; really then, a social constructionist identity-consciousness would be transmitted which is always, so to say, on the edge, always foregrounded in the balance of contradictory possibilities. A somewhat extended restatement of a similar intention is available from Lisa Lowe's *Immigrant Acts* (1996) at the other end of that decade:

I want to cast the project of securing the conditions for teaching U.S. racialized minority, postcolonial, and women's literatures in the contemporary university as [...] a collection of linked alternative pedagogies central to contesting both the traditional function of the educational apparatus to incorporate students as subjects of the state, and the narratives through which that socialization takes place. [...] [It] is a set of links that is not predicated on notions of similarity or identity but is a project built out of material, historical and topical differentiation. [...] Through concerted pedagogical and curricular changes taking place in different institutional sites, we can locate and displace the powerful ideological narratives that traditionally structure the current university [...]. The teaching of an immigrant female and postcolonial text [...] decentres the autonomous notion of Western culture by recentering the complexities of racialized female and postcolonial collectives and unmasks the developmental narrative as a fiction designed to justify the histories of colonialism, neo-colonialism, and forced labour and to erase the dislocations and hybridities that are the resulting conditions of those histories.[71]

The social constructionist impetus is identified in the emphasis on 'material, historical and topical differentiation', and its identity-based grounding in the pre-allocation of identified racial and gender minorities with radical possibilities. It is at the nexus of curriculum and pedagogy – in the classroom within the current university, in other words – that Lowe, like Spivak, seeks to instigate this process.

With the intention naturally comes the act, and the act of teaching-learning in the classroom was under scrutiny as soon as the canon debates came to a head in the 1990s, and identity-based anthological production got underway. Two volumes in the series the *Wellesley Studies in Critical Theory, Literary History and Culture*, from the mid-1990s, present some observations arising from such scrutiny. Volume 3 in this, Alberti's edited *The Canon in the Classroom*,[72] contains thoughtful self-reflexive papers on the experience of teaching an opened-up and revised canon – along social constructionist identity lines – in the classroom. These papers are all worthy of careful attention in this context, but, for the sake of economy, I focus on just one observation in Lauter's 'Afterword' (comparing the current to an earlier 1960s classroom):

> The problematic of classroom processes was, over time further complicated by the emergence of difference – in gender, race, class, and sexuality – as pivotal to the dynamics that mark faculty-student interactions. I think it is fair to say that few of the earlier reformers recognized the centrality of what today we refer to as 'subject position' in the organization of power in schools and colleges. Particularly when the subject matter involves multiculturalism or gender, questions of subject position becomes critical to any honest dialogue. These problems of power, discourse, subject position, so deeply woven into the fabric of institutional learning, undo naïve assumptions that some of us made about 'building socialism in one classroom,' to use a joking phrase of that earlier time.[73]

It is not just the intention of the teacher but the very mode of structuring classroom exchange that enjoins identity-based thinking, a compulsory logic of embodiment, a penchant for speaking with the whole *identified* being (to echo that quotation from Adorno in Chapter 2) on students now. At the deepest level, if Lauter's observation was correct then and still obtains, social constructionist identity politics engulfs and colours interpersonal relations in the institutional practice of literary studies.

It seems appropriate to conclude this textual tracing of the entrenchment of identity politics in literary studies by going back to Gerald Graff, with whom I began this part of the present study in Chapter 6. In the early 1990s he had evidently kept up with the profession of literary studies, the subject of his history in 1987, and written a series of articles on the canon debates. Three of these were collected in Volume 2 of the *Wellesley Studies*, Cain's edited *Teaching the Conflicts*, and made the subject of a collection of responses from teachers, with a final say being given to Graff.[74] Again these responses are all of great interest in this context, but a full discussion of these is beyond the scope of this study. Of immediate interest is the argument of those three essays that were debated in the responses. The gist if these are best summarized in Graff's own words:

> I would argue that the primary weakness of the humanities curriculum [...] is no longer its failure to embrace cultural and ideological difference, but its failure to take maximum educational advantage of the impressive range of difference that it now does embrace. The curriculum encompasses a far wider range of cultural differences than in the past but instead of engaging those differences it still tends to keep their components in non-communicating courses and their departments. As a result students are often unable to recognize difference *as* difference, since they experience its components only in separation.[75]

Graff went on to recommend a 'dialogic curriculum' where the differences and polarities of the curriculum debate would not simply be confined to teachers but opened to students, by curricular and pedagogic adjustments that overcome compartmentalization. This is a far cry from the ghettoization of identity-based political positions in literary studies that Graff had anticipated in 1987. In the 1990s he was advocating bringing different identity-based sections of the academy into conversation with each other through curricular revision and teaching practice – as a salutary development precisely along the lines of social constructionist identity politics. Perhaps there was some possibility in Graff's notion of a 'dialogic curriculum' that differences would not simply be perpetually held and multiplied and spread within the embracing structure of social constructionist identity politics, but dissolved through conversation. But if that was so, there was little sign of it. The institutional structure that Graff's programme of conflictual curriculum and teaching reform suggested immediately was a social constructionist programme that brings difference together, in ever expanding and enlightening and engaged conversation, *as* difference.

Whether anything like a conflictual curriculum and pedagogy has emerged anywhere in the institutional practice of literary studies in Graff's programmatic fashion is a moot question. But this study argues that something akin to that does now obtain through a range of complex processes, some of which are discerned here by following certain lines of textual enquiry (self-announcements, narrative theory text-books, anthologies, and the canon debates). Social constructionist identity politics has indeed become enmeshed into the institutional practice of literary studies, percolating down to the very structure of interpersonal exchanges in classrooms. And this study argues that while this has been an enlightening and expansive process in some respects, it has also emphatically been one that has spread limits and constraints across literary studies generally, curtailing free debate and exchange in significant ways. Further, I suspect that would prove to be the case in other humanistic and social sciences disciplines too, if the matter is examined carefully.

9
Conclusion: Questions and Prospects

Beyond textual expressions which chart the entrenchment of social constructionist identity politics in literary studies – and arguably more widely in the humanities and social sciences – lie other relatively intractable, unrecorded, transient, and yet familiarly institutional expressions. The recorded tracings of Theory-'against Theory'-'after Theory' developments, of self-announcements, of textbook and anthology production, of canon debates, constantly emanate from and return within such a diffuse hum of numerous untextualized exchanges and communications and gestures. Ultimately, such untextualized exchanges moderate the everyday life of academic institutional spaces amidst other kinds of institutional spaces and within the broader life of society. So, beyond those textual traces that the previous three chapters are devoted to there is this larger field of everyday institutional expressions, and it may be expected that just as identity politics is entrenched within and structures the disposition of textualized expressions of literary studies, it is so too for untextualized expressions. If identity politics is institutionalized, it is as much within the ebb and flow of the untextualized everyday life of literary studies as within the textualized archive. To try to render this everyday institutional life tractable, to categorize and analyse its nuances, to collect observations about it and systematize them, would be akin to what Geertz described as collecting 'convergent data' from a wider range of sources than this study can attend to. This study has attended to a narrowly circumscribed and limited range of observations, drawing on a particular kind of source – but the inferences available from that seem to me to be sufficiently indicative.

Though a systematic exploration of the everyday institutional life of literary studies and the place of identity politics therein is outside the scope of this study, a few habitual and typified questions of transient everyday occurrence can be noted to gesture towards the disposition therein. For those readers who, like the present author, are within the academy, and particularly within the institutional practice of literary studies, the occurrence of such questions might seem commonplace. The answers to such questions are most immediately a matter of recognizing patterns and tacit or agreed assumptions and associations and experiences that *are* the everyday life of literary studies. And such questions are in fact not simply a trigger to recognizing something that already obtains; such questions are often within the interstices of the institutional practice of literary studies *as* interrogatives, as moments of self-reckoning, doubt, indecision, prickliness. That such questions are not just after-the-fact or retrospective modes of seeking direction but constant nudges and winks within the everyday life of literary studies gives some indication of their relevance for gauging the institutional disposition of the discipline, the entrenchment of identity politics therein.

I have in mind such questions as may arise in a literature department meeting devoted to discussing curricular issues. 'Why aren't there any women/black/gay authors in this genre or period based course?'; 'Would it be possible to increase our student intake by making the curriculum more inclusive?'; 'Surely, any respectable undergraduate programme for English must have courses in postcolonial literature, immigrant writing, women's literature and so on?'; 'Can't we follow a conventional syllabus and yet acknowledge the great importance of neglected minorities and their writings?'; 'How can we find a text that fits all aspects of the core course in Theory – can *Pride and Prejudice* be used to explain gay theory/ postcolonial theory/black writing ... ?'; 'Who will teach that course on gay literature/women's writing/postcolonial literature?'. Then there are questions about appointments and academic responsibilities. 'The employment prospects for gay/ethnic minority/women academics have improved with the advent of Theory, haven't they?'; 'Do we have any black or coloured applicants for this post of Lecturer in Postcolonial Studies?'; 'As the only gay person in this department does it fall to me to offer a course in Queer Studies?'; 'She is not the obvious person for it, but perhaps we can ask her to supervise this dissertation on feminist literature?'; 'Is it true that somehow, as much through choice as through the amenability of the environment, women tend to research and teach in areas related to women's writing, immigrants tend to research and teach in postcolonial literature, black academics tend to have research and teaching interests in black writing and criticism, and so on?'; 'Though not quite in my area, perhaps I should apply for that Lectureship in Postcolonial Studies? – after all, I am obviously a postcolonial subject'; 'Wonder whether the promotion committee/interview panel knew I am gay?'; 'Wonder whether I wasn't short-listed because I am what I am?'. Students and researchers revolve questions in a similar mould too. 'Should I speak as a woman/gay person/ethnic minority person in this discussion on literary theory?'; 'When the lecturer talked about neglect of minority writers did my classmates glance meaningfully at me? – speak to me particularly sympathetically? – address me especially cautiously?'; 'Does my being a student from India reading literature in Britain give me a privileged status in classroom discussions of the postcolonial novel?'; 'Given my sex/sexual orientation/appearance would it be advantageous for me to write a dissertation on novels by women/gay writers/black writers?'; 'Given that I am a female student, surely I have an edge over that male lecturer in my reading of this poem by a woman writer?'; 'Am I being asked to read these books because they are worth reading or because they are by writers from Third World countries?'; 'Of course he doesn't understand the notion of "otherness" as well as I do – how could he?'; 'As the only other minority classmate perhaps I can expect him to be sympathetic to my reading'? There are those questions that might surface, or be quietly suppressed, in professional relations between academic peers. 'Perhaps we should invite him to present a paper at this conference? ... to collaborate in this project? ... to join us in making this funding bid? ... to contribute to this edited volume? – we need more minority faces/voices'; 'Why didn't they ask me to contribute to that edited volume? – after all I am a Muslim/black/transsexual ...'; 'How can I show them how open-minded and radical I am despite being white, middle class male?'; 'Do they think they can climb academic ladders just because they belong to some minority or the other?'; 'Isn't it absurd of the personnel office to send me this diversity booklet?'; 'The question is, how can we register our awareness of diversity issues and respect for differences in our mission statement? ... in the aims and outcomes of programmes? ... in the prospectus? ... in conducting development courses for research supervisors?'; 'How should we take account of the multiculturalist bent of the ethics framework for research adopted by this university?'. There are also questions that crop up when students and researchers browse in libraries or bookshops, or flip through publisher's catalogues. 'Where might I find this book? ... under black writers/women's studies/Queer studies? Or might it be simply under "literary fiction"?'; 'Under which category can this monograph most advantageously be placed?'; 'Do I need to consult *all* these books and journals with the word "identity" in their titles?'; 'Perhaps I should throw "identity" or "marginality" into the title of my book? – it will come up often as a search term on Amazon.com then or on a Google search, won't it? – perhaps that will encourage such-and-such prestigious publisher to consider it for publication?'. Questions such as these lie transparently in media coverage of academic pursuits, in the *Times Higher Education Supplement* or *Chronicle of Higher Education*, for instance. Questions such as these have to be negotiated (with difficulty) when British or North American literary scholars attend academic events in African or Asian or South American countries.

Each of these questions may well be a perfectly necessary one when placed in its immediate context. These are all transient interrogatives which revolve specific situations in specific places, occupying the sphere of informal exchanges that constitute the everyday institutional life of literary studies. But when dislocated from their particularities and brought together (as above), these are also – and that is the point here – indicative of the habitual concerns of institutional literary studies now, and are recognizable as such. Indeed such questions are likely to be received as symptomatic of the institutional practice of the social sciences and humanities at large in academia. A systematic study and analysis of such questions, in their particularity and their general coherence, may convey the depth of the institutionalization of identity politics. Somewhere in the interstices of such questions and their locations lies a fuller realization of the entrenchment of the logic of embodiment than a study such as the present can convey.

It remains to be seen whether the reservations that have been raised here about social constructionist identity politics need to be refined in view of a deeper understanding of the everyday life of academic institutions, and of institutional practice in and with regard to the social and political world. It is possible that these reservations will dissolve through such sustained attention to the matter – either by registering facets of the developments outlined above which are not sufficiently registered yet, or by questioning the spreading of limits in open discussion and debate *through* such attention itself. I suspect the latter is likely to be an important part of addressing and overcoming those reservations. To a great extent the spreading of limits through the institutionalization of social constructionist identity politics, the pervasiveness of the logic of embodiment to encompass different identity-based political positions, the entrenchment of identity politics in disciplines of knowledge have occurred in the flow of practice and within contingent drives of conceptualization. These have come to be ensconced, with extraordinary expedition, through the heat of debates, discussions, doubts, and the need for immediate effects and actions over a few decades. These developments have also been normalized almost before they could be fully grasped by the speed with which they have been assimilated within the market and disposed for consumption. The unease and enthusiasm which have constantly attended these developments have themselves become marketable factors, markers of controversy or interest, and rapidly structured for transmission – capitalizing (with capitalist verve) on a politically and socially amenable environment. Perhaps an effort at retrospection and stocktaking (largely the enterprise of this study), a careful consideration of the nuances of disciplinary pursuits *apropos* identity politics, an attempt at reconsidering and reformulating ideas that now seem like foregone conclusions – a sure sign of institutionalization – will themselves act as a remedy for what appears to me amiss in the institutional entrenchment of social constructionist identity politics.

This can be hoped for because ultimately such an effort is most likely to cohere with the worldliness of intellectual work itself, attending to the dimensions of both intellectual work with regard to the world and intellectual work as of the world. Just as scholarly texts mediate worldly desires between academia and the socio-political environment that contains it, so the everyday life of academic institutions and disciplinary institutional practice is constantly and constitutively penetrated by the social and political world and *vice versa*. It is, I think, clear in this study that the whole development of social constructionist identity politics to its current institutionalized pre-eminence is the result of powerful worldly desires and awareness. Perhaps even closer and deeper engagement with such worldly desires will disengage social constructionist identity politics from its limitations and extend the politics of social constructionism beyond embodied identities.

Notes

1 Introduction: Prelude to Definitive Elaborations

1. This is characterized as a 'culture of critical discourse' which: '(1) is concerned to *justify* its assertions, but (2) whose *mode* of justification does not proceed by evoking authorities, and (3) prefers to elicit the voluntary consent of those addressed solely on the basis of arguments adduced' – Alvin Gouldner, *The Future of Intellectuals and the Rise of the New Class* (London: Macmillan, 1979), p. 28.

2 Identity-Based Political Positions

1. W.J.M. Mackenzie, *Political Identity* (Manchester: Manchester University Press, 1978).
2. Particularly in Jean-Paul Sartre, *Between Existentialism and Marxism*, trans. John Matthews (London: NLB, 1974), and also in his *Critique of Dialectical Reason*, Vol. 1: *Theory of Practical Ensembles*, trans. Alan Sheridan-Smith (London: NLB, 1976).
3. F.A. Hayek, *The Constitution of Liberty* (London: Routledge and Kegan Paul, 1960).
4. Robert Nozick, *Anarchy, State and Utopia* (Oxford: Basil Blackwell, 1974). Incidentally, Nozick discusses the individual identity question in the form given above in *Philosophical Explanations* (Oxford: Clarendon, 1981).
5. John Rawls, *A Theory of Justice* (Oxford: Oxford University Press, 1971); John Rawls, *Political Liberalism* (New York: Columbia University Press, 1993).
6. Derek Parfit, *Reasons and Persons* (Oxford: Clarendon, 1984), Chapters 14–15.
7. Kathleen Wallace, 'Autonomous "I" of an Intersectional Self', *The Journal of Speculative Philosophy* 17:3, 2003, 177.
8. Ibid., p. 187.
9. See Amin Maalouf, *On Identity*, trans. Barbara Bray (London: Harvill, 2000), particularly Chapters 1–2; Caryl Phillips, 'Necessary Journeys', *Guardian* (Review Section) 11 December 2004, pp. 4–6.
10. Eric Hobsbawm, 'Identity Politics and the Left', *New Left Review* 217, May/June 1996, p. 43.
11. Todd Gitlin, 'From Universality to Difference: Notes on the Fragmentation of the Idea of the Left', in Craig Calhoun (ed.), *Social Theory and the Politics of Identity* (Oxford: Blackwell, 1994), p. 169.
12. David Palumbo-Liu, 'Assumed Identities', *New Literary History* 31, 2000, p. 766.
13. Stuart Hall, 'Introduction: Who Needs "Identity"?', in Stuart Hall and Paul du Gay (eds), *Questions of Cultural Identity* (London: Sage, 1996), p. 4.
14. Kwame Anthony Appiah, *The Ethics of Identity* (Princeton: Princeton University Press, 2004), p. 23 and pp. 162–165.

15. Niklas Luhmann, 'The Individuality of the Individual: Historical Meanings and Contemporary Problems', *Essays in Self-Reference* (New York: Columbia University Press, 1990), pp. 118–119.
16. Norbert Elias, *The Society of Individuals*, trans. Edmund Jephcott (Oxford: Blackwell, 1991).
17. George Herbert Mead, *Mind, Self and Society* (Chicago: University of Chicago Press, 1934).
18. Marcel Mauss, 'A Category of the Human Mind: The Notion of Person, the Notion of "Self"', *Sociology and Psychology* (1950), trans. Ben Brewster (London: Routledge & Kegan Paul, 1979).
19. Erik Erikson, *Identity: Youth and Culture* (New York: Norton, 1968).
20. Kenneth R. Hoover, *A Politics of Identity: Liberation and the Natural Community* (Urbana: University of Illinois Press, 1975).
21. Peter du Preez, *The Politics of Identity: Ideology and the Human Image* (Oxford: Basil Blackwell, 1980), p. 50.
22. Henri Tajfel, *The Social Psychology of Minorities* (London: Minority Rights Group, 1978); Henri Tajfel, *Human Groups and Social Categories: Studies in Social Psychology* (Cambridge: Cambridge University Press, 1981). Henri Tajfel was probably the first to offer a definition of social identity from a social psychologist's perspective in 'La catégorisation socialé', in S. Moscovici (ed.), *Introduction à la Psychologie Sociale*, Vol. 1 (Paris: Larousse, 1972), pp. 272–302.
23. Best exemplified in the collection of papers, John J. Gumperz (ed.), *Language and Social Identity* (Cambridge: Cambridge University Press, 1982). In the introduction to this, Gumperz states: 'We customarily take gender, ethnicity, and class as given parameters and boundaries within which we create our own social identities. The study of language as interactional discourse demonstrates that these parameters are not constants that can be taken for granted but are communicatively produced' (p. 1).
24. It was broadcast as one in a series of ten programmes entitled *Multiracial Britain*.
25. Monique Wittig, 'The Mark of Gender', in Nancy K. Miller (ed.), *The Poetics of Gender* (New York: Columbia University Press, 1986), p. 67.
26. The identification of instrumentalist reason (sometimes taken as reason itself) as being rooted in Western Enlightenment and imperialism – at the expense of the kind of apprehension that a mythic consciousness allowed – is generally derived from Max Horkheimer and Theodor Adorno, *Dialectic of Enlightenment*, trans. John Cumming (London: Verso, 1979 [1st German publication 1947]).
27. Jürgen Habermas's attempts to come up with universal sociological formulations of communicative action and deliberative democracy, while largely confining his frame of scholarly reference and political engagement to Europe, has naturally raised occasional questions about the tacit Eurocentrism of his approach. See, for instance, Ilan Kapoor, 'Deliberative Democracy or Agonistic Pluralism? The Relevance of the Habermas-Mouffe Debate for Third World Politics', *Alternatives: Global, Local, Political* 27:4, October–December 2002, p. 477.
28. I have in mind the teleology of history that G.W.F. Hegel tried to flesh out in his lectures, collected as *The Philosophy of History*, trans. J. Sibree

(New York: Dover, 1956), where the propensity of cultures at different stages of development to move towards self-consciousness is argued, but is not extended to black Africans, for whom, Hegel feels, slavery is justified.

29. The distinction I have made here between *being marginalized* and *being threatened*, and the polarization of emancipative and protectionist politics with that terminology, is a deliberate and convenient move. These terms are used more loosely in research in this area. For example, in Xenia Chryssochoou, *Cultural Diversity: Its Social Psychology* (Malden, MA: Blackwell, 2004), a study primarily of the social psychology of migration, threat to identity is perceived both by the minority migrants and the majority that receives migrants.

30. Theodor W. Adorno, *The Jargon of Authenticity*, trans. Knut Tarnowski and Fredric Will (London: Routledge & Kegan Paul, 1973), pp. 13–14.

3 Embodying Identity-Based Political Positions

1. Stephan Fuchs, *Against Essentialism: A Theory of Culture and Society* (Cambridge, MA: Harvard University Press, 2001), p. 12.
2. Ibid., p. 13.
3. Ibid., p. 15.
4. Ibid., p. 15.
5. Karl Marx, 'Concerning Feuerbach' [1845] (better known by the title given by Engels, 'Theses on Feuerbach'), in *Marx: Early Writings*, trans. Rodney Livingstone and Gregory Benton (Harmondsworth: Penguin, 1975), p. 423.
6. Glenn Loury, *The Anatomy of Racial Inequality* (Cambridge, MA: Harvard University Press, 2002), pp. 157–158.
7. Paul C. Taylor, *Race: A Philosophical Introduction* (Cambridge: Polity, 2004), pp. 116–117.
8. Kenneth J. Gergen, *Social Construction in Context* (London: Sage, 2001), p. 170.
9. Linda Nicholson and Steve Seidman (eds), *Social Postmodernism: Beyond Identity Politics* (Cambridge: Cambridge University Press, 1995).
10. J.L. Austin, *How to Do Things With Words* (Oxford: Oxford University Press, 1962). For Austin, a *performative sentence*: 'indicates that the issuing of the utterance is the performing of an action – it is not normally thought of as just saying something' (pp. 6–7).
11. Richard Dyer, *The Culture of Queers* (London: Routledge, 2002), p. 3.
12. Jacques Derrida, *Of Grammatology*, trans. Gayatri Chakravorty Spivak (Baltimore: Johns Hopkins University Press, 1974), p. 22.
13. Michel Foucault, *Discipline and Punish: The Birth of the Prison*, trans. Alan Sheridan (London: Allen Lane, 1977).
14. Elias Canetti, *Crowds and Power*, trans. Carol Stewart (Harmondsworth: Penguin, 1973); José Ortega y Gasset, *Man and People*, trans. Willard R. Trask (London: George Allen & Unwin, 1959).
15. José Ortega y Gasset, *The Revolt of the Masses*, trans. Andrew Kerrigan (Notre Dame, Indiana: University of Notre Dame Press, 1965), p. 6.
16. Daphni Patai, 'The Struggle for Feminist Purity Threatens the Goals of Feminism', *Chronicle of Higher Education*, 5 February 1992, p. 1B – rpt.

In Barbara Ryan (ed.), *Identity Politics in the Women's Movement* (New York: New York University Press, 2001), p. 40.

17. Rosi Braidotti, *Metamorphoses: Toward a Materialist Theory of Becoming* (Cambridge: Polity, 2002), pp. 20–21.

18. Jamilah Ahmed, 'Reaching the Body: Future Directions', in Helen Thomas and Jamilah Ahmed (eds), *Cultural Bodies: Ethnography and Theory* (Malden, MA: Blackwell, 2004), p. 289.

19. Ibid., p. 286.

20. Stuart Hall, 'New Ethnicities', in David Morley and Kuan-Hsing Chen (eds), *Stuart Hall: Critical Dialogues in Cultural Studies* (London: Routledge, 1996), pp. 441–449.

4   Analogues and Equivalences

1. See Gayatri Chakravorty Spivak on the dangers of conflating the two meanings of 'represent' – represent-as-portrait in art, literature or philosophy (*darstellen*) and represent-as-proxy in politics (*vertreten*) – in 'Can the Subaltern Speak?' in Carey Nelson and Lawrence Greenberg (eds), *Marxism and the Interpretation of Culture* (Basingstoke: Macmillan, 1988), pp. 275–277.

2. Comparatively less, but not altogether overlooked. In fact 'analogy' is used precisely for the kind of identity politics I have in mind for this study, in Rita Felski, *Literature after Feminism* (Chicago: University of Chicago, 2003), p. 16.

3. Stokely Carmichael and Charles V. Hamilton, *Black Power: The Politics of Liberation in America* (New York: Random House, 1967), pp. 79–80.

4. See, for instance, Wilbur C. Rich (ed.) *The Politics of Minority Coalitions: Race, Ethnicity and Shared Uncertainties* (Westport, Connecticut: Praeger, 1996).

5. Bernice Johnson Reagon, 'Coalition Politics: Turning the Century', in Barbara Smith (ed.), *Home Girls* (New York: Kitchen Table Press, 1983), 356–357.

6. Shane Phelan, *Identity Politics: Lesbian Feminism and the Limits of Community* (Philadelphia: Temple University Press, 1989), p. 127.

7. See, for instance, Barbara Ryan (ed.), *Identity Politics in the Women's Movement* (New York: New York University Press, 2001). This interesting collection which raises many of the complexities and misgivings about essentialist feminist politics and the feminist politics of embodiment, ends with essays and extracts by Diane L. Fowlkes, Shane Phelan, and the editor, which seem to reach a consensus on continuing coalitional efforts.

8. Jerry Gafio Watts, 'Black and Coalition Politics: A Theoretical Reconceptualization', in Rich (ed.), *The Politics of Minority Coalitions*, p. 40.

9. Jacques Derrida, *Of Grammatology*, trans. Gayatri Chakravorty Spivak (Baltimore: Johns Hopkins University Press, 1974/1976), pp. 62–63.

10. Steven Seidman, *Difference Troubles: Queering Social Theory and Sexual Politics* (Cambridge: Cambridge University Press, 1997), p. 257.

11. Ibid., p. 258.

12. Both Morgenthau's and Berki's writings on political realism accept the need for a developed ethical perspective without adhering to any absolute moral norms. See, Hans J. Morgenthau, *Politics among Nations: The Struggle for Power and Peace* (New York: Alfred A. Knopf, 1954), Chapter 1; and R.N. Berki, *On Political Realism* (London: Dent, 1981).

13. Ernesto Laclau, *Emancipation(s)* (London: Verso, 1996), p. 35.
14. See notes 16 and 17.
15. Michel de Certeau, *Culture in the Plural*, trans. Om Conley (Minneapolis: University of Minnesota Press, 1997), pp. 71–72.
16. John Rawls, *Theory of Justice* (Oxford: Oxford University Press, 1971), p. 375.
17. John Rawls, *Political Liberalism* (New York: Columbia University Press, 1993), p. 12.
18. Ibid., p. 36.
19. Ibid., Lecture 4.
20. John Rawls, *The Law of Peoples with 'The Idea of Public Reason Revisited'* (Cambridge, MA: Harvard University Press, 1999).
21. See Jürgen Habermas, 'Popular Sovereignty as Procedure', in James Bohman and William Rehg (eds), *Deliberative Democracy: Essays on Reason and Politics* (Cambridge, MA: MIT Press, 1997); Jürgen Habermas, 'Three Models of Democracy', in *The Inclusion of the Other: Studies in Political Theory*, trans. Ciaran Cronin (Cambridge: Polity, 1998/1st pub. in German 1996); Jürgen Habermas, 'The Postnational Constellation and the Future of Democracy', *The Postnational Constellation: Political Essays*, trans. Max Pensky (Cambridge: Polity, 2001).
22. David Held and Anthony McGrew, 'Globalization and the Liberal Democratic State', in Yoshikazu Sakamoto (ed.), *Global Transformation: Challenges to the State System* (Tokyo and New York: United Nations University Press, 1994); David Held, 'Democracy: From City States to a Cosmopolitan Order?' in David Held (ed.), *Prospects for Democracy: North South East West* (Cambridge: Polity, 1993); David Held, 'Democracy and the New International Order', in Daniele Archibugi and David Held (eds), *Cosmopolitan Democracy: An Agenda for a New World Order* (Cambridge: Polity, 1995); David Held and Anthony McGrew, *Globalization/Anti-Globalization* (Cambridge: Polity, 2002); David Held, *Global Covenant: The Social Democratic Consensus to the Washington Consensus* (Cambridge: Polity, 2004).
23. Davina Cooper, *Challenging Diversity: Rethinking Equality and the Value of Difference* (Cambridge: Cambridge University Press, 2004), p. 7.
24. Ibid., p. 8.
25. Kenneth J. Gergen, *Social Construction in Practice* (London: Sage, 2001), p. 175.
26. Ibid., p. 178.
27. Ibid., pp. 181–182.
28. The papers in Mario Diani and Doug McAdam (eds), *Social Movements and Networks: Relational Approaches to Collective Action* (Oxford: Oxford University Press, 2003) are good examples of such efforts. In particular Ann Mische's contribution, 'Cross-talk in Movements: Reconceiving the Culture-Network Link', pp. 258–280, presents exactly the kind of strategic formulations I have in mind here.
29. R.D. Grillo, *Pluralism and the Politics of Difference: State, Culture, and Ethnicity in Comparative Perspective* (Oxford: Clarendon, 1998).
30. Discussed in Michael Walzer, *On Toleration* (New Haven: Yale University Press, 1997); Anna E. Galeotti, *Toleration as Recognition* (Cambridge: Cambridge University Press, 2002).
31. Usefully discussed from various perspectives in Paul Berman (ed.), *Debating P.C.* (New York: Dell, 1992).

32. On this see Ilan Kapoor, 'Deliberative Democracy or Agonistic Pluralism? The Relevance of the Habermas–Mouffe Debate for Third World Politics', *Alternatives: Global, Local, Political* 27:4, October–December 2002, p. 477.

33. The argument against deep individualism in modern culture is made by Charles Taylor in *The Ethics of Authenticity* (Cambridge, MA: Harvard University Press, 1991). Interestingly he presents this as an excess of individualism in apprehending identity: 'I can define my identity only against the background of things that matter. But to bracket out history, nature, society, the demands of solidarity, everything but what I find in myself, would be to eliminate all candidates for what matters' (p. 40).

34. Charles Taylor, 'The Politics of Recognition', in Charles Taylor with Amy Gutmann (ed.), *Multiculturalism: Examining the Politics of Recognition* (Princeton: Princeton University Press, 1994), p. 71.

35. Jürgen Habermas, 'Struggles for Recognition in the Democratic Constitutional State', trans. Shierry Weber Nicholsen, in ibid., p. 119.

36. Amy Gutmann, *Identity in Democracy* (Princeton: Princeton University Press, 2003).

37. See, for instance, Steve Fenton, *Ethnicity* (Cambridge: Polity, 2003), or Miri Song, *Choosing Ethnic Identity* (Cambridge: Polity, 2003).

38. Stuart Hall, 'New Ethnicities', in David Morley and Kuan-Hsing Chen (eds), *Stuart Hall: Critical Dialogues in Cultural Studies* (London: Routledge, 1996), p. 447.

39. I have in mind: Alain Touraine's *The Voice and the Eye: An Analysis of Social Movements*, trans. Alan Duff (Cambridge: Cambridge University Press, 1981), followed soon after by Alain Touraine et al., *Solidarity: The Analysis of a Social Movement, Poland 1980–1981*, trans. David Denby (Cambridge: Cambridge University Press, 1983) and Alain Touraine, Michel Wieviorka, and François Dubet, *The Workers' Movement*, trans. Ian Patterson (Cambridge: Cambridge University Press and Paris: Editions de la Maison des Sciences de l'Homme, 1987 [first published 1984]); and Jürgen Habermas's 'New Social Movements', *Telos* 49, Fall 1981, pp. 33–37, followed soon after by his *The Theory of Communicative Action Vol 1: Reason and the Rationalization of Society*, trans. Thomas McCarthy (Cambridge: Polity, 1984) and *The Theory of Communicative Action Vol. 2: Lifeworld and System: A Critique of Functionalist Reason*, trans. Thomas McCarthy (Cambridge: Polity, 1987). By the time the special edition of *Social Research* on Social Movements was published, Jean L. Cohen (guest ed.), 52:4, Winter 1985, with contributions by Alain Touraine, Charles Tilly, Alberto Melucci, Claus Offe, and Klaus Eder, the early discourse of new social movements, not complicit with identity politics, has reached a peak.

40. Alain Touraine, Michel Wieviorka, and François Dubet, *The Workers' Movement* (1987), p. 278.

41. Associated with the publication of such works as Régis Debray, *Teachers, Writers, Celebrities: The Intellectuals of Modern France*, trans. David Macey (London: New Left Books, 1981); Alvin W. Gouldner, *The Future of Intellectuals and the Rise of the New Class* (London: Macmillan, 1979); Pierre Bourdieu, *Homo Academicus*, trans. Peter Collier (Cambridge: Polity, 1988 [first published 1984]).

42. Chantal Mouffe, 'Radical Democracy or Liberal Democracy', in David Trend (ed.) *Radical Democracy: Identity, Citizenship, and the State* (New York: Routledge, 1996), p. 24.

43. Ernesto Laclau and Chantal Mouffe, *Hegemony and Socialist Strategy: Towards a Radical Democratic Politics* (London: Verso, 1985).

44. Chantal Mouffe, 'Democratic Citizenship and Political Community', *The Return of the Political* (London: Verso, 1993), p. 70.

45. Mouffe, 'Radical Democracy: Modern or Postmodern?', ibid., p. 12.

46. Indicative studies include: Margaret E. Keck and Kathryn Sikkink, *Activists Beyond Borders* (Ithaca, NY: Cornell University Press, 1998); Veronika Bennholdt-Thomsen, Nick Fraaclas, and Claudia Von Werlhof (eds), *There is an Alternative* (London: Zed, 2001); Amory Starr, *Naming the Enemy* (London: Zed, 2000); Tim Jordan, *Activism! Direct Action, Hacktivism and the Future of Society* (London: Reaktion Books, 2002); John Holloway, *Change the World Without Taking Power* (London: Pluto, 2002); William F. Fisher and Thomas Pooniah (eds), *Another World is Possible* (London: Zed, 2003); *We are Everywhere* (London: Verso, 2004); David Graeber, 'The New Anarchists' (in the 'A Movement of Movements' series, 5), *New Left Review* Vol. 13, Jan/Feb 2002, pp. 61–74.

47. I use *implicature* and *relevance* with the sense of precision that analytical philosophers like Paul Grice and Dan Sperber/Deirdre Wilson give them, and with the awareness that the distance I have assumed in this exposition of clusters of terms is not unlike that of an analytical philosophical perspective. But that is where the resemblance ends – I have no desire here to pull the consideration of postcolonialism and postmodernism, or identity politics for that matter, into the ahistorical environment of cognitive linguistics, and every intention of seeing these as firmly grounded in the social, historical, political, and material conditions that this study is interested in.

48. See, Paul Lamy, 'The Globalization of American Sociology: Excellence or Imperialism?', *American Sociologist* 11:2, May 1976, pp. 104–113; Fredrick H. Goreau, 'The Multinational Version of Social Sciences', *International Social Science Journal* 35:2, May 1983, pp. 379–390; Walter Parker, 'Globalizing the Social Studies Curriculum', *Educational Leadership* 42:2, October 1984, p. 92.

49. In tune with the ringing appeal made by Jay Van Andel, co-founder of the Amway Corp. and then Chairman of the Board of the US Chamber of Commerce, in February 1980, 'The Markets of the World: New Economic Frontiers', *Vital Speeches of the Day* 46:11, 15 March 1980, pp. 338–342.

50. See, Raymond F. Hopkins, 'Global Management Networks: The Internationalization of Domestic Bureaucracies', *International Social Science Journal* 30:1, February 1978, pp. 31–46; and particularly the influential article, Theodore Levitt, 'The Globalization of Markets', *Harvard Business Review* 61:3, May–June 1983, pp. 92–102.

51. Robert J.C. Young, *Postcolonialism: An Historical Introduction* (Oxford: Blackwell, 2001), p. 11.

52. Graham Huggan, *The Postcolonial Exotic: Marketing the Margins* (London: Routledge, 2001), pp. 4–8. The parenthetical quotations are from p. 6.

53. Jean-François Lyotard, 'Answering the Question: What is Postmodernism?', trans. Régis Durand, in Lyotard, *The Postmodern Condition: A Report on*

Knowledge, trans. Geoff Bennington and Brian Massumi (Manchester: Manchester University Press, 1984), p. 81.

54. David Held and Anthony McGrew, *Globalization/Anti-Globalization* (Cambridge: Polity, 2002), p. 131.

55. Sara Suleri, 'Woman Skin Deep: Feminism and the Postcolonial Condition', in Kwame Anthony Appiah and Henry Louis Gates Jr. (eds), *Identities* (Chicago: University of Chicago Press, 1995), pp. 133–146.

56. Aijaz Ahmad, *In Theory: Classes, Nations, Literatures* (London: Verso, 1992).

5 Identity Politics at Work

1. Peter Berger and Thomas Luckmann, *The Social Construction of Reality: A Treatise in the Sociology of Knowledge* (Harmondsworth: Penguin, 1966), p. 72.

2. Max Weber, *Economy and Society*, Vol. 1 (eds) Guenther Roth and Claus Wittich (Berkeley: University of California Press, 1978), p. 48.

3. Volume 31:4, Special issue *Is There Life after Identity Politics*, 2000, of the journal *New Literary History* presents some useful historicizing efforts proclaimedly from within the new left (and with a view to resisting any closure of the new left's association with identity politics), notably: Grant Farred, 'Endgame Identity?: Mapping the New Left Roots of Identity Politics', 627–648; and David Palumbo-Liu, 'Assumed Identities', 765–780. Also of interest in the context of this study is Eric Lott, 'After Identity Politics: The Return of Universalism', 665–678, which takes not quite the reverse view (as the title might suggest) but a grudging alternative of recommending a new 'ventilat[ion of] the willed universalisms of both the social-democratic *and* Leninist variety' (p. 678). All this amounts to is a clearer apprehension of the distinction made here between social constructionist identity politics and identity-based political positions than is usual, and a recognition (perhaps acceptance) of the universalism implicit in the former and its akinness to other leftwing 'willed universalisms'.

4. Andrei S. Markovits, 'The European and American Left since 1945', *Dissent* 52:1, Winter 2005.

5. Ibid., p. 10.

6. 'The Kansas *Telos* Conference (December 4–6, 1980)' – Special Symposium section, *Telos* no. 74, Winter 1980–1981, pp. 81–111.

7. Jonathan Rutherford (ed.), *Identity: Community, Culture, Difference* (London: Lawrence & Wishart, 1990).

8. Jonathan Rutherford, 'A Place Called Home: Identity and the Cultural Politics of Difference', ibid., p.10.

9. 'Forum: Liberalism and the Left: Rethinking the Relationship', *Radical History Review* 71, Spring 1998, pp. 3–51.

10. Amber Hollibaugh, 'Liberalism and the Left: An Activist's Perspective', ibid., p. 30.

11. Todd Gitlin, 'From Universality to Difference: Notes on the Fragmentation of the Idea of the Left', in Craig Calhoun (ed.), *Social Theory and the Politics of Identity* (Oxford: Blackwell, 1994), p. 169.

12. Robert Nesbit, 'The Decline and Fall of Social Class', *Pacific Sociological Review* 2, 1959, pp. 11–17.

13. Debate: 'Are Social Classes Dying?', Issue of *International Sociology* 8:3, September 1993.
14. Jan Pakulski, 'The Dying of Class or of Marxist Class Theory?', ibid., pp. 279–292.
15. Jan Pakulsi and Malcolm Waters, *The Death of Class* (London: Sage, 1995).
16. 'Symposium on Class', *Theory and Society* 25:5, 1996.
17. Ernest Mandel, *Late Capitalism*, trans. Joris de Bres (London: Verso, 1972/1975).
18. Henri Lefebvre, *The Survival of Capitalism: Reproduction and the Relations of Production*, trans. Frank Bryant (London: Allison and Busby, 1973/1976).
19. Michel Foucault, *'Society Must be Defended': Lectures at the College de France 1975–76*, trans. David Macey (London: Allen Lane, 1997/2003) – mainly in the first lecture.
20. Herbert Marcuse's *One-Dimensional Man* (London: Sphere, 1964), p. 13, confessedly vacillated between the ability of industrialized capitalism to contain all qualitative changes into its one-dimensionality, and the existence of forces that could destroy it by refusing to conform. The attribution of *one*-dimensionality that industrial capitalism was amenable to is, however, conquered by the containment of multidimensionality (what I think identity politics is) in late capitalism.
21. This is evidenced in relation to focused contexts in, for instance: Christopher J. Williams, 'In Defence of Materialism: A Critique of Afrocentric Ontology', *Race and Class* 47:1, July–September 2005, 35–48; Juanita Elias, 'Stitching-Up the Labour Market', *International Feminist Journal of Politics* 7:1, March 2005, 90–111; John Hutnyk, 'Hybridity', *Ethnic and Racial Studies* 28:1, January 2005, 79–102; and most of the essays in Richard Harvey Brown (ed.) *The Politics of Selfhood: Bodies and Identities in Global Capitalism* (Minneapolis: University of Minnesota press, 2003). Within a broader canvas the place of identity politics in the recent history of capitalism is noted in: Ingolfur Blühdorn, 'Self-Experience in the Theme Park of Radical Action? Social Movements and Political Articulation in the Late-Modern Condition', *European Journal of Social Theory* 9:1, February 2006, 23–42; Adam D. Morton, 'The Grimly Comic Riddle of IPE: Where is the Class Struggle?' *Politics* 26:9, February 2006, 62–72; David Harvey, *A Brief History of Neoliberalism* (Oxford: Oxford University Press, 2003); David Harvey, *The New Imperialism* (Oxford: Oxford University Press, 2003); Perry Anderson, *Spectrum: From Right to Left in the World of Ideas* (London: Verso, 2003); Perry Anderson, *The Origin of Postmodernity* (London: Verso, 1998).
22. Stuart Hall, *The Hard Road to Renewal: Thatcherism and the Crisis of the Left* (London: Verso, 1988); Stuart Hall, 'The Toad in the Garden: Thatcherism among the Theorists', in C. Nelson and L. Grossberg (eds), *Marxism and the Interpretation of Culture* (Basingstoke: Macmillan, 1988).
23. Intro. Willy Brandt, *North South: A Programme for Survival: The Report of the Independent Commission on International Development Issues under the Chairmanship of Willy Brandt* (London: Pan, 1980), p. 219.
24. Joseph Stiglitz, *Globalization and its Discontents* (Harmondsworth: Penguin, 2002).
25. Fredric Jameson, *Postmodernism, or, The Cultural Logic of Late Capitalism* (London: Verso, 1991).

26. Jürgen Habermas, 'Popular Sovereignty as Procedure' in James Bohman and William Rehg (eds), *Deliberative Democracy: Essays on Reason and Politics* (Cambridge, MA: MIT Press, 1997); Jürgen Habermas, 'Three Models of Democracy' in *The Inclusion of the Other: Studies in Political Theory*, trans. Ciaran Cronin (Cambridge: Polity, 1998/1st pub. in German 1996). These points are also covered in Habermas's *Between Facts and Norms: Contributions to a Discourse Theory of Law and Democracy*, trans. William Rehg (Cambridge, MA: MIT Press, 1996). Joshua Cohen, 'Deliberation and Democratic Legitimacy', in Bohman and Rehg (eds), *Deliberative Democracy*; Joshua Cohen, 'Democracy and Liberty' in Jon Elster (ed.), *Deliberative Democracy* (Cambridge: Cambridge University Press, 1998).

6   Theory, Institutional Matters, Identity Politics

1. Gerald Graff, *Professing Literature: An Institutional History* (Chicago: University of Chicago Press, 1987), pp. 249–250.
2. Gerald Graff, *Literature Against Itself: Literary Ideas in Modern Society* (Chicago: University of Chicago Press, 1979).
3. Terry Eagleton, *After Theory* (London: Allen Lane, 2003), p. 29.
4. Gerald Graff, *Literature Against Itself*, p. 25.
5. Gerald Graff, 'The Future of Theory in the Teaching of Literature', in Ralph Cohen (ed.) *The Future of Literary Theory* (New York: Routledge, 1989), p. 266.
6. Stanley Fish, *Professional Correctness: Literary Studies and Political Change* (Oxford: Clarendon, 1995), p. 48.
7. Paul de Man, 'The Resistance to Theory', in Paul de Man, *The Resistance to Theory* (Manchester: Manchester University Press, 1986), pp. 4–5.
8. Ibid., p. 7.
9. Ibid., p. 8.
10. Paul de Man, 'The Return to Philology', in de Man, *The Resistance to Theory*, p. 24.
11. Paul de Man, *Blindness and Insight: Essays in the Rhetoric of Contemporary Criticism* (New York: Oxford University Press, 1971).
12. Geoffrey H. Hartman, *Criticism in the Wilderness: The Study of Literature Today* (New Haven: Yale University Press, 1980), p. 41.
13. Ibid., p. 85.
14. Frank Lentricchia, *Criticism and Social Change* (Chicago: University of Chicago Press, 1983), p. 13.
15. Susan Horton, 'The Institution of Literature and the Cultural Community', in Joseph Natoli (ed.), *Literary Theory's Future(s)* (Urbana: University of Illinois Press, 1989), p. 277.
16. Ralph Cohen, 'Introduction', in Frank Cohen (ed.) *The Future of Literary Theory*, p. vii.
17. The irony is tacitly brought out in the survey of the 'rhetorical turn', and the political aspirations that were inserted into it, given by Michael Bernard-Donals, *The Practice of Theory: Rhetoric, Knowledge, and Pedagogy in the Academy* (Cambridge: Cambridge University Press, 1998).
18. Edward Said, 'Introduction: Secular Criticism', in Edward Said, *The World, the Text, and the Critic* (London: Vintage, 1983), p. 3.

19. Edward Said, 'Religious Criticism', ibid., p. 292.
20. Hartman, *Criticism in the Wilderness*, p. 111.
21. Edward Said, 'American "Left" Literary Criticism', *The World, the Text, and the Critic*, p. 162.
22. Edward Said, 'Traveling Theory', ibid., p. 246.
23. Edward Said, *Representations of the Intellectual: The 1993 Reith Lectures* (London: Vintage, 1994).
24. Edward Said, *Orientalism* (London: Routledge and Kegan Paul, 1978); Edward Said, *The Question of Palestine* (London: Routledge and Kegan Paul, 1980).
25. Edward Said, 'Traveling Theory Reconsidered', *Reflections on Exile* (Cambridge, MA: Harvard University Press, 2000), pp. 438–439.
26. Hartman, *Criticism in the Wilderness*, p. 9.
27. Lentricchia, *Criticism and Social Change*, p. 13.
28. Ibid., p. 7.
29. Ralph Cohen, 'Introduction', *The Future of Literary Theory*, p. x.
30. Terry Eagleton, *The Significance of Theory* (Oxford: Basil Blackwell, 1990), p. 26.
31. G.V. Plekhanov, *Art and Social Life.* (London: Lawrence and Wishart, 1953).
32. Graff, *Literature against Itself*, p. 26.
33. Eugene Goodheart, *The Skeptic Disposition in Contemporary Criticism* (Princeton: Princeton University Press, 1984), p. 175.
34. William E. Cain, *The Crisis in Criticism: Theory, Literature and Reform in English Studies* (Baltimore: Johns Hopkins University Press, 1984), p. xiv.
35. Howard Felperin, *Beyond Deconstruction: The Uses and Abuses of Literary Theory* (Oxford: Clarendon, 1985), p. 214.
36. Art Berman, *From the New Criticism to Deconstruction: The Reception of Structuralism and Post-Structuralism* (Urbana: University of Illinois Press, 1988), p. 302.
37. Cohen, 'Introduction', *The Future of Literary Theory*, p. x.
38. Denis Donoghue, *The Pure Good of Theory* (Oxford: Blackwell, 1992), p. 47.
39. Catherine Belsey, *Critical Practice* (London: Methuen, 1980), p. 129.
40. Gayatri Chakravorty Spivak, 'Reading the World: Literary Studies in the Eighties' (1985), in Gayatri Chakravorty Spivak, *In Other Worlds: Essays in Cultural Politics* (New York: Methuen, 1987), p. 100.
41. Lentricchia, *Criticism and Social Change*, p. 13.
42. J. Hillis Miller, *The Ethics of Reading: Kant, de Man, Eliot, Trollope, James, and Benjamin* (New York: Columbia University Press, 1987), p. 45.
43. J. Hillis Miller, 'The Function of Literary Theory at the Present Time', in Cohen (ed.), *The Future of Literary Theory*, p. 103.
44. Ibid., p. 110.
45. J. Hillis Miller, *On Literature* (London: Routledge, 2002), p. 1.
46. Fish, *Professional Correctness*, pp. 44–45.
47. Peter Davison, Rolf Meyersohn, and Edward Shils (eds), *Literary Taste, Culture and Mass Communications* (Cambridge: Chadwyck-Healey/Teaneck NJ: Somerset House, 1978) – in 14 volumes.
48. Anthony Easthope, *Literary into Cultural Studies* (London: Routledge, 1991), p. 180.
49. Belsey, *Critical Practice*, p. 144.
50. Jonathan Culler, *The Pursuit of Signs: Semiotics, Literature, Deconstruction* (London: Routledge and Kegan Paul, 1981), p. 221.

51. Cain, *The Crisis in Criticism*, p. 263.
52. Joseph Natoli, 'Prefacing *Future*(s)/Mediating on One Future', in Natoli (ed.), *Literary Theory's Future(s)*, p. 2.
53. Graff, 'The Future of Theory in the Teaching of Literature', in Cohen (ed.) *The Future of Literary Theory*, p. 266.
54. Christopher Norris, *Deconstruction and the Interests of Theory* (London: Pinter, 1988), p. 14.
55. Patrick Parrinder, *The Failure of Theory: Essays in Criticism and Contemporary Fiction* (Brighton: Harvester, 1987), p. 11.
56. Felperin, *Beyond Decosntruction*, p. 28.
57. Jacques Derrida, 'Mochlos: or, the Conflict of Faculties' (1980), in Richard Rand (ed.), *Logomachia: The Conflict of Faculties* (Lincoln: University of Nebraska Press, 1992), pp. 1–34.
58. Fredric Jameson, 'Periodizing the Sixties' (1984), in Fredric Jameson, *The Ideologies of Theory: Essays 1971–1986* (London: Routledge, 1988), pp. 178–208.
59 Aijaz Ahmad, *In Theory: Nations, Classes, Nations, Literatures* (London: Verso, 1992).
60. Wlad Godzich, 'Introduction', *The Culture of Literacy* (Cambridge, MA: Harvard University Press, 1994), pp. 1–35.
61. US National Association of Scholars (NAS), *Losing the Big Picture: The Fragmentation of the English Major since 1964* (Princeton: NAS, 2000).
62. For example, in Nicholas Trendell, 'Post-Theory', *The Critical Decade: Culture in Crisis* (London: Carcanet, 1993).
63. Thomas Docherty, *After Theory* (London: Routledge, 1990), p. 1.
64. Paul A. Bové, *In the Wake of Theory* (Hanover: Wesleyan University Press, 1992), p. 26.
65. Docherty, *After Theory*, p. 213.
66. Bové, *In the Wake of Theory*, p. 47.
67. Donoghue, *The Pure Good of Theory*, pp. 47–48.
68. Ibid., p. 49.
69. Denis Donoghue, *The Practice of Reading* (New Haven: Yale University Press, 1998), p. 100.
70. Fish, *Professional Correctness*, pp. 85–86.
71. John M. Ellis, *Literature Lost: Social Agendas and the Corruption of the Humanities* (New Haven: Yale University Press, 1997).
72. Valentine Cunningham, *Reading after Theory* (Oxford: Blackwell, 2002), p. 42.
73. Ibid., pp. 148–149.
74. David Bordwell and Noël Carroll, *Post-Theory: Reconstructing Film Studies* (Madison: University of Wisconsin Press, 1996); Martin McQuillan, *Post-Theory* (Edinburgh: Edinburgh University Press, 1999); Judith Butler, John Guillory, Kendall Thomas (eds), *What's Left of Theory?: New Work in the Politics of Literary Theory* (New York: Routledge, 2000); Eduard Strauch, *Beyond Literary Theory* (Lanham: University Press of America, 2001); Terry Eagleton, *After Theory* (London: John Allen, 2003); Michael Payne and John Schad (eds), *Life after Theory* (London: Continuum, 2003); Ivan Callus and Stefan Herbrechter, *Post-Theory, Culture, Criticism* (Amsterdam: Rodopi, 2004); Gavin Butt (ed.), *After Criticism* (Oxford: Blackwell, 2004); Vincent Leitch and Jeffrey Williams, *After Theory* (London: Routledge, 2005).
75. Terry Eagleton, *After Theory*, p. 12.

76. Ibid., p. 49.

77. Richard Ohmann, *English in America: A Radical View of the Profession* (New York: Oxford University Press, 1976), p. 303.

78. Robert Scholes, *The Rise and Fall of English: Reconstructing English as a Discipline* (New Haven: Yale University Press, 1998), p. 120.

79. Robert Scholes, *Textual Power: Literary Theory and the Teaching of English* (New Haven: Yale University Press, 1985), p. 16.

80. D.J. Palmer, *The Rise of English Studies* (London: Oxford University Press, 1965), pp. 39–40.

81. Chris Baldick, *The Social Mission of English Criticism, 1848–1932* (Oxford: Clarendon, 1983), p. 61.

82. Brian Doyle, *English and Englishness* (London: Routledge, 1989).

83. Gauri Vishwanathan, *Masks of Conquest: Literary Study and British Rule in India* (London: Faber and Faber, 1989).

84. Svati Joshi (ed.), *Rethinking English: Essays in Literature, Language, History* (New Delhi: Trianka, 1991); Rajeshwari Sunder Rajan (ed.), *The Lie of the Land* (Delhi: Oxford University Press, 1992); and Harish Trivedi, *Colonial Transactions* (Calcutta: Papyrus, 1993).

85. John Dixon, *A Schooling in 'English'* (Buckingham: Open University Press, 1991).

86. Robert Crawford, *Devolving English Literature* (Oxford: Clarendon, 1992), p. 11.

87. David Johnson, *Shakespeare and South Africa* (Oxford: Clarendon, 1996).

88. Josephine Guy and Ian Small, *Politics and Value in English Studies: A Discipline in Crisis?* (Cambridge: Cambridge University Press, 1993).

89. Patrick Cohn Hogan, *The Politics of Interpretation: Ideology, Professionalism, and the Study of Literature* (New York: Oxford University Press, 1990); Carl Woodring, *Literature: An Embattled Profession* (New York: Columbia University Press, 1990); Harold Fromm, *Academic Capitalism and Literary Value* (Athens, GA: University of Georgia Press, 1991); Susan Gubar and Jonathan Kamholtz (eds), *English Inside and Out: The Places of Literary Criticism* (New York: Routledge, 1993); Robert Heilman, *The Professor and the Profession* (Columbia: University of Mississippi Press, 1999); Donald Hall (ed.), *Professions: Conversations on the Future of Literary and Cultural Studies* (Urbana: University of Illinois Press, 2001); Jeffrey J. Williams (ed.), *The Institution of Literature* (Albany: State University of New York Press, 2002).

90. Tilottama Rajan, 'In the Wake of Cultural Studies: Globalization, Theory, and the University', *Diacritics* 31:1, Fall 2001, p. 68.

91. Ibid., p. 77.

7   Self-Announcements and Institutional Realignments

1. Steven Lynn, *Texts and Contexts: Writing about Literature with Critical Theory* (New York: Harper Collins, 1994), p. xiv.

2. Raman Selden, *A Reader's Guide to Contemporary Literary Theory* (Brighton: Harvester, 1985), p. 3. In Eagleton's *Literary Theory: An Introduction* (Oxford: Blackwell, 1983), at the end of Chapter 2, 'Phenomenology, Hermeneutics, Reception Theory', appears the following observation: 'Most of us recognize that no reading is innocent or without presuppositions. But fewer people pursue the full implications of this readerly guilt' (p. 89). What in Eagleton

is an observation relevant to certain critical theoretical approaches is for Selden a general statement about the field of literary theory as a whole.

3. This is charted particularly in linguistic analysis of academic writing, as in books and papers by Ken Hyland: *Hedging in Scientific Research Articles* (Amsterdam: John Benjamins, 1998); *Disciplinary Discourses: Social Interactions in Academic Writing* (Harlow: Pearson, 2000); 'Self-Citation and Self-Reference: Credibility and Promotion in Academic Publication', *Journal of the American Society for Information Science and Technology* 54:3, 2003, 251–291; 'What Do They Mean? Questions in Academic Writing', *Text* 22:4, 2002, 529–558; 'Options of Identity in Academic Writing', *ELT Journal* 56:4, October 2002, 35–43; 'Bumping into the Reader: Addressee Features in Academic Articles', *Written Communication* 18:4, October 2001, 549–575. Also relevant here are such analysis of student academic writing as: Roz Ivanic, *Writing and Identity: The Discoursal Construction of Identity in Academic Writing* (Amsterdam: John Benjamin, 1997), and in most of the essays in Mary R. Lea and Barry Stierer (eds), *Student Writing in Higher Education* (Buckingham: Open University Press and The Society for Research in Higher Education, 2000).

4. The phrase 'academic tribes and territories' is a reference to Tony Becher and Paul R. Trowler, *Academic Tribes and Territories* (Second Edition – First Edition 1989) (Buckingham; Open University Press and The Society for Research into Higher Education, 2001). Other well-known references here: Pierre Bourdieu, Jean-Claude Passeron, Monique de Saint Martin, *Academic Discourse: Linguistic Misunderstanding and Professorial Power* (1965), trans. Richard Teese (Cambridge: Polity, 1994); Pierre Bourdieu, *Homo Academicus*, trans. Peter Collier (Cambridge: Polity, 1988 [Fr. edn, 1984]); Marjorie Garber, *Academic Instincts* (Princeton: Princeton University Press, 2001).

5. Peter Berger and Thomas Luckmann, *The Social Construction of Reality: A Treatise in the Sociology of Knowledge* (Harmondsworth: Penguin, 1966), p. 72.

6. Jean Michel Rabaté, *The Future of Theory* (Oxford: Blackwell, 2002), p. 140.

7. Ibid.

8. Mary Louise Pratt, *Imperial Eyes: Travel Writing and Transculturation* (London: Routledge, 1992), p. 7.

9. James Buzard, 'On Auto-Ethnographic Authority', *Yale Journal of Criticism* 16:1, 2003, 61–91.

10. Clifford Geertz, 'The Way We Think Now: Toward an Ethnography of Modern Thought', *Local Knowledge* (London: Fontana, 1983), p. 155.

11. In this context, there is a relevant essay that is worthy of mention: Richard van Oort, 'The Critics as Ethnogapher', *New Literary History* 35:4, Autumn 2004, 621–661. This deals with the sympathy that literary scholars with an interest in charting and analysing 'otherness' feel for Clifford Geertz's formulations. Van Oort pays particular attention to Stephen Greenblatt's references to Geertz, and makes that the occasion for a discernment of deep epistemological assumptions that are shared by ethnography and literary studies. The essay also presents a sceptical analysis of the sentiments expressed in the passage from Geertz quoted here.

12. Ibid., p. 156.

13. Terry Castle, *Clarissa's Ciphers: Meaning and Disruption in Richardson's 'Clarissa'* (Ithaca: Cornell University Press, 1982); Terry Castle, *Masquerade*

and Civilization: The Carnivalesque in Eighteenth-Century English Culture and Fiction (Stanford, CA: Stanford University Press, 1986).

14. Terry Castle, *The Apparitional Lesbian: Female Homosexuality and Modern Culture* (New York: Columbia University Press, 1993), pp. 3–4.
15. Ibid., p. 4.
16. Ibid., p. 28.
17. Ibid., pp. 30–31.
18. Ibid., p. 34.
19. Jacques Derrida, *Specters of Marx; The State of the Debt, the Work of Mourning, and the New International*, trans. Peggy Kamuf (New York: Routledge, 1994).
20. Shoshanna Felman, *What Does a Woman Want? Reading and Sexual Difference* (Baltimore: Johns Hopkins University Press, 1993), p. 3.
21. Ibid., p. 10.
22. Ibid., pp. 12–13.
23. Ibid., p. 14.
24. Gregory Woods, *A History of Gay Literature: The Male Tradition* (New Haven: Yale University Press, 1998), p. 3.
25. Ibid., p. 10.
26. Ibid., p. 11.
27. 'Social communication [...] arises out of contingency [...], not out of the common situation or out of the conventions that join both partners together. The situation and conventions regulate the manner in which gaps are filled, but the gaps in turn arise out of contingency and inexperienceability and, consequently, function as a basic inducement to communication. Similarly, it is the gaps, the fundamental symmetry between text and reader, that give rise to communication in the reading process; the lack of a common situation and a common frame of reference corresponds to the contingency and the "no-thing" which brings about the interaction between persons. Asymmetry, contingency, the "no-thing" – these are all different forms of an indeterminate, constitutive blank which underlies all processes of interaction. [...] Balance can only be attained if the gaps are filled, and so the constitutive blank is continually bombarded with projections.' – Wolfgang Iser, *The Act of Reading: A Theory of Aesthetic Response* (Baltimore: Johns Hopkins University Press, 1978), pp. 166–167.
28. Walter Benn Michaels, 'Race into Culture: A Critical Genealogy of Cultural Identity', in Kwame Anthony Appiah and Henry Louis Gates Jr. (eds), *Identities* (Chicago: University of Chicago Press, 1995), p. 60.
29. Toril Moi, *Sexual/Textual Politics* (London: Routledge, 1985), p. xiv.
30. Sara Mills, Lynne Pearce, Sue Spaull and Elaine Millard, *Feminist Readings/Feminists Reading* (New York: Harvester Wheatsheaf, 1989), p. 219.
31. Mary Eagleton, 'Introduction', in Mary Eagleton (ed.), *Feminist Literary Criticism* (London: Longman, 1991), p. 11.
32. Maggie Humm, *Feminist Criticism: Women as Contemporary Critics* (New York: Harvester Wheatsheaf, 1986), p. x.
33. Maggie Humm, *Practising Feminist Criticism* (London: Prentice Hall/Harvester Wheatsheaf, 1995), p. xiv.
34. Gayatri Chakravorty Spivak, 'Marginality in the Teaching Machine', *Outside in the Teaching Machine* (New York: Routledge, 1993), p. 53.
35. Ibid., p. 54.

36. Ibid., p. 55.
37. Gayatri Chakravorty Spivak, 'Post-structuralism, Marginality, Postcoloniality and Value' in P. Collier and H. Geyer-Ryan (eds), *Literary Theory Today* (Ithaca, NY: Cornell University Press, 1990), pp. 219–244.
38. Graham Huggan, *The Post-Colonial Exotic: Marketing the Margins* (London: Routledge, 2001), p. 23.
39. Sandra M. Gilbert and Susan Gubar, *The Madwoman in the Attic: The Woman Writer and the Nineteenth Century Imagination* (New Haven: Yale University Press, 1979).
40. Susan Gubar, *Critical Condition: Feminism at the Turn of the Century* (New York: Columbia University Press, 2000), p. 5.
41. Ibid., p. 9.
42. Ibid., pp. 11–12.
43. Ibid., p. 14.
44. Shelly Eversley, *The 'Real' Negro: The Question of Authenticity in Twentieth-Century African American Literature* (New York: Routledge, 2004), p. 79.
45. Ibid., p. 80.
46. Ibid., p. 80.

8   Theory Textbooks and Canons

1. John Issitt, 'Reflections on the Study of Textbooks', *History of Education* 33:6, November 2004, p. 685.
2. Ibid., p. 685.
3. Ibid., p. 688.
4. Ibid., p. 688.
5. Ibid., p. 689.
6. Thomas S. Kuhn, *The Structure of Scientific Revolutions* (Chicago: University of Chicago Press, 1970, first edition 1962), particularly pp. 138–140.
7. Patrick Parrinder, 'Having Your Assumptions Questioned: A Guide to the "Theory Guides"', in Richard Bradford (ed.), *The State of Theory* (London: Routledge, 1993), p. 133.
8. David B. Downing, 'The "Mop-up" Work of Theory Anthologies: Theorizing the Discipline and the Disciplining of Theory', *Symploke* 8:1–21, 2000, 135.
9. Stein Haugom Olsen, 'Progress in Literary Studies', *New Literary History* 36:3, Summer 2005, 341–358.
10. Patrick Parrinder, *The Failure of Theory: Essays on Criticism and Contemporary Fiction* (Brighton: Harvester, 1987), pp. 18–38.11. Gerald Graff and Jeffrey Di Leo, 'Anthologies, Literary Theory, and the Teaching of Literature: An Exchange', *Symploke* 8:1–2, 2000, 113.
12. Jonathan Culler, *The Pursuit of Signs: Semiotics, Literature, Deconstruction* (London: Routledge & Kegan Paul, 1981), p. 220.
13. Belsey's first substantive comments on the 'new critical practice' appear after summarizing New Criticism, reader-response, and Saussurean and post-Saussurean linguistics – Catherine Belsey, *Critical Practice* (London: Routledge, 1980), p. 55.
14. Terry Eagleton, *Literary Theory: An Introduction* (Oxford: Blackwell, 1983), p. vii.

15. Ibid., the three chapters mentioned here are: 'Introduction: What is Literature?', 'Ch.1: The Rise of English', and 'Conclusion: Political Criticism'.
16. Raman Selden, *A Reader's Guide to Contemporary Literary Theory* (Brighton: Harvester, 1985), pp. 3–4.
17. Brendan Gill, *Here at the New Yorker* (London: Joseph, 1975).
18. Steven Lynn, *Texts and Contexts: Writing about Literature with Critical Theory* (New York: Harper Collins, 1994), p. xviii.
19. Michael Ryan, *Literary Theory: A Practical Introduction* (Oxford: Blackwell, 1999), p. viii.
20. Peter Barry, *Beginning Theory: An Introduction to Literary and Cultural Theory* (Manchester; Manchester University Press, 1995).
21. Catherine Belsey, *Critical Practice*, 2nd edition (London: Routledge, 2002), p. xii.
22. Terry Eagleton, *Literary Theory: An Introduction*, 2nd edition (Oxford: Blackwell, 1996), pp.190–205.
23. Catherine Belsey, *Critical Practice*, 2nd edition (2002), p. xii.
24. Catherine Belsey, *Critical Practice* (1980), p. 66.
25. Catherine Belsey, *Critical Practice*, 2nd edition (2002), p. 61.
26. Terry Eagleton, *Literary Theory* (1983), p. 150 [1996 edition, p. 130].
27. Terry Eagleton, *The Illusions of Postmodernism* (Oxford: Blackwell, 1996).
28. Terry Eagleton, *Literary Theory* (1996), p. 190.
29. Ibid., p. 194.
30. Raman Selden, *Practising Theory and Reading Literature: An Introduction* (New York: Harvester Wheatsheaf, 1989).
31. Raman Selden, Peter Widdowson, and Peter Brooker (eds), *A Practical Reader in Contemporary Literary Theory* (Hemel Hempstead: Prentice Hall/Harvester Wheatsheaf, 1996).
32. Raman Selden, *A Reader's Guide to Contemporary Literary Theory* (Brighton: Harvester, 1985), p. 146.
33. Raman Selden, *A Reader's Guide to Contemporary Literary Theory*, 2nd edition (Hemel Hempstead: Harvester Wheatsheaf, 1989).
34. Raman Selden and Peter Widdowson, *A Reader's Guide to Contemporary Literary Theory*, 3rd edition (Hemel Hampstead: Harvester Wheatsheaf, 1993).
35. Ibid., p. 188.
36. Raman Selden, *A Reader's Guide to Contemporary Literary Theory* (1985), p. 128.
37. Raman Selden and Peter Widdowson, *A Reader's Guide to Contemporary Literary Theory*, 3rd edition (1993), p. 203.
38. Raman Selden, Peter Widdowson, and Peter Brooker, *A Reader's Guide to Contemporary Literary Theory*, 4th edition (Hemel Hempstead: Prentice Hall/Harvester Wheatsheaf, 1997).
39. Steven Lynn, *Texts and Contexts: Writing about Literature with Critical Theory* (New York: Harper Collins, 1994), p. 21.
40. Ibid., p. 195.
41. Steven Lynn, *Texts and Contexts*, 2nd edition (New York: Longman, 1998), p. xiii.
42. Steven Lynn, *Texts and Contexts*, 3rd edition (New York: Longman, 2001), p. 135.

43. Patrick Parrinder, 'Having Your Assumptions Questioned: A Guide to the "Theory Guides"', in Richard Bradford (ed.), *The State of Theory* (London: Routledge, 1993), p. 127.
44. William J. Bennett, *To Reclaim a Legacy: A Report on the Humanities in Higher Education*, National Endowment of Humanities USA, 1984, at http://www.higher-ed.org/resources/legacy.htm; Harold Bloom, *The Western Canon: The Books and School of the Ages* (New York: Harcourt Brace, 1994).
45. Paul Lauter, *Canons and Contexts* (New York: Oxford University Press, 1991); John Guillory, *Cultural Capital: The Problem of Literary Canon Formation* (Chicago: University of Chicago Press, 1993); Gregory S. Jay, *Taking Multiculturalism Seriously: Ethnos and Ethos in the Classroom* (New York: Cornell University Press, 1997).
46. Matthew Arnold, 'The Study of Poetry' (1880), *Matthew Arnold's Essays in Criticism: First and Second Series* (London: Dent, 1964), pp. 237–238; F.R. Leavis, *The Great Tradition* (London: Chatto & Windus, 1948).
47. Harold Bloom, *The Western Canon*, p. 17.
48. Paul Lauter, 'Canon Theory and Emergent Practice', *Canons and Contexts*, p. 165.
49. John Guillory, *Cultural Capital*, p. 56.
50. Ibid., p. 59.
51. E. Dean Kolbas, *Critical Theory and the Literary Canon* (Boulder, CO: Westview, 2001), p. 2.
52. Sandra M. Gilbert and Susan Gubar (eds), *The Norton Anthology of Literature by Women: The Tradition in English* (New York: W.W. Norton, 1985); Marian Arkin and Barbara Shollar (eds), *Longman Anthology of World Literature by Women 1875–1975* (New York: Longman, 1985); Dale Spender and Janet Todd (eds), *Anthology of British Women Writers* (London: Pandora, 1989).
53. Virginia Blain, Isobel Grundy, and Patricia Clements (eds), *The Feminist Companion to Literature in English: Women Writers from the Middle Ages to the Present* (New Haven: Yale University Press, 1990); Sandra M. Gilbert and Susan Gubar (eds), *The Norton Anthology of Literature by Women: The Traditions in English*, 2nd edition (New York: W.W. Norton, 1996); Deborah H. Holdstein (ed.) *The Prentice Hall Anthology of Women's Literature* (Upper Saddle River NJ: Prentice Hall, 1999); Mary K. DeShazer, *The Longman Anthology of Women's Literature* (New York: Longman, 2001).
54. Ethan Mordden (ed.), *Waves: An Anthology of Gay Literature* (London: Vintage, 1994); Lillian Federman, *Chloe plus Olivia: An Anthology of Lesbian Literature from the Seventeenth Century to the Present* (London: Viking, 1994); Brett Beemyn and Mickey Eliason (eds), *Queer Studies: A Lesbian, Gay, Bisexual and Transgender Anthology* (New York: New York University Press, 1996); Byrne R.S. Fone (ed.), *The Columbia Anthology of Gay Literature* (New York: Columbia University Press, 1998); Robert Drake (ed.), *The Gay Canon: Great Books Every Gay Man Should Read* (New York: Doubleday, 1998).
55. Gregory Woods, *A History of Gay Literature: The Male Tradition* (New Haven: Yale University Press, 1998).
56. And interestingly this is a tradition in which the anthological enterprise has been informed from an early period by an explicitly social constructionist apprehension of black identity. Memorably, in the introduction to Abraham Chapman (ed.), *Black Voices* (New York: Mentor, 1968), the editor had

observed: 'I have no special thesis about Negro American Literature to advance or prove. If there's anything I would like to emphasize, it is the plural *Voices* in the title of this book, the individuality of each and every black writer, the diversity of styles and approaches to literature, the conflict of ideas, values, and varying attitudes to life, within black America. In my reading and experience I simply have not found any such thing as "the Negro"' (p. 27).

57. Henry Louis Gates Jr. and Nellie McKay (eds), *The Norton Anthology of African-American Literature* (New York: W.W. Norton, 1996); Al Young (ed.), *African American Literature: A Brief Introduction and Anthology* (New York: Harper Collins College, 1996); Patricia Liggins Hill et al. (eds), *Call and Response: The Riverside Anthology of the African American Tradition* (Boston: Houghton Mifflin, 1998); Kevin Powell (ed.), *Step into a World: A Global Anthology of New Black Literature* (Hoboken, NJ: John Wiley, 2000).

58. Margaret Busby (ed.) *Daughters of Africa: An International Anthology of Words and Writings by Women of African Descent from Ancient Egyptian to the Present* (London: Jonathan Cape, 1992); Valorie Lee (ed.), *The Prentice Hall Anthology of African American Women's Literature* (Upper Saddle River, NJ: Prentice Hall, 2005).

59. Joseph Beam (ed.), *In the Life: A Black Gay Anthology* (Boston: Alyson, 1986); Catherine E. Mckinley (ed.), *Afrekete: An Anthology of Black Lesbian Writing* (New York: Anchor, 1995); Devon W. Carbado, Dwight A. McBride, and Donald Weise (eds), *Black Like Us: A Century of Lesbian, Gay, and Bisexual African American Fiction* (San Francisco: Cleis Press, 2002).

60. Denis Lynn Daly Heyek (ed.), *Barrios and Borderlands: Cultures of Latinos and Latinas in the United States* (New York: Routledge, 1994); Eduardo R. del Rio (ed.), *The Prentice Hall Anthology of Latino Literature* (Upper Saddle River NJ: Prentice Hall, 2001); Shawn Wong (ed.), *Asian American Literature: A Brief Introduction and Anthology* (New York: Harper Collins College, 1996); Shirley Geok-Lin Lim (ed.), *Asian-American Literature: An Anthology* (Chicago: NTC/Contemporary, 1999).

61. John Thieme (ed.), *The Arnold Anthology of Postcolonial Literatures in English* (London: Arnold, 1996); Robert L. Ross (ed.), *Colonial and Postcolonial Fiction in English* (New York: Garland, 1999).

62. The sixth edition – Nina Baym (ed.), *The Norton Anthology of American Literature* (Vols A–E) (New York: W.W. Norton, 2003).

63. The seventh edition – M.H. Abrams (gen. ed.) and Stephen Greenblatt (assoc. ed.), *The Norton Anthology of English Literature* (New York: W.W. Norton, 2000).

64. Sarah N. Lawall and Maynard Mack (eds), *The Norton Anthology of World Masterpieces*, 7th edition (New York: W.W. Norton, 1997/1999); David Damrosch (ed.), *Longman Anthology of World Literature* (New York: Longman, 2003/2004); Paul Davis, Gary Harrison, and David M. Johnson (eds), *Bedford Anthology of World Literature* (New York: Bedford/St. Martin's, 2002/2003).

65. Alfred David, *Teaching with the Norton Anthology of English Literature*, Fifth edition (New York: W.W. Norton, 1988) – this was updated with Kelly Hurley and Philip Schwyzer for the seventh edition in 2000; Bruce Michelson, *Teaching with the Norton Anthology of American Literature Fifth edition* (New York: W.W. Norton, 1998) – updated for the sixth edition in 2003; Sandra

M. Gilbert, Susan Gubar, and Lisa C. Harper, *Teaching with the Norton Anthology of Literature by Women: The Traditions in English Second edition: A Guide for Instructors* (New York: W.W. Norton, 1996); David Damrosch, *Teaching World Literature: A Companion to the Longman Anthology of World Literature* (New York: Pearson Education, 2005).

66. Ilan Stavans, 'The Quest for a Latino Literary Tradition', *Chronicle of Higher Education* 47:14, 1 December 2000, p. B13.

67. Marjorie Perloff, 'Why Big Anthologies Make Bad Textbooks', *Chronicle of Higher Education* 45:32, 14 April 1999, pp. B6–B7; Marjorie Perloff, 'Whose New American Poetry? Anthologizing in the Nineties', *Diacritics* 26:3–4, 1996, 104–123.

68. *Symploke* 8:1–2, 2000, Jeffrey R. DiLeo (ed.); *Symploke* 11:1–2, 2003, Ian Buchanan and Jeffrey R. Di Leo (ed.), special edition 'Theory Trouble'. Discussion in the latter is of: Vincent B. Leitch (ed.) *The Norton Anthology of Theory and Criticism* (New York: W.W. Norton, 2001).

69. Waïl S. Hassan, 'World Literature in the Age of Globalization: Reflections on an Anthology', *College English* 63:1, September 2000, p. 40.

70. Gayatri Chakravorty Spivak, 'Marginality in the Teaching Machine', *Outside in the Teaching Machine* (New York: Routledge, 1993), p. 63.

71. Lisa Lowe, *Immigrant Acts: On Asian American Cultural Politics* (Durham, NC: Duke University Press, 1996), p. 58.

72. John Alberti (ed.), *The Canon in the Classroom: The Pedagogical Implications of Canon Revision in American Literature* (Wellesley Studies in Critical Theory, Literary History and Culture Volume 3) (New York: Garland, 1995).

73. Paul Lauter, 'Afterword', ibid., p. 322.

74. William E. Cain (ed.), *Teaching the Conflicts: Gerald Graff, Curricular Reform, and the Culture Wars (Wellesley Studies in Critical Theory, Literary History and Culture, Volume 2)* (New York: Garland, 1994). The writings by Graff included here are: 'Taking Cover in Coverage' (pp. 3–16), 'Other Voices, Other Rooms: Organizing and Teaching the Humanities Conflict' (pp. 17–44), 'How Curricular Disconnection Disempowers Students' (pp. 45–52), and 'Afterword: In Defense of Teaching the Conflicts' (pp. 219–228).

75. Gerald Graff, 'Other Voices, Other Rooms', ibid., p. 27.

Bibliography

Abrams, M.H. (gen.ed.) and Stephen Greenblatt (assoc. ed.). *The Norton Anthology of English Literature*, 7th edition. New York: W.W. Norton, 2000.

Adorno, Theodor W. *The Jargon of Authenticity*. Trans. Knut Tarnowski and Fredric Will. London: Routledge & Kegan Paul, 1973.

Ahmad, Aijaz. *In Theory: Classes, Nations, Literatures*. London: Verso, 1992.

Ahmed, Jamilah. 'Reaching the Body: Future Directions'. In Thomas and Ahmed (eds), *Cultural Bodies*, 2004, 283–300.

Alberti, John (ed.). *The Canon in the Classroom: The Pedagogical Implications of Canon Revision in American Literature (Wellesley Studies in Critical Theory, Literary History and Culture Volume 3)*. New York: Garland, 1995.

Andel, Jay Van. 'The Markets of the World: New Economic Frontiers'. *Vital Speeches of the Day* 46:11, 15 March 1980, 338–342.

Anderson, Perry. *The Origin of Postmodernity*. London: Verso, 1998.

Anderson, Perry. *Spectrum: From Right to Left in the World of Ideas*. London: Verso, 2003.

Appiah, Kwame Anthony. *The Ethics of Identity*. Princeton: Princeton University Press, 2004.

Appiah, Kwame Anthony and Henry Louis Gates Jr. (eds), *Identities*. Chicago: University of Chicago Press, 1995.

Arkin, Marian and Barbara Shollar (eds). *Longman Anthology of World Literature by Women 1875–1975*. New York: Longman, 1985.

Austin, J.L. *How to Do Things with Words*. Oxford: Oxford University Press, 1962.

Archibugi, Daniele and David Held (eds), *Cosmopolitan Democracy: An Agenda for a New World Order*. Cambridge: Polity, 1995.

Arnold, Matthew. *Matthew Arnold's Essays in Criticism: First and Second Series*. London: Dent, 1964.

Baldick, Chris. *The Social Mission of English Criticism, 1848–1932*. Oxford: Clarendon, 1983.

Barry, Peter. *Beginning Theory: An Introduction to Literary and Cultural Theory*. Manchester: Manchester University Press, 1995.

Baym, Nina (ed.). *The Norton Anthology of American Literature*, 6th edition (Vols. A–E). New York: W.W. Norton, 2003.

Beam Weise, Joseph (ed.). *In the Life: A Black Gay Anthology*. Boston: Alyson, 1986.

Becher, Tony and Paul R. Trowler. *Academic Tribes and Territories*, 2nd edition. Buckingham: Open University Press and The Society for Research into Higher Education, 2001.

Beemyn, Brett and Mickey Eliason (eds), *Queer Studies: A Lesbian, Gay, Bisexual and Transgender Anthology*. New York: New York University Press, 1996.

Belsey, Catherine. *Critical Practice*. London: Methuen, 1980.

Belsey, Catherine. *Critical Practice*, 2nd edition. London: Routledge, 2002.

Bennett, William J. *To Reclaim a Legacy: A Report on the Humanities in Higher Education*. Washington DC National Endowment of Humanities, 1984. At http://www.higher-ed.org/resources/legacy.htm.

Bennholdt-Thomsen, Veronika Nick Fraaclas, and Claudia Von Werlhof (eds). *There is an Alternative*. London: Zed, 2001.

Berger, Peter and Thomas Luckmann. *The Social Construction of Reality: A Treatise in the Sociology of Knowledge*. Harmondsworth: Penguin, 1966.

Berki, R.N. *On Political Realism*. London: Dent, 1981.

Berman, Art. *From the New Criticism to Deconstruction: The Reception of Structuralism and Post-Structuralism*. Urbana: University of Illinois Press, 1988.

Berman, Paul (ed.). *Debating P.C.* New York: Dell, 1992.

Bernard-Donals, Michael. *The Practice of Theory: Rhetoric, Knowledge, and Pedagogy in the Academy*. Cambridge: Cambridge University Press, 1998.

Blain, Virginia, Isobel Grundy, and Patricia Clements (eds). *The Feminist Companion to Literature in English: Women Writers from the Middle Ages to the Present*. New Haven: Yale University Press, 1990.

Bloom, Harold. *The Western Canon: The Books and School of the Ages*. New York: Harcourt Brace, 1994.

Blühdorn, Ingolfur. 'Self-Experience in the Theme Park of Radical Action? Social Movements and Political Articulation in the Late-Modern Condition'. *European Journal of Social Theory* 9:1, February 2006. 23–42.

Bohman, James and William Rehg (eds). *Deliberative Democracy: Essays on Reason and Politics*. Cambridge, MA: MIT Press, 1997.

Bordwell, David and Noël Carroll. *Post-Theory: Reconstructing Film Studies*. Madison: University of Wisconsin Press, 1996.

Bourdieu, Pierre, Jean-Claude Passeron, and Monique de Saint Martin. *Academic Discourse: Linguistic Misunderstanding and Professorial Power* (1965). Trans. Richard Teese. Cambridge: Polity, 1994.

Bourdieu, Pierre. *Homo Academicus*. Trans. Peter Collier. Cambridge: Polity, 1988.

Bové, Paul A. *In the Wake of Theory*. Hanover: Wesleyan University Press, 1992.

Bradford, Richard (ed.). *The State of Theory*. London: Routledge, 1993.

Braidotti, Rosi. *Metamorphoses: Toward a Materialist Theory of Becoming*. Cambridge: Polity, 2002.

Brandt, Willy. *North South: A Programme for Survival: The Report of the Independent Commission on International Development Issues under the Chairmanship of Willy Brandt*. London: Pan, 1980.

Brown, Richard Harvey (ed.). *The Politics of Selfhood: Bodies and Identities in Global Capitalism*. Minneapolis: University of Minnesota press, 2003.

Buchanan, Ian and Jeffrey R. Di Leo (eds). Special Issue *Theory Trouble*. *Symploke* 11:1–2, 2003.

Busby, Margaret (ed.). *Daughters of Africa: An International Anthology of Words and Writings by Women of African Descent from Ancient Egyptian to the Present*. London: Jonathan Cape, 1992.

Butler, Judith, John Guillory, and Kendall Thomas (eds). *What's Left of Theory?: New Work in the Politics of Literary Theory*. New York: Routledge, 2000.

Butt, Gavin (ed.) *After Criticism*. Oxford: Blackwell, 2004.

Buzard, James. 'On Auto-Ethnographic Authority'. *Yale Journal of Criticism* 16:1, 2003, 61–91.

Cain, William E. *The Crisis in Criticism: Theory, Literature and Reform in English Studies*. Baltimore: Johns Hopkins University Press, 1984.

Cain, William E. (ed.). *Teaching the Conflicts: Gerald Graff, Curricular Reform, and the Culture Wars (Wellesley Studies in Critical Theory, Literary History and Culture, Volume 2)*. New York: Garland, 1994.

Calhoun, Craig (ed.). *Social Theory and the Politics of Identity.* Oxford: Blackwell, 1994.

Callus, Ivan and Stefan Herbrechter. *Post-Theory, Culture, Criticism.* Amsterdam: Rodopi, 2004.

Canetti, Elias. *Crowds and Power.* Trans. Carol Stewart. Harmondsworth: Penguin, 1973.

Carbado, Devon W., Dwight A. McBride, and Donald Weise (eds). *Black Like Us: A Century of Lesbian, Gay, and Bisexual African American Fiction.* San Francisco: Cleis Press, 2002.

Carmichael, Stokely and Charles V. Hamilton. *Black Power: The Politics of Liberation in America.* New York: Random House, 1967.

Castle, Terry. *Clarissa's Ciphers: Meaning and Disruption in Richardson's 'Clarissa'.* Ithaca: Cornell University Press, 1982.

Castle, Terry. *Masquerade and Civilization: The Carnivalesque in Eighteenth-Century English Culture and Fiction.* Stanford, CA: Stanford University Press, 1986.

Castle, Terry. *The Apparitional Lesbian: Female Homosexuality and Modern Culture.* New York: Columbia University Press, 1993.

Certeau, Michel de. *Culture in the Plural.* Trans. Om Conley. Minneapolis: University of Minnesota Press, 1997.

Chapman, Abraham (ed.). *Black Voices.* New York: Mentor, 1968.

Chryssochoou, Xenia. *Cultural Diversity: Its Social Psychology.* Malden, MA: Blackwell, 2004.

Cohen, Jean L. (guest ed.). *Social Research.* Special issue *Social Movements.* 52:4, Winter 1985.

Cohen, Joshua. 'Deliberation and Democratic Legitimacy'. In Bohman and Relig (eds), *Deliberative Democracy*, 1997, 67–91.

Cohen, Joshua. 'Democracy and Liberty'. In Elster (ed.), *Deliberative Democracy*, 1998, 185–231.

Cohen, Ralph (ed.). *The Future of Literary Theory.* New York: Routledge, 1989.

Collier, P. and H. Geyer-Ryan (eds). *Literary Theory Today.* Ithaca, NY: Cornell University Press, 1990.

Cooper, Davina. *Challenging Diversity: Rethinking Equality and the Value of Difference.* Cambridge: Cambridge University Press, 2004.

Crawford, Robert. *Devolving English Literature.* Oxford: Clarendon, 1992.

Culler, Jonathan. *The Pursuit of Signs: Semiotics, Literature, Deconstruction.* London: Routledge and Kegan Paul, 1981.

Cunningham, Valentine. *Reading after Theory.* Oxford: Blackwell, 2002.

Damrosch, David (ed.). *Longman Anthology of World Literature.* New York: Longman, 2003/2004.

Damrosch, David. *Teaching World Literature: A Companion to the Longman Anthology of World Literature.* New York: Pearson Education, 2005.

David, Alfred, Kelly Hurley, and Philip Schwyzer. *Teaching with the Norton Anthology of English Literature*, 7th edition. New York: W.W. Norton, 2000.

Davis, Paul, Gary Harrison, and David M. Johnson (eds). *Bedford Anthology of World Literature.* New York: Bedford/St. Martin's, 2002/2003.

Davison, Peter, Rolf Meyersohn, and Edward Shils (eds). *Literary Taste, Culture and Mass Communications.* Cambridge: Chadwyck-Healey/Teaneck, NJ: Somerset House, 1978, 14 volumes.

Debray, Régis. *Teachers, Writers, Celebrities: The Intellectuals of Modern France.* Trans. David Macey. London: New Left Books, 1981.

Derrida, Jacques. *Of Grammatology*. Trans. Gayatri Chakravorty Spivak. Baltimore: Johns Hopkins University Press, 1974.

Derrida, Jacques. 'Mochlos: or, the Conflict of Faculties'. In Rand (ed.). *Logomachia: The Conflict of Faculties*, 1992. 1–34.

Derrida, Jacques. *Specters of Marx; The State of the Debt, the Work of Mourning, and the New International*. Trans. Peggy Kamuf. New York: Routledge, 1994.

DeShazer, Mary K. *The Longman Anthology of Women's Literature*. New York: Longman, 2001.

Diani, Mario and Doug McAdam (eds). *Social Movements and Networks: Relational Approaches to Collective Action*. Oxford: Oxford University Press, 2003.

Dixon, John. *A Schooling in 'English'*. Buckingham: Open University Press, 1991.

Docherty, Thomas. *After Theory*. London: Routledge, 1990.

Donoghue, Denis. *The Pure Good of Theory*. Oxford: Blackwell, 1992.

Donoghue, Denis. *The Practice of Reading*. New Haven: Yale University Press, 1998.

Downing, David B. 'The "Mop-up" Work of Theory Anthologies: Theorizing the Discipline and the Disciplining of Theory'. *Symploke* 8: 1–21, 2000, 129–150.

Doyle, Brian. *English and Englishness*. London: Routledge, 1989.

Drake, Robert (ed.). *The Gay Canon: Great Books Every Gay Man Should Read*. New York: Doubleday, 1998.

Dyer, Richard. *The Culture of Queers*. London: Routledge, 2002.

Eagleton, Mary (ed.). *Feminist Literary Criticism*. London: Longman, 1991.

Eagleton, Terry. *Literary Theory: An Introduction*. Oxford: Blackwell, 1983.

Eagleton, Terry. *The Illusions of Postmodernism* (Oxford: Blackwell, 1996).

Eagleton, Terry. *Literary Theory: An Introduction*, 2nd edition. Oxford: Blackwell, 1996.

Eagleton, Terry. *The Significance of Theory*. Oxford: Basil Blackwell, 1990.

Eagleton, Terry. *After Theory*. London: Allen Lane, 2003.

Easthope, Anthony. *Literary into Cultural Studies*. London: Routledge, 1991.

Elias, Juanita. 'Stitching-Up the Labour Market'. *International Feminist Journal of Politics* 7:1, March 2005, 90–111.

Elias, Norbert. *The Society of Individuals*. Trans. Edmund Jephcott. Oxford: Blackwell, 1991.

Ellis, John M. *Literature Lost: Social Agendas and the Corruption of the Humanities*. New Haven: Yale University Press, 1997.

Elster, Jon (ed.). *Deliberative Democracy*. Cambridge: Cambridge University Press, 1998.

Erikson, Erik. *Identity: Youth and Culture*. New York: Norton, 1968.

Eversley, Shelly. *The 'Real' Negro: The Question of Authenticity in Twentieth-Century African American Literature*. New York: Routledge, 2004.

Farred, Grant. 'Endgame Identity?: Mapping the New Left Roots of Identity Politics'. *New Literary History* 31:4, 2000, 627–648.

Federman, Lillian (ed.). *Chloe plus Olivia: An Anthology of Lesbian Literature from the Seventeenth Century to the Present*. London: Viking, 1994.

Felman, Shoshanna. *What Does a Woman Want? Reading and Sexual Difference*. Baltimore: Johns Hopkins University Press, 1993.

Felperin, Howard. *Beyond Deconstruction: The Uses and Abuses of Literary Theory*. Oxford: Clarendon, 1985.

Felski, Rita. *Literature after Feminism*. Chicago: University of Chicago, 2003.

Fenton, Steve. *Ethnicity.* Cambridge: Polity, 2003.

Fish, Stanley. *Professional Correctness: Literary Studies and Political Change.* Oxford: Clarendon, 1995.

Fisher, William F. and Thomas Pooniah (eds). *Another World is Possible.* London: Zed, 2003.

Fone, Byrne R.S. (ed). *The Columbia Anthology of Gay Literature.* New York: Columbia University Press, 1998.

Foucault, Michel. *Discipline and Punish: The Birth of the Prison.* Trans. Alan Sheridan. London: Allen Lane, 1977.

Foucault, Michel. *'Society Must be Defended': Lectures at the College de France 1975–76.* Trans. David Macey.) London: Allen Lane, 1997.

Fromm, Harold. *Academic Capitalism and Literary Value.* Athens, GA: University of Georgia Press, 1991.

Fuchs, Stephan. *Against Essentialism: A Theory of Culture and Society.* Cambridge, MA: Harvard University Press, 2001.

Galeotti, Anna E. *Toleration as Recognition.* Cambridge: Cambridge University Press, 2002.

Garber, Marjorie. *Academic Instincts.* Princeton: Princeton University Press, 2001.

Gasset, José Ortega y. *Man and People.* Trans. Willard R. Trask. London: George Allen & Unwin, 1959.

Gasset, José Ortega y. *The Revolt of the Masses.* Trans. Andrew Kerrigan. Notre Dame, IN: University of Notre Dame Press, 1965.

Gates Jr., Henry Louis, and Nellie McKay (eds). *The Norton Anthology of African-American Literature.* New York: W.W. Norton, 1996.

Geertz, Clifford. *Local Knowledge.* London: Fontana, 1983.

Gergen, Kenneth J. *Social Construction in Context.* London: Sage, 2001.

Gill, Brendan. *Here at the New Yorker.* London: Joseph, 1975.

Gilbert, Sandra M. and Susan Gubar. *The Madwoman in the Attic: The Woman Writer and the Nineteenth Century Imagination.* New Haven: Yale University Press, 1979.

Gilbert, Sandra M. and Susan Gubar (eds). *The Norton Anthology of Literature by Women: The Tradition in English.* New York: W.W. Norton, 1985.

Gilbert, Sandra M. and Susan Gubar (eds). *The Norton Anthology of Literature by Women: The Traditions in English,* 2nd edition. New York: W.W. Norton, 1996.

Gilbert, Sandra M., Susan Gubar, and Lisa C. Harper. *Teaching with the Norton Anthology of Literature by Women: The Traditions in English Second edition: A Guide for Instructors.* New York: W.W. Norton, 1996.

Gitlin, Todd. 'From Universality to Difference: Notes on the Fragmentation of the Idea of the Left'. In Calhoun (ed.), *Social Theory and the Politics of Identity,* 1994, 150–174.

Godzich, Wlad. *The Culture of Literacy.* Cambridge, MA: Harvard University Press, 1994.

Goodheart, Eugene. *The Skeptic Disposition in Contemporary Criticism.* Princeton: Princeton University Press, 1984.

Goreau, Fredrick H. 'The Multinational Version of Social Sciences'. *International Social Science Journal* 35:2, May 1983, 379–390.

Gouldner, Alvin. *The Future of Intellectuals and the Rise of the New Class.* London: Macmillan, 1979.

Graeber, David. 'The New Anarchists'. *New Left Review*. 13, Jan/Feb 2002, 61–74.

Graff, Gerald. *Literature against Itself: Literary Ideas in Modern Society*. Chicago: University of Chicago Press, 1979.

Graff, Gerald. *Professing Literature: An Institutional History*. Chicago: University of Chicago Press, 1987.

Graff, Gerald. 'The Future of Theory in the Teaching of Literature'. In Cohen (ed.), *The Future of Literary Theory*, 1989, 250–267.

Graff, Gerald, 'Afterword: In Defense of Teaching the Conflicts'. In Cain (ed.), *Teaching the Conflicts*, 1994, 219–228.

Graff, Gerald. 'How Curricular Disconnection Disempowers Students'. In Cain (ed.), *Teaching the Conflicts*, 1994, 45–52.

Graff, Gerald. 'Other Voices, Other Rooms: Organizing and Teaching the Humanities Conflict'. In Cain (ed.), *Teaching the Conflicts*, 1994, 17–44.

Graff, Gerald. 'Taking Cover in Coverage'. In Cain (ed.), *Teaching the Conflicts*, 1994, 3–16.

Graff, Gerald and Jeffrey R. Di Leo. 'Anthologies, Literary Theory, and the Teaching of Literature: An Exchange'. *Symploke* 8: 1–2, 2000, 113–128.

Grillo, R.D. *Pluralism and the Politics of Difference: State, Culture, and Ethnicity in Comparative Perspective*. Oxford: Clarendon, 1998.

Gubar, Susan. *Critical Condition: Feminism at the Turn of the Century*. New York: Columbia University Press, 2000.

Gubar, Susan and Jonathan Kamholtz (eds). *English Inside and Out: The Places of Literary Criticism*. New York: Routledge, 1993.

Guillory, John. *Cultural Capital: The Problem of Literary Canon Formation*. Chicago: University of Chicago Press, 1993.

Gumperz, John J. (ed.). *Language and Social Identity*. Cambridge: Cambridge University Press, 1982.

Gutmann, Amy. *Identity in Democracy*. Princeton: Princeton University Press, 2003.

Guy, Josephine and Ian Small. *Politics and Value in English Studies: A Discipline in Crisis?* Cambridge: Cambridge University Press, 1993.

Habermas, Jürgen. 'New Social Movements'. *Telos* 49, Fall 1981, 33–37.

Habermas, Jürgen. *The Theory of Communicative Action Vol. 1: Reason and the Rationalization of Society*. Trans. Thomas McCarthy. Cambridge: Polity, 1984.

Habermas, Jürgen. *The Theory of Communicative Action Vol. 2: Lifeworld and System: A Critique of Functionalist Reason*. Trans. Thomas McCarthy. Cambridge: Polity, 1987.

Habermas, Jürgen. 'Struggles for Recognition in the Democratic Constitutional State'. Trans. Shierry Weber Nicholsen. In Taylor with Gutmann (eds), *Multiculturalism*, 1994, 107–148.

Habermas, Jürgen. *Between Facts and Norms: Contributions to a Discourse Theory of Law and Democracy*. Trans. William Relig. Cambridge, MA: MIT Press, 1996.

Habermas, Jürgen. *Inclusion of the Other: Studies in Political Theory*. Trans. Ciaran Cronin. Cambridge: Polity, 1998.

Habermas, Jürgen. 'Popular Sovereignty as Procedure'. In Bohman and Rehg (eds), *Deliberative Democracy*, 1997, 35–66.

Habermas, Jürgen. *The Postnational Constellation: Political Essays*. Trans. Max Pensky. Cambridge: Polity, 2001.

Hall, Donald (ed.). *Professions: Conversations on the Future of Literary and Cultural Studies.* Urbana: University of Illinois Press, 2001.

Hall, Stuart. 'Cultural Identity and Diaspora'. In Rutherford (ed.). *Identity,* 1990, 222–237.

Hall, Stuart. 'The Toad in the Garden: Thatcherism among the Theorists'. In Nelson and Grossberg (eds), *Marxism and the Interpretation of Culture,* 1988, 35–73.

Hall, Stuart. *The Hard Road to Renewal: Thatcherism and the Crisis of the Left.* London: Verso, 1988.

Hall, Stuart. 'New Ethnicities'. In Morley and Chen (eds), *Stuart Hall,* 1996, 441–449.

Hall, Stuart and Paul du Gay (eds). *Questions of Cultural Identity.* London: Sage, 1996.

Hartman, Geoffrey H. *Criticism in the Wilderness: The Study of Literature Today.* New Haven: Yale University Press, 1980.

Harvey, David. *A Brief History of Neoliberalism.* Oxford: Oxford University Press, 2003.

Harvey, David. *The New Imperialism.* Oxford: Oxford University Press, 2003.

Hassan, Waïl S. 'World Literature in the Age of Globalization: Reflections on an Anthology'. *College English* 63:1, September 2000, 38–47.

Hayek, F.A. *The Constitution of Liberty.* London: Routledge and Kegan Paul, 1960.

Hegel, G.W.F. *The Philosophy of History.* Trans. J. Sibree. New York: Dover, 1956.

Heilman, Robert. *The Professor and the Profession.* Columbia: University of Mississippi Press, 1999.

Held, David (ed.) *Prospects for Democracy: North South East West.* Cambridge: Polity, 1993.

Held, David. 'Democracy and the New International Order'. In Archibugi and Held (eds.). *Cosmopolitan Democracy: An Agenda for a New World Order,* 1995, 96–120.

Held, David. *Global Covenant: The Social Democratic Consensus to the Washington Consensus.* Cambridge: Polity, 2004.

Held, David and Anthony Mc Grew. 'Globalization and the Liberal Democratic State'. In Sakamoto (ed.), *Global Transformation,* 1994, 57–84.

Held, David and Anthony McGrew. *Globalization/Anti-Globalization.* Cambridge: Polity, 2002.

Heyek, Denis Lynn Daly (ed.). *Barrios and Borderlands: Cultures of Latinos and Latinas in the United States.* New York: Routledge, 1994.

Hill, Patricia (gen. ed.). *Call and Response: The Riverside Anthology of the African American Tradition.* Boston: Houghton Mifflin, 1998.

Hobsbawm, Eric. 'Identity Politics and the Left'. *New Left Review* 217, May/June 1996, 38–47.

Hogan, Patrick Cohn. *The Politics of Interpretation: Ideology, Professionalism, and the Study of Literature.* New York: Oxford University Press, 1990.

Holdstein, Deborah H. (ed.). *The Prentice Hall Anthology of Women's Literature.* Upper Saddle River, NJ: Prentice Hall, 1999.

Hollibaugh, Amber. 'Liberalism and the Left: An Activist's Perspective'. *Radical History Review* 71, Spring 1998, 29–33.

Holloway, John. *Change the World without Taking Power.* London: Pluto, 2002.

Hoover, Kenneth R. *A Politics of Identity: Liberation and the Natural Community.* Urbana: University of Illinois Press, 1975.

Hopkins, Raymond F. 'Global Management Networks: The Internationalization of Domestic Bureaucracies'. *Internatioal Social Science Journal* 30:1, February 1978, 31–46.

Horkheimer, Max and Theodor Adorno. *Dialectic of Enlightenment.* Trans. John Cumming. London: Verso: 1979.

Horton, Susan. 'The Institution of Literature and the Cultural Community'. In Natoli (ed.), *Literary Theory's Future(s)*, 1989, 267–320.

Huggan, Graham. *The Postcolonial Exotic: Marketing the Margins.* London: Routledge, 2001.

Humm, Maggie. *Feminist Criticism: Women as Contemporary Critics.* New York: Harvester Wheatsheaf, 1986.

Humm, Maggie. *Practising Feminist Criticism.* London: Prentice Hall/Harvester Wheatsheaf, 1995.

Hutnyk, John. 'Hybridity'. *Ethnic and Racial Studies* 28:1, January 2005, 79–102.

Hyland, Ken. *Hedging in Scientific Research Articles.* Amsterdam: John Benjamins, 1998.

Hyland, Ken. *Disciplinary Discourses: Social Interactions in Academic Writing.* Harlow: Pearson, 2000.

Hyland, Ken. 'Bumping into the Reader: Addressee Features in Academic Articles'. *Written Communication* 18:4, October 2001, 549–575.

Hyland, Ken. 'Options of Identity in Academic Writing'. *ELT Journal* 56:4, October 2002, 35–43.

Hyland, Ken. 'What Do They Mean? Questions in Academic Writing'. *Text* 22:4, 2002, 529–558.

Hyland, Ken. 'Self-Citation and Self-Reference: Credibility and Promotion in Academic Publication'. *Journal of the American Society for Information Science and Technology* 54:3, 2003, 251–291.

International Sociology. 'Debate: Are Social Classes Dying?'. Issue. *International Sociology* 8:3, September 1993, 259–316.

Iser, Wolfgang. *The Act of Reading: A Theory of Aesthetic Response.* Baltimore: Johns Hopkins University Press, 1978.

Issitt, John. 'Reflections on the Study of Textbooks'. *History of Education* 33:6, November 2004, 683–696.

Ivanic, Roz. *Writing and Identity: The Discoursal Construction of Identity in Academic Writing.* Amsterdam: John Benjamin, 1997.

Jameson, Fredric. *The Ideologies of Theory: Essays 1971–1986.* London: Routledge, 1988.

Jameson, Fredric. *Postmodernism, or, The Cultural Logic of Late Capitalism.* London: Verso, 1991.

Jay, Gregory S. *Taking Multiculturalism Seriously: Ethnos and Ethos in the Classroom.* New York: Cornell University Press, 1997.

Johnson, David. *Shakespeare and South Africa.* Oxford: Clarendon, 1996.

Jordan, Tim. *Activism! Direct Action, Hacktivism and the Future of Society.* London: Reaktion Books, 2002.

Joshi, Svati (ed.) *Rethinking English: Essays in Literature, Language, History.* New Delhi: Trianka, 1991.

Kapoor, Ilan. 'Deliberative Democracy or Agonistic Pluralism? The Relevance of the Habermas-Mouffe Debate for Third World Politics'. *Alternatives: Global, Local, Political* 27:4, October–December 2002, 459–487.

Keck, Margaret E. and Kathryn Sikkink. *Activists Beyond Borders*. Ithaca, NY: Cornell University Press, 1998.

Kolbas, E. Dean. *Critical Theory and the Literary Canon*. Boulder, CO: Westview, 2001.

Kuhn, Thomas S. *The Structure of Scientific Revolutions*. Chicago: University of Chicago Press, 1970.

Laclau, Ernesto. *Emancipation(s)*. London: Verso, 1996.

Laclau, Ernesto and Chantal Mouffe. *Hegemony and Socialist Strategy: Towards a Radical Democratic Politics*. London: Verso, 1985.

Lamy, Paul. 'The Globalization of American Sociology: Excellence or Imperialism?'. *American Sociologist* 11:2, May 1976. 104–113.

Lauter, Paul. *Canons and Contexts*. New York: Oxford University Press, 1991.

Lauter, Paul. 'Afterword'. In Alberti (ed.), *The Canon and the Classroom*, 1995, 313–327.

Lawall, Sarah N. and Maynard Mack (eds). *The Norton Anthology of World Masterpieces*, 7th edition. New York: W.W. Norton, 1997/1999.

Lea, Mary R. and Barry Stierer (eds). *Student Writing in Higher Education*. Buckingham: Open University Press and The Society for Research in Higher Education, 2000.

Leavis, F.R. *The Great Tradition*. London: Chatto & Windus, 1948.

Lee, Valorie (ed.). *The Prentice Hall Anthology of African American Women's Literature*. Upper Saddle River, NJ: Prentice Hall, 2005.

Lefebvre, Henri. *The Survival of Capitalism: Reproduction and the Relations of Production*. Trans. Frank Bryant. London: Allison and Busby, 1976.

Leitch, Vincent (ed.). *The Norton Anthology of Theory and Criticism*. New York: W.W. Norton, 2001.

Leitch, Vincent and Jeffrey Williams. *After Theory*. London: Routledge, 2005.

Lentriccia, Frank. *Criticism and Social Change*. Chicago: University of Chicago Press, 1983.

Levitt, Theodore. 'The Globalization of Markets'. *Harvard Business Review* 61:3, May–June 1983, 92–102.

Lim, Shirley Geok-Lin (ed.) *Asian-American Literature: An Anthology*. Chicago: NTC/Contemporary, 1999.

Lott, Eric. 'After Identity Politics: The Return of Universalism'. *New Literary History* 31:4, 2000, 665–678.

Loury, Glenn. *The Anatomy of Racial Inequality*. Cambridge, MA: Harvard University Press, 2002.

Lowe, Lisa. *Immigrant Acts: On Asian American Cultural Politics*. Durham, NC: Duke University Press, 1996.

Luhmann, Niklas. *Essays in Self-Reference*. New York: Columbia University Press, 1990.

Lynn, Steven. *Texts and Contexts: Writing about Literature with Critical Theory*. New York: Harper Collins, 1994.

Lynn, Steven. *Texts and Contexts*, 2nd edition. New York: Longman, 1998.

Lynn, Steven. *Texts and Contexts*, 3rd edition. New York: Longman, 2001.

Lyotard, Jean-François. *The Postmodern Condition: A Report on Knowledge*. Trans. Geoff Bennington and Brian Massumi. Manchester: Manchester University Press, 1984.

Maalouf, Amin. *On Identity*. Trans. Barbara Bray. London: Harvill, 2000.

Mackenzie, W.J.M. *Political Identity.* Manchester: Manchester University Press, 1978.

Mckinley, Catherine E. (ed.). *Afrekete: An Anthology of Black Lesbian Writing.* New York: Anchor, 1995.

McQuillan, Martin. *Post-Theory.* Edinburgh: Edinburgh University Press, 1999.

Man, Paul de. *Blindness and Insight: Essays in the Rhetoric of Contemporary Criticism.* New York: Oxford University Press, 1971.

Man, Paul de. *The Resistance to Theory.* Manchester: Manchester University Press, 1986.

Mandel, Ernest. *Late Capitalism.* Trans. Joris de Bres. London: Verso, 1972.

Marcuse, Herbert. *One-Dimensional Man.* London: Sphere, 1964.

Markovits, Andrei S. 'The European and American Left since 1945'. *Dissent* 52:1, Winter 2005, 5–13.

Marx, Karl. 'Concerning Feuerbach' [1845]. In *Marx: Early Writings*. Trans. Rodney Livingstone and Gregory Benton. Harmondsworth: Penguin, 1975, 421–423.

Mauss, Marcel. *Sociology and Psychology.* Trans. Ben Brewster. London: Routledge & Kegan Paul, 1979.

Mead, Geroge Herbert. *Mind, Self and Society.* Chicago: University of Chicago Press, 1934.

Michaels, Walter Benn. 'Race into Culture: A Critical Genealogy of Cultural Identity'. In Appiah and Gates Jr. (eds), *Identities*, 1995. 32–62.

Michelson, Bruce. *Teaching with the Norton Anthology of American Literature*, 5th edition. New York: W.W. Norton, 1998.

Miller, J. Hillis. *The Ethics of Reading: Kant, de Man, Eliot, Trollope, James, and Benjamin.* New York: Columbia University Press, 1987.

Miller, J. Hillis. 'The Function of Literary Theory at the Present Time'. In Cohen (ed.), *The Future of Literary Theory*, 1989, 102–111.

Miller, J. Hillis. *On Literature.* London: Routledge, 2002.

Miller, Nancy K. (ed.). *The Poetics of Gender.* New York: Columbia University Press, 1986.

Mills, Sara, Lynne Pearce, Sue Spaull, and Elaine Millard. *Feminist Readings/ Feminists Reading.* New York: Harvester Wheatsheaf, 1989.

Moi, Toril. *Sexual/Textual Politics.* London: Routledge, 1985.

Mordden, Ethan (ed.). *Waves: An Anthology of Gay Literature.* London: Vintage, 1994.

Morgenthau, Hans J. *Politics Among Nations: The Struggle for Power and Peace.* New York: Alfred A. Knopf, 1954.

Morley, David and Kuan-Hsing Chen (eds). *Stuart Hall: Critical Dialogues in Cultural Studies.* London: Routledge, 1996.

Morton, Adam D. 'The Grimly Comic Riddle of IPE: Where is the Class Struggle?' *Politics* 26:9, February 2006. 62–72.

Mouffe, Chantal. *The Return of the Political.* London: Verso, 1993.

Mouffe, Chantal. 'Radical Democracy or Liberal Democracy'. In Trend (ed.), *Radical Democracy*, 1996, 19–26.

National Association of Scholars (NAS). *Losing the Big Picture: The Fragmentation of the English Major since 1964.* Princeton: NAS, 2000.

Natoli, Joseph (ed.). *Literary Theory's Future(s).* Urbana: University of Illinois Press, 1989.

Nelson, Carey and Lawrence Greenberg (eds). *Marxism and the Interpretation of Culture*. Basingstoke: Macmillan, 1988.

Nesbit, Robert. 'The Decline and Fall of Social Class'. *Pacific Sociological Review* 2, 1959, 11–17.

Nicholson, Linda and Steve Seidman (eds). *Social Postmodernism: Beyond Identity Politics*. Cambridge: Cambridge University Press, 1995.

Norris, Christopher. *Deconstruction and the Interests of Theory*. London: Pinter, 1988.

Nozick, Robert. *Anarchy, State and Utopia*. Oxford: Basil Blackwell, 1974.

Nozick, Robert. *Philosophical Explanations*. Oxford: Clarendon, 1981.

Ohmann, Richard. *English in America: A Radical View of the Profession*. New York: Oxford University Press, 1976.

Oort, Richard van. 'The Critics as Ethnographer'. *New Literary History* 35:4, Autumn 2004, 621–661.

Olsen, Stein Haugom. 'Progress in Literary Studies'. *New Literary History* 36:3, Summer 2005, 341–358.

Pakulski, Jan. 'The Dying of Class or of Marxist Class Theory?'. *International Sociology* 8:3, September 1993, 279–292.

Pakulsi, Jan and Malcolm Waters. *The Death of Class*. London: Sage, 1995.

Palmer, D.J. *The Rise of English Studies*. London: Oxford University Press, 1965.

Palumbo-Liu, David. 'Assumed Identities'. *New Literary History* 31, 2000, 765–780.

Parfit, Derek. *Reasons and Persons*. Oxford: Clarendon, 1984.

Parker, Walter. 'Globalizing the Social Studies Curriculum'. *Educational Leadership* 42:2, October 1984, 92.

Parrinder, Patrick. *The Failure of Theory: Essays in Criticism and Contemporary Fiction*. Brighton: Harvester, 1987.

Parrinder, Patrick. 'Having your Assumptions Questioned: A Guide to the 'Theory Guides'. In Bradford (ed.), *The State of Theory*, 1993, 127–144.

Patai, Daphni. 'The Struggle for Feminist Purity Threatens the Goals of Feminism'. *Chronicle of Higher Education* 5 February 1992, 1B.

Payne, Michael and John Schad (eds). *Life after Theory*. London: Continuum, 2003.

Perloff, Marjorie. 'Whose New American Poetry? Anthologizing in the Nineties'. *Diacritics* 26:3–4, 1996, 104–123.

Perloff, Marjorie. 'Why Big Anthologies Make Bad Textbooks'. *Chronicle of Higher Education* 45:32, 14 April 1999, B6–B7.

Phelan, Shane. *Identity Politics: Lesbian Feminism and the Limits of Community*. Philadelphia: Temple University Press, 1989.

Phillips, Caryl. 'Necessary Journeys'. *Guardian* (Review Section) 11 December 2004, 4–6.

Plekhanov, G.V. *Art and Social Life*. London: Lawrence and Wishart, 1953.

Powell, Kevin (ed.). *Step into a World: A Global Anthology of New Black Literature*. Hoboken, NJ: John Wiley, 2000.

Pratt, Mary Louise. *Imperial Eyes: Travel Writing and Transculturation*. London: Routledge, 1992.

Preez, Peter du. *The Politics of Identity: Ideology and the Human Image*. Oxford: Basil Blackwell, 1980.

Rabaté, Jean Michele. *The Future of Theory*. Oxford: Blackwell, 2002.

Radical History Review. 'Forum: Liberalism and the Left: Rethinking the Relationship'. *Radical History Review* 71, Spring 1998, 3–51.

Rajan, Rajeshwari Sunder (ed.). *The Lie of the Land*. Delhi: Oxford University Press, 1992.

Rajan, Tilottama. 'In the Wake of Cultural Studies: Globalization, Theory, and the University'. *Diacritics* 31:1, Fall 2001, 67–88.

Rand, Richard (ed.) *Logomachia: The Conflict of Faculties*. Lincoln: University of Nebraska Press, 1992.

Rawls, John. *A Theory of Justice*. Oxford: Oxford University Press, 1971.

Rawls, John. *Political Liberalism*. New York: Columbia University Press, 1993.

Rawls, John. *The Law of Peoples with 'The Idea of Public Reason Revisited'*. Cambridge, MA: Harvard University Press, 1999.

Reagon, Bernice Johnson. 'Coalition Politics: Turning the Century'. In Smith (ed.), *Home Girls*. 1983, 356–357.

Rich, Wilbur C. (ed.) *The Politics of Minority Coalitions: Race, Ethnicity and Shared Uncertainties*. Westport, CT: Praeger, 1996.

Rio, Eduardo R. del (ed.). *The Prentice Hall Anthology of Latino Literature*. Upper Saddle River, NJ: Prentice Hall, 2001.

Ross, Robert L. (ed.), *Colonial and Postcolonial Fiction in English*. New York: Garland, 1999.

Rutherford, Jonathan (ed.) *Identity: Community, Culture, Difference*. London: Lawrence & Wishart, 1990.

Ryan, Barbara (ed.). *Identity Politics in the Women's Movement*. New York: New York University Press, 2001.

Ryan, Michael. *Literary Theory: A Practical Introduction*. Oxford: Blackwell, 1999.

Said, Edward. *Orientalism*. London: Routledge and Kegan Paul, 1978.

Said, Edward. *The Question of Palestine*. London: Routledge and Kegan Paul, 1980.

Said, Edward. *The World, the Text, and the Critic*. London: Vintage, 1983.

Said, Edward. *Representations of the Intellectual: The 1993 Reith Lectures*. London: Vintage, 1994.

Said, Edward. *Reflections on Exile*. Cambridge, MA: Harvard University Press, 2000.

Sakamoto, Yoshikazu (ed.). *Global Transformation: Challenges to the State System*. Tokyo and New York: United Nations University Press, 1994.

Sartre, Jean-Paul. *Between Existentialism and Marxism*. Trans. John Matthews. London: NLB, 1974.

Sartre, Jean-Paul. *Critique of Dialectical Reason Vol.1: Theory of Practical Ensembles*. Trans. Alan Sheridan-Smith. London: NLB, 1976.

Scholes, Robert. *Textual Power: Literary Theory and the Teaching of English*. New Haven: Yale University Press, 1985.

Scholes, Robert. *The Rise and Fall of English: Reconstructing English as a Discipline*. New Haven: Yale University Press, 1998.

Seidman, Steven. *Difference Troubles: Queering Social Theory and Sexual Politics*. Cambridge: Cambridge University Press, 1997.

Selden, Raman. *A Reader's Guide to Contemporary Literary Theory*. Brighton: Harvester, 1985.

Selden, Raman. *Practising Theory and Reading Literature: An Introduction*. New York: Harvester Wheatsheaf, 1989.

Selden, Raman. *A Reader's Guide to Contemporary Literary Theory*, 2nd edition. Hemel Hempstead: Harvester Wheatsheaf, 1989.

Selden, Raman and Peter Widdowson. *A Reader's Guide to Contemporary Literary Theory*, 3rd edition. Hemel Hampstead: Harvester Wheatsheaf, 1993.

Selden, Raman, Peter Widdowson, and Peter Brooker (eds). *A Practical Reader in Contemporary Literary Theory.* Hemel Hempstead: Prentice Hall/Harvester Wheatsheaf, 1996.

Selden, Raman, Peter Widdowson, and Peter Brooker. *A Reader's Guide to Contemporary Literary Theory,* 4th edition. Hemel Hempstead: Prentice Hall/ Harvester Wheatsheaf, 1997.

Smith, Barbara (ed.). *Home Girls.* New York: Kitchen Table Press, 1983.

Song, Miri. *Choosing Ethnic Identity.* Cambridge: Polity, 2003.

Spender, Dale and Janet Todd (eds). *Anthology of British Women Writers.* London: Pandora, 1989.

Spivak, Gayatri Chakravorty. *In Other Worlds: Essays in Cultural Politics.* New York: Methuen, 1987.

Spivak, Gayatri Chakravorty. 'Can the Subaltern Speak?'. In Nelson and Greenberg (eds), *Marxism and the Interpretation of Culture,* 1988, 271–313.

Spivak, Gayatri Chakravorty. 'Post-structuralism, Marginality, Postcoloniality and Value'. In Collier and Geyer-Ryan (eds), *Literary Theory Today,* 1990, 219–244.

Spivak, Gayatri Chakravorty. *Outside in the Teaching Machine.* New York: Routledge, 1993.

Starr, Amory. *Naming the Enemy.* London: Zed, 2000.

Stavans, Ilan. 'The Quest for a Latino Literary Tradition'. *Chronicle of Higher Education* 47:14, 1 December 2000, B13.

Stiglitz, Joseph. *Globalization and its Discontents.* Harmondsworth: Penguin, 2002.

Strauch, Eduard. *Beyond Literary Theory.* Lanham: University Press of America, 2001.

Suleri, Sara. 'Woman Skin Deep: Feminism and the Postcolonial Condition'. In Appiah and Gates Jr. (eds), *Identities,* 1995, 133–146.

Tajfel, Henri. 'La catégorisation socialé'. In S. Moscovici (ed.), *Introduction à la Psychologie Sociale, Vol.1.* Paris: Larousse, 1972, 272–302.

Tajfel, Henri. *The Social Psychology of Minorities.* London: Minority Rights Group, 1978.

Tajfel, Henri. *Human Groups and Social Categories: Studies in Social Psychology.* Cambridge: Cambridge University Press, 1981.

Taylor, Charles. *The Ethics of Authenticity.* Cambridge, MA: Harvard University Press, 1991.

Taylor, Charles. 'The Politics of Recognition' (1992). In Taylor with Gutmann (ed.), *Multiculturalism,* 1994, 25–73.

Taylor, Charles with Amy Gutmann (ed.). *Multiculturalism: Examining the Politics of Recognition.* Princeton: Princeton University Press, 1994.

Taylor, Paul C. *Race: A Philosophical Introduction.* Cambridge: Polity, 2004.

Telos. 'The Kansas *Telos* Conference (December 4–6, 1980)' – Special Symposium section. *Telos* 74, Winter 1980–1981, pp. 81–111.

Theory and Society. 'Symposium on Class'. *Theory and Society* 25:5, 1996, 667–736.

Thieme, John (ed.). *The Arnold Anthology of Postcolonial Literatures in English.* London: Arnold, 1996.

Thomas, Helen and Jamilah Ahmed (eds). *Cultural Bodies: Ethnography and Theory.* Malden, MA: Blackwell, 2004.

Touraine, Alain. *The Voice and the Eye: An Analysis of Social Movements.* Trans. Alan Duff. Cambridge: Cambridge University Press, 1981.

Touraine, Alain Francois Dubet, Michel Wieviorska, and Jan Strzelecki. *Solidarity: The Analysis of a Social Movement, Poland 1980–1981.* Trans. David Denby.) Cambridge: Cambridge University Press, 1983.

Touraine, Alain, Michel Wieviorka, and François Dubet. *The Workers' Movement*. Trans. Ian Patterson. Cambridge: Cambridge University Press and Paris: Editions de la Maison des Sciences de l'Homme, 1987.

Trend, David (ed.). *Radical Democracy: Identity, Citizenship, and the State*. New York: Routledge, 1996.

Trendell, Nicholas. *The Critical Decade: Culture in Crisis*. London: Carcanet, 1993.

Trivedi, Harish. *Colonial Transactions*. Calcutta: Papyrus, 1993.

Vishwanathan, Gauri. *Masks of Conquest: Literary Study and British Rule in India*. London: Faber and Faber, 1989.

Wallace, Kathleen. 'Autonomous 'I' of an Intersectional Self'. *The Journal of Speculative Philosophy* 17:3, 2003, 176–191.

Walzer, Michael. *On Toleration*. New Haven: Yale University Press, 1997.

Watts, Jerry Gafio. 'Black and Coalition Politics: A Theoretical Reconceptualization'. In Rich (ed.), *The Politics of Minority Coalitions*, 1996, 35–51.

We are Everywhere. London: Verso, 2004.

Weber, Max. *Economy and Society*, Vol. 1. Guenther Roth and Claus Wittich (eds), Berkeley: University of California Press, 1978.

Weeks, Jeffrey. 'The Value of Difference'. In Rutherford (ed.), *Identity*, 1990. 88–100.

Williams, Christopher J. 'In Defence of Materialism: A Critique of Afrocentric Ontology' *Race and Class* 47:1, July–September 2005, 35–48.

Williams, Jeffrey J. (ed.). *The Institution of Literature*. Albany: State University of New York Press, 2002.

Wittig, Monique. 'The Mark of Gender'. In Miller (ed.), *The Poetics of Gender*, 1986. 63–73.

Wong, Shawn (ed.). *Asian American Literature: A Brief Introduction and Anthology*. New York: Harper Collins College, 1996.

Woodring, Carl. *Literature: An Embattled Profession*. New York: Columbia University Press, 1990.

Woods, Gregory. *A History of Gay Literature: The Male Tradition*. New Haven: Yale University Press, 1998.

Young, Al (ed.) *African American Literature: A Brief Introduction and Anthology*. New York: Harper Collins College, 1996.

Young, Robert J.C. *Postcolonialism: An Historical Introduction*. Oxford: Blackwell, 2001.

Index

Adorno, Theodor, 20–21, 42, 43, 76, 151, 213
Ahmad, Aijaz, 79, 84, 119
Ahmed, Jamilah, 43–44
Alberti, John, 213
Althusser, Louis, 30, 76, 101, 119
Altizer, Thomas, 108
analytical philosophy, 9, 227n
Appiah, Kwame Anthony, 13–14, 31
Arnold, Matthew, 133, 207
Aronowitz, Stanley, 31, 85
Austin, J.L., 33, 34
autoethnography, 140–42, 178

Baldick, Chris, 133, 134
Barry, Peter, 190
Barthes, Roland, 101, 116
Baudrillard, Jean, 76
Beauvoir, Simone de, 45, 119
Belsey, Catherine, 104, 113, 117, 185, 186–87, 188, 191–96, 197, 198, 199, 204
Bennett, William, 206
Berger, Peter, and Luckmann, 81–82, 138
Berki, R.N., 57
Berman, Art, 113
Bhabha, Homi, 79, 86
Blair, Tony, 18
Bloom, Harold, 108, 206, 207
Bourdieu, Pierre, 101, 131
Bové, Paul, 121–23, 127, 130
Braidotti, Rosi, 41–42
Brandt, Willy, 91
Breines, Paul, 86
Brooker, Peter and Selden and Widdowson, 201–02
Brooks, Cleanth and Wimsatt, 102
Burke, Kenneth, 104
Bush, George, 18
Buzard, James, 142

Cain, William E., 113, 117, 213–14
Cannetti, Elias, 35–36
Carmichael, Stokely (Kwame Ture) and Hamilton 51, 53
Castle, Terry, 144–49, 151, 152, 155, 156, 158, 166, 172
Certeau, Michel de, 59
Chomsky, Noam, 108
Chryssochoou, Xenia, 223n
Cixous, Hélène, 101, 119
class, 3, 7, 9, 11, 13, 18, 23, 32, 40, 44, 46–47, 83–86, 88–89, 127, 195, 212, 213
coalition politics, 51–53
Cohen, Joshua, 95
Cohen, Ralph, 106, 110, 113, 117, 118
Cook, Blanche, 87
Cooper, Davina, 61–63
Crawford, Robert, 133–34
Culler, Jonathan, 117, 186
cultural studies, 115–17, 125, 129–30, 135
Cunningham, Valentine, 127–28

D'Amico, Robert, 86
deconstructionist criticism, 104–06, 108, 112, 114, 117, 118, 125
democracy, 58, 59–61, 72–74, 78
Derrida, Jacques, 30, 34, 50, 53–55, 57, 58, 101, 102, 109, 116, 119, 140, 148–49
Di Leo, Jeffrey R, and Graff, 185–86, 189
difference, 30, 53–58, 59, 74, 82, 214
diversity, 61–63, 207
Dixon, John, 133
Docherty, Thomas, 121–23, 130
Donoghue, Denis, 113, 124–25, 126, 129
Downing, David, 182–83, 184, 185, 189
Doyle, Brian, 133, 134
Dyer, Richard, 34

Eagleton, Mary, 161, 162, 169, 173
Eagleton, Terry, 100, 101, 102, 103,
      106, 111, 117, 119, 129–30,
      137, 185, 186–87, 188, 191–93,
      196–98, 199, 204, 233–34n
Easthope, Anthony, 116–17
Elias, Norbert, 15
Eliot, T.S., 133
Ellis, John, 127–28
Erikson, Erik, 15
essentialism, 1, 3, 19, 22, 23–26,
      37–38, 39, 40, 41, 44, 45,
      52–53, 153, 158, 159–160,
      171
ethnicity, 7, 8, 9, 11, 13, 17, 23, 24,
      32, 40, 44, 65–66, 68–69, 83,
      119, 129; new 45, 68–69, 195,
      217–19
Evans, Sara, 87
Eversley, Shelly, 173–78
existentialism, 8, 20–21, 151

Fanon, Frantz, 76
Felman, Shoshanna, 149–54, 155,
      156, 158, 166, 172
Felperin, Howard, 113, 118
feminism, 8, 11–12, 16–17, 18, 19,
      39, 45–46, 51–52, 83, 113,
      118, 125, 150–54, 158–163,
      168–73, 175–76, 193, 194,
      196–97, 199–201; second
      wave, 45, 119, 168–69
Fish, Stanley, 101–02, 106, 115,
      125–26, 129
Forner, Eric, 87
Foucault, Michel, 30, 35, 50, 76,
      89–90, 101, 102, 108, 109,
      119, 166, 196
French, Marilyn, 45
Friedan, Betty, 45, 119
Frye, Northrope, 104
Fuchs, Stephan, 25–26

Gasset, José Ortega y, 36
Gates Jr., Henry Louis, 118
Geertz, Clifford, 142–43, 216, 234n
gender studies/politics, 7, 9, 11, 13,
      23, 24, 25, 26, 31–32, 44,
      94–95, 99–101, 115, 119, 120,

      125, 127, 134, 143, 149–154,
      158–163, 164, 165, 168–73,
      195, 212, 213, 217–19
Gergen, Kenneth J., 30, 62–63
Giddens, Anthony, 76
Gilbert, Sandra and Gubar, 45, 119,
      168
Gitlin, Todd, 10, 84, 88
globalization, 74, 76–79, 88, 89–90,
      135
Godzich, Wlad, 120
Goldmann, Lucien, 108, 111
Goodheart, Eugene, 113
Gouldner, Alvin, 2–3, 221n
Graff, Gerald, 99–101, 103, 104, 113,
      115, 117, 118, 131–2, 134,
      213–14; and Di Leo 185–86,
      189
Gramsci, Antonio, 72, 123
Greenblatt, Stephen, 234n
Grillo, R.D., 65
Gubar, Susan, 168–73; and Gilbert
      45, 119, 168
Guillory, John, 207–08
Gumperz, John J., 15, 222n
Gutmann, Amy, 68
Guy, Josephine and Small 134

Habermas, Jürgen, 17, 61, 67, 68, 69,
      71, 95, 101, 222n
Hall, Stuart, 12, 45, 68–69, 86, 91
Hamilton, Charles V. and
      Carmichael, 51, 53
Hartman, Geoffrey, 103, 104, 106,
      108, 109–10, 118
Hassan, Waïl S., 211
Hayek, Fredrick, 9
Hegel, G.W.F., 18, 222–23n
Heidegger, Martin, 34, 53, 54
Held, David, 61; and McGrew, 78
Hennessy, Rosemary, 31
Hobsbawm, Eric, 10, 84
Hollibaugh, Amber, 87
Hoover, Kenneth, 15, 59
Horne, Gerald, 87
Horton, Susan, 106
Huggan, Graham, 77, 167–68
Humm, Maggie, 161–62, 169, 173
Hurston, Zora Neale, 175

Ingarden, Roman, 104
institutionalization, 81–82, 181–82;
    in literary studies, 114–17,
    130–36, 138–39, 147, 150,
    152–53, 156–57, 158, 167–68,
    169, 172, 174, 184, 187,
    204–05, 216–20
Irigaray, Luce, 101, 119
Iser, Wolfgang, 155, 235n
Issitt, John, 180–82, 184, 188

Jacoby, Russell, 86
Jameson, Fredric, 93, 101, 111, 119
Jay, Gregory S., 207
Johnson, David, 134
Joshi, Svati, 133

Kautsky, Karl, 123
Kelly, Joan, 45
Kierkegaard, Søren, 33
Kolbas, E. Dean, 208
Kristeva, Julia, 101, 119
Kuhn, Thomas, 182–83

Lacan, Jacques, 101, 119
Laclau, Ernesto, 57–58; and Mouffe
    72, 122
Lauter, Paul, 207, 213
Leavis, F.R, 104, 133, 207
Lefebvre, Henri, 89
Lenin, V.I., 123
Lentricchia, Frank, 104, 106, 110, 113
Lévi-Strauss, Claude, 101
Locke, Alain, 177–78
Lott, Eric, 228n
Loury, Glenn, 27–29
Lowe, Lisa, 212
Luckmann, Thomas, and Berger,
    81–82, 138
Luhmann, Niklas, 14–15
Lukács, Georg, 104, 108, 111
Luke, Tim, 86
Lynn, Steven, 137, 189, 202–04
Lyotard, Jean-François, 75, 77–78

Maalouf, Amin, 10
McGrew, Anthony, and Held, 78
Mackenzie, W.J.M., 7
McNamara, Robert, 91

Man, Paul de, 103–07, 108, 109, 111,
    112, 113, 114, 121, 124
Mandel, Ernest, 89
Marable, Manning, 87
Marcuse, Herbert, 90, 229n
marginality, 163–68
Markovits, Andrei, 85
Marx, Karl, 27
Marxism, 8, 42, 46–47, 71–72, 83–90,
    119–20, 121–22, 125, 135,
    148–49
Mauss, Marcel, 15
Mead, George Herbert, 15
Mercer, Kobena, 86
Michaels, Walter Benn, 159
Mill, John Stuart, 13
Millard, Elaine and Mills, Pearce,
    Spaull, 160–61
Miller, J. Hillis, 106, 113–14, 118
Millett, Kate, 119
Mills, Sara and Pearce, Spaull,
    Millard, 160–61
Moi, Toril, 160, 161
Mouffe, Chantal, 31, 72–74, 196; and
    Laclau, 72, 122
Morgenthau, Hans, 57
multiculturalism, 65–68, 88, 203–04,
    206, 211, 213, 217–19

nationality/nationalism, 7, 8, 17,
    18, 19, 23, 24, 40, 44, 83,
    119
Natoli, Joseph, 117, 118
Nesbit, Robert, 89
New Criticism, 99, 104, 107, 112,
    135, 140, 184, 187, 193
New Historicism, 125
Nicholson, Linda and Seidman,
    30–31
Norris, Christopher, 118
Nozick, Robert, 9

Ohmann, Richard, 131–32, 134
Olsen, Stein Haugom, 183
Oort, Richard van, 234n
Orientalism, 108, 119

Pakulski, Jan, 89
Palmer, D.J., 132

Palumbo-Liu, David, 11
Parfit, Derek, 9
Parmar, Pratibha, 86
Parrinder, Patrick, 118, 182, 183, 184–85, 205–06
Patai, Daphni, 40
Pearce, Lynne and Mills, Spaull, Millard, 160–61
performative articulation, 33–34
Perloff, Marjorie, 211
Phelan, Shane, 31, 52
Phillips, Caryl, 10
Piccone, Paul, 86
Plekhanov, G.V., 111
pluralism, 58–61, 67, 88, 159
postcolonialism, 74–79, 88, 100, 113, 125, 129, 134, 165, 167–68, 193, 194, 212, 217–19
postmodernism, 74–79, 88
poststructuralism, 99, 112, 116, 196
Pratt, Mary Louise, 140–42
Preez, Peter du, 15, 59

Rabaté, Jean Michel, 140
race studies/politics, 7, 8, 9, 11, 13, 17, 18, 19, 23, 24, 27–29, 31–32, 39, 44, 45–46, 51–52, 69, 83, 99–101, 113, 115, 118, 119, 120, 125, 127, 143, 159, 163, 164, 165, 169, 170, 173–78, 212, 213, 217–19
Rajan, Rajeshwari Sunder, 133
Rajan, Tilottama, 135
Rawls, John, 9, 59–61, 67
Reagan, Ronald, 90–91
Reagon, Bernice Johnson, 52
relational politics, 62–63
religion, 7, 11–12, 13, 17, 18, 19, 23, 32–33, 40, 44, 169, 170, 217–19
Richards, I.A., 104, 133
Rutherford, Jonathan, 86–87
Ryan, Michael, 189–90

Said, Edward, 76, 101, 102, 103, 107–10, 111, 112, 119, 121, 124

Sartre, Jean Paul, 8
Scholes, Robert, 131–32, 134
Seidman, Steven, 55–57; and Nicholson 30–31
Selden, Raman, 137, 187–89, 190, 198–202, 204; and Widdowson, 199, 200–01, 202, 203; and Widdowson and Brooker, 199, 201–02
sexuality, 7, 11, 13, 23, 25, 26, 119, 213, 217–19; gay 17, 18, 32, 83, 100, 113, 125, 143, 154–58; lesbian 32, 83, 125, 144–49, 170, 171; Queer 33–34, 193, 194
Showalter, Elaine, 118, 119
Small, Ian and Guy, 134
social constructionism, 1, 3, 22, 26–31, 37–38, 40, 41, 44–47, 82, 93–95, 153, 158, 159–60, 171, 174
social movements, 63, 69–74
Spaull, Sue and Mills, Pearce, Millard, 160–61
Spillers, Hortense, 177–78
Spivak, Gayatri Chakravorty, 113, 158, 162–68, 175, 211–12, 224n
Stevens, Ilan, 210–11
Stiglitz, Joseph, 92
Stimpson, Catherine, 118
structuralism, 111
Stuart, Andrea, 86
Suleri, Sara, 79

Tajfel, Henri, 15, 222n
Taylor, Charles, 67–68, 69, 226n
Taylor, Paul C., 27–29
textbooks, 137, 159–163, 179–86
Thatcher, Margaret, 90–91
Touraine, Alain, 71–72, 85
Trivedi, Harish, 133
Trudeau, Pierre, 66

Vishwanathan, Gauri, 133, 134

Wallace, Kathleen, 9–10
Waltz, Kenneth, 57

Watts, Jerry Gafio, 53
Weber, Max, 81–82
Weeks, Jeffrey, 86
Westbrooke, Robert, 87
Widdowson, Peter and Selden 199,
    200–01, 202, 203; and Selden
    and Brooker, 201–02

Williams, Raymond, 101, 108,
    111
Wimsatt, William and Brooks, 102
Wittig, Monique, 16–17
Woods, Gregory, 154–58, 166

Young, Robert, 77, 79